MW00397788

INSTITUTIONAL PATHWAYS TO EQUITY

NEW FRONTIERS OF SOCIAL POLICY

INSTITUTIONAL PATHWAYS TO EQUITY

ADDRESSING INEQUALITY TRAPS

Anthony J. Bebbington, Anis A. Dani,
Arjan de Haan, and Michael Walton, Editors

© 2008 The International Bank for Reconstruction and Development / The World Bank

1818 H Street NW
Washington DC 20433
Telephone: 202-473-1000
Internet: www.worldbank.org
E-mail: feedback@worldbank.org

All rights reserved

1 2 3 4 11 10 09 08

This volume is a product of the staff of the International Bank for Reconstruction and Development / The World Bank. The findings, interpretations, and conclusions expressed in this volume do not necessarily reflect the views of the Executive Directors of The World Bank or the governments they represent.

The World Bank does not guarantee the accuracy of the data included in this work. The boundaries, colors, denominations, and other information shown on any map in this work do not imply any judgement on the part of The World Bank concerning the legal status of any territory or the endorsement or acceptance of such boundaries.

Rights and Permissions

The material in this publication is copyrighted. Copying and/or transmitting portions or all of this work without permission may be a violation of applicable law. The International Bank for Reconstruction and Development / The World Bank encourages dissemination of its work and will normally grant permission to reproduce portions of the work promptly.

For permission to photocopy or reprint any part of this work, please send a request with complete information to the Copyright Clearance Center Inc., 222 Rosewood Drive, Danvers, MA 01923, USA; telephone: 978-750-8400; fax: 978-750-4470; Internet: www.copyright.com.

All other queries on rights and licenses, including subsidiary rights, should be addressed to the Office of the Publisher, The World Bank, 1818 H Street NW, Washington, DC 20433, USA; fax: 202-522-2422; e-mail: pubrights@worldbank.org.

ISBN: 978-0-8213-7013-1
eISBN: 978-0-8213-7014-8
DOI: 10.1596/978-0-8213-7013-1

Cover photo: Health workers in Mali by Giacomo Pirozzi / Panos
Cover design: Naylor Design, Washington, DC

Library of Congress Cataloging-in-Publication Data

Institutional pathways to equity : addressing inequality traps / edited by Anthony J. Bebbington ... [et al.].
p. cm.
Includes bibliographical references and index.
ISBN 978-0-8213-7013-1 — ISBN 978-0-8213-7014-8 (electronic)
1. Income distribution. 2. Institutional economics. 3. Income distribution—Cross-cultural studies. 4. Equality. 5. Poverty. I. Bebbington, Anthony, 1962-
HC79.151497 2007
339.2—dc22

2007041564

NEW FRONTIERS OF SOCIAL POLICY

In many developing countries, the mixed record of state effectiveness, market imperfections, and persistent structural inequities has undermined the effectiveness of social policy. To overcome these constraints, social policy needs to move beyond conventional social service approaches toward development's goals of equitable opportunity and social justice. This series has been created to promote debate among the development community, policy makers, and academia and to broaden understanding of social policy challenges in developing country contexts.

The books in the series are linked to the World Bank's Social Development Strategy. The strategy is aimed at empowering people by transforming institutions to make them more inclusive, responsive, and accountable. This involves the transformation of subjects and beneficiaries into citizens with rights and responsibilities. Themes in this series will include equity and development, assets and livelihoods, and citizenship and rights-based social policy, as well as the social dimensions of infrastructure and climate change.

Other titles in the series:

- *Assets, Livelihoods, and Social Policy*
- *Inclusive States: Social Policy and Structural Inequalities*

Anis Dani
Series Editor
Adviser, Social Policy

CONTENTS

PART III. INSTITUTIONAL TRANSITIONS AND PATHWAYS TOWARD EQUITY

BOXES

FIGURES

TABLES

PREFACE

This collection grows out of thinking linked to the preparation of the *World Development Report 2006: Equity and Development*. The *World Development Reports (WDRs)* are arguably the most publicly visible of the World Bank's flagship publications. While they are not statements of Bank policy, they are generally taken to be a good reflection of emerging thinking in the institution. They are also understood to be relatively formative, indeed powerful, and there are many cases in which one can associate *WDRs* with shifts in the ways that the Bank understands and engages in development. For all these reasons, these reports are often hotly debated both internally and externally with government, civil society, and academic actors.

WDRs are exercises in synthesis—they draw on existing work, both inside and outside the Bank, in order to craft an argument about the theme of the report. However, in many cases the team preparing the reports commissions background papers from people outside the core team and generally outside the Bank. Authors of these background papers are asked to synthesize material and craft an argument on the way in which the overall theme of the report (in this case, equity) plays out the thematic, disciplinary, geographic, and policy contexts of which the author is an expert. These background papers serve as focused sub-syntheses upon which the core team then may or may not draw.

These two antecedents are relevant for understanding the collection presented in this book. In the case of *WDR 2006*, once the theme, directors, and core writing team had been defined, and as the process of preparation got underway in the first half of 2004, the U.K. Department for International Development (DfID) decided that it wanted both to support the report writing process (for it found the theme important) and at the same time to have some influence over the positions that the report would take. In essence, the hope was to inject more social science (beyond economics) into the report's preparation and nudge the report toward engaging in depth the themes of politics, social structure, and political economy. Such negotiations are always sensitive. On the one hand, *WDR* writing teams welcome support, but they are less keen on the idea that they need to be pushed in a particular direction by a third party. On the other hand, team members—let alone the broad set of internal and external reviewers—are themselves never always of completely the same mind. Additional work is often used to bring new ideas and perspectives to the table. In this case, the resolution of these tensions was that DfID would support the preparation of a number of background papers on themes that DfID would have some say in identifying (in coordination with the *WDR* team).

This book brings together a number of these background papers. The thrust of their argument is very similar to that of *WDR*, although they bring slightly different emphases. Analytically, there is a particular emphasis on political economy, social identity, and social mobilization—in order to understand what causes and perpetuates inequity, as well as understand the processes through which it is contested and might be changed. Methodologically, the papers are not grounded in quantitative social science and economics—although there are economists among our authors, and indeed among us; the papers also come from political scientists, historians, and regional development specialists. Among other things, this diversity gives the papers a more contextualized flavor and approach than was feasible in *WDR*—that is, they seek to understand inequity and the processes through which it has been challenged and reduced within particular geographic and sociopolitical contexts. Our hope is that these characteristics will make this collection a companion volume to *WDR*, one that can be used alongside *WDR* in teaching; at the same time, it has a purpose of its own, which is to illustrate the range of ways—analytically, methodologically, disciplinarily—in which inequity can be tackled as a research and policy problem.

The essays were first presented and discussed at a workshop help in Washington, D.C., in November 2004, and we are grateful to the Social Development Department and the many people who helped in the preparation of that event. The papers have since been commented on and revised at least twice before reaching this publication stage. This process has, of course, involved many people and, in alphabetical order, we would particularly like to thank the following: Yvonne Byron-Smith, Joyce Chinsen, Bridget Dillon, Francisco H. G. Ferreira, Charlotte Heath, Liane Lohde, Steen L. Jorgensen, Stephen Kidd, Keith Mackiggan, Tamar

Manuelyan-Atinc, Kirsty Mason, Anna Morris, Andrew Norton, Berk Ozler, Giovanna Prennushi, Vijayendra Rao, Ana Revenga, Christian Rogg, Rebecca Sugui, Arthur van Diesen, Adrian Wood, and Michael Woolcock, for the many different ways in which they contributed to this process.

We also wish to acknowledge formally the financial support of the U.K. Department for International Development for production of the background papers and the Trust Fund for Environmentally and Socially Sustainable Development, financed by the governments of Norway and Finland, for underwriting the publication of this book.

Editors
November 2007

ABOUT THE EDITORS

Anthony J. Bebbington is Professor of Nature, Society, and Development and is ESRC professorial research fellow at the School for Environment and Development, University of Manchester. He spent several years at the World Bank as senior social scientist developing pioneering work on social capital and local level institutions and later taught and conducted research at the University of Colorado. He was a member of the team that prepared the World Development Report on *Equity and Development.* His recent publications include forthcoming *Development Success: Statecraft in the South* (edited with W. McCourt, London: Palgrave Macmillan) and *The Search for Empowerment. Social Capital as Idea and Practice at the World Bank* (edited with M. Woolcock, S. Guggenheim, and E. Olson, West Hartford: Kumarian, 2006). His research interests are rural development and rural livelihoods, nongovernmental organizations, social movements and indigenous organizations, political ecology, and policy processes within development bureaucracies, including the World Bank.

Anis A. Dani is Adviser, Social Policy in the Sustainable Development Network, World Bank. An anthropologist by training, he worked on development research and rural development projects and the nongovernmental organizations sector in South Asia, as well as China before joining the World Bank in 1995. At the World Bank, he was engaged in operations in South Asia, East Asia, and Eastern Europe while conducting social research, overseeing social impact assessments, and managing projects. He then coordinated the Bank's work on social analysis, adapting it into an instrument for upstream, ex-ante, poverty, and social impact analysis of policy reforms. He has been leading the conceptual work on social policy as a follow-up to the formulation of the World Bank's social development strategy. His recent publications include *Poverty and Social Impact Analysis of Reforms: Lessons and Examples from*

Implementation, co-edited with Aline Coudouel and Stefano Paternostro, World Bank (2006), and *Poverty and Social Impact Analysis of Mining Sector Reform in Romania: A Policy Note* (Social Development Department, World Bank 2005). His current research interests include social policy, social impacts of policy reforms, inequality, migration, and social dimensions of infrastructure.

Arjan de Haan is Social Development Adviser, Department for International Development (DFID), Beijing Office. By training and profession, he is a social historian and social policy specialist. He is social development adviser at DFID's Beijing Office. Earlier, he served as the social development adviser on DFID's Growth and Investment Group and as adviser, Research and Social Policy at DFID headquarters. In between, he also worked as social development adviser in DFID's India Office. During his years at DFID headquarters, he played a key role in DFID's support for the PRSP process and in mobilizing background analytical work for the World Development Report on *Equity and Development.* He took a year off from DFID to teach and conduct research on social policy as a visiting professor at the Department of Sociology and Anthropology, University of Guelph, Ontario. Before joining DFID, he taught at the Department of History, Erasmus University, Rotterdam, and served as a research fellow and acting director at the Poverty Research Unit, University of Sussex. His research interests are poverty, inequality, and social policy.

Michael Walton is Senior Visiting Fellow at the Centre for Policy Research, Delhi, and adjunct lecturer at the Kennedy School of Government, Harvard University. From 1980 to 2004, Michael Walton worked at the World Bank, where his positions included chief economist for East Asia and the Pacific (1995–97), director for Poverty Reduction (1997–2000), and chief economist for human development (1999–2000). Recent publications include co-editor (with Vijayendra Rao) of *Culture and Public Action* (Stanford University Press, 2004), co-author of *Inequality in Latin America and the Caribbean: Breaking with History* (World Bank, 2004), and co-director of *World Development Report 2005/06 on Equity and Development.* He is currently undertaking research on education in India and on the relationship among equity, institutions, and growth. Michael Walton has a bachelor's degree in philosophy and economics and a master's degrees in economics from Oxford University.

ABOUT THE AUTHORS

Armando Barrientos, Ph.D., is a Senior Research Fellow at the Brooks World Poverty Institute, the University of Manchester, United Kingdom, and senior researcher with the Chronic Poverty Research Centre.

Carles Boix, Ph.D., is Professor of Politics and Public Affairs at the Department of Politics and the Woodrow Wilson School of Public and International Affairs, Princeton University.

Arjan de Haan, Ph.D., is a social historian and social policy specialist and is Social Development Adviser, Department for International Development, Beijing Office.

José Antonio Lucero, Ph.D., is Assistant Professor of Political Science at Temple University, where he works and publishes on indigenous politics and social movements in Latin America. In 2008, he will join the faculty of the Henry M. Jackson School of International Studies at the University of Washington.

Joy M. Moncrieffe, Ph.D., is a political sociologist and Fellow at the Institute of Development Studies. She is working on issues of accountability, citizenship, and power, and she has a special interest in working with children who are growing up in violent and other fragile contexts.

Michael L. Ross, Ph.D., is an Associate Professor of Political Science and Chairman of the International Development Studies program at the University of California–Los Angeles.

Rachel Sabates-Wheeler, Ph.D., is Research Fellow and a Co-Director of the Centre for Social Protection at the Institute of Development Studies at the University of Sussex, United Kingdom.

ABBREVIATIONS

ADAPT	Area Development Approach for Poverty Termination (India)
APWDW	Assistance Program for Widowed and Destitute Women (Bangladesh)
BCL	Bougainville Copper Limited
BPC	Beneficio de Prestação Continuada (urban old-age pension) (Brazil)
CIDOB	Confederación de Pueblos Indígenas de Bolivia (Confederation of Indigenous Peoples of Eastern Bolivia)
CODENPE	Consejo de Desarrollo de las Nacionalidades y Pueblos de Ecuador (Development Council of the Nationalities and Peoples of Ecuador)
CONAIE	Confederación de Nacionalidades Indígenas del Ecuador (Confederation of Indigenous Nationalities of Ecuador)
CONAMAQ	Consejo Nacional de Ayllus y Markas de Qullasuyu (National Council of Ayllus and Markas of Qullasuyu) (Bolivia)
CONFENIAE	Confederación de Nacionalidades Indígenas de la Amazonia Ecuatoriana (Confederation of Amazonian Nationalities of Ecuador)
CSUTCB	Confederación Sindical Única de Trabajadores Campesinos de Bolivia (Sole Confederation of Rural Workers of Bolivia)
DANIDA	Danish International Development Agency
DfID	Department for International Development (United Kingdom)
ECUARUNARI	Awakening of the Ecuadorian Indian (Kichwa)

EU	European Union
FEI	Federación Ecuatoriana de Indios (Ecuadorian Federation of Indians)
FEINE	Consejo de Pueblos Indígenas Evangélicos del Ecuador (formerly the Federación de Evangélicos Indígenas del Ecuador, or Evangelical Indigenous Federation of Ecuador)
FENOCIN	Federación Nacional de Organizaciones Indígenas y Negras (Federation of Peasant, Indigenous, and Black Organizations) (Ecuador)
FUNRURAL	Fundo de Assistência e Previdência do Trabalhador Rural (Assistance Fund for Rural Workers) (Brazil)
GAM	Gerakan Aceh Merdeka (Aceh Freedom Movement) (Indonesia)
GDP	gross domestic product
HDI	Human Development Index
INRA	Ley del Instituto Nacional de Reforma Agraria (Agrarian Reform Law) (Bolivia)
IUH	impuesto a la utilidades de empresa (capital tax on corporations) (Bolivia)
KBK	Kalahandi-Bolangir-Koraput
LC	local council
LPP	Ley de Participación Popular (Law of Popular Participation) (Bolivia)
MAS	Movimiento al Socialismo (Movement toward Socialism) (Bolivia)
MNR	Movimiento Nacionalista Revolucionario (Nationalist Revolutionary Movement) (Bolivia)
NBER	National Bureau of Economic Research
NFHS	National Family Health Survey (India)
NGO	nongovernmental organization
NRM	National Resistance Movement (Uganda)
NSS	National Statistical Survey (India)
NTFP	nontimber forest products
OAAS	Old-Age Allowance Scheme (Bangladesh)
OECD	Organisation for Economic Co-operation and Development
PEAP	Poverty Eradication Action Plan (Uganda)
PESA	Panchayat Extension to Scheduled Areas

PPA	participatory poverty appraisal
PR	Prêvidencia Rural (rural old-age pension) (Brazil)
PRI	panchayati raj institution
PRODEPINE	Program for the Development of Indigenous and Afro-Ecuadorian Peoples
PRORURAL	Programa de Assistência ao Trabalhador Rural (Rural Workers' Assistance Program) (Brazil)
RC	resistance council
RMV	Renda Mensal Vitalícia (old-age pension) (Brazil)
SC	scheduled caste
SRS	Sample Registration Survey (India)
ST	scheduled tribe
TCO	tierra comunitaria de origen (indigenous territory)
TFESSD	Trust Fund for Environmentally and Socially Sustainable Development
TIP	"Three 'I's of Poverty" (incidence, intensity, and inequality)
UNDP	United Nations Development Programme

PART I

INTRODUCTION

CHAPTER 1

Inequalities and Development: Dysfunctions, Traps, and Transitions

Anthony J. Bebbington, Anis A. Dani, Arjan de Haan, and Michael Walton

This book is a cross-disciplinary exploration of the ways in which inequalities affect development. *Inequalities* are understood as differences in people's access to economic opportunities, sociopolitical participation, and ability to live a fulfilling life; they would often be considered unjustified on ethical grounds. *Development* is understood as a process of societal change that combines economic growth, poverty reduction, and enhanced abilities to exercise voice. Although the chapters emphasize one or another dimension of inequality, they share the view that these dimensions are mutually reinforcing, and while they emphasize one or another face of development, they consider each as important in its own right. Likewise, although the contributors take as a given the *normative* view that the inequalities they explore are unacceptable, they explore different *instrumental* dimensions of the importance of these inequalities. In other words, they discuss different ways in which inequalities lead to dysfunctions in development. At the same time, each chapter explores how, through both political economy and policy processes, these dysfunctional arrangements might be broken. In short, the book offers analytically grounded observations and suggestions for thinking through policies that might break the varying ways in which social groups are trapped in inequitable relationships and might rupture

---

Anthony J. Bebbington acknowledges with thanks a U.K. Economic and Social Science Research Council Professorial Research Fellowship (RES-051-27-0191) that supported much of his time in the joint preparation of this chapter and completion of the book. The authors are grateful to the comments of two anonymous reviewers on this chapter and the collection.

the pathways that lead from inequalities to failures in growth, poverty reduction, and sociopolitical participation.

Our emphasis is on national development processes, national institutions, and national policies.[1] The decision to focus on inequalities stems not from an ideological commitment that sees inequality as more politically significant than poverty, growth, or some other concern,[2] but rather from the analytical argument that in many respects inequality—or more precisely, the social processes that create it—precedes poverty or growth. Thus, inequalities exist with or without growth and in the presence or absence of poverty, and the nature of these inequalities will influence the nature of growth and poverty in the future. Put idiomatically, if "the poor will always be with us," inequalities will always be with us. There is also a second analytical reason for focusing on inequalities: empirically, inequality appears more resistant to change than does poverty.[3] If it is indeed more resistant, and if inequality has causal influences on poverty or growth, understanding the factors that sustain continued inequality is essential to understanding how the poverty-reducing effects of growth might increase.

With these statements of intent in mind, this opening chapter has three purposes. The first is analytical; therefore, in the first two sections, we elaborate on the arguments that suggest the importance of inequality for development processes, as well as on those arguments that help explain why inequality is so "sticky." Phrased in more formal terms, the emphasis here is on how "inequality traps" emerge and are sustained over time. Our second purpose is also analytical—while being motivated by a commitment to policy. It is to explore the different conditions under which the institutional arrangements that underlie these fixed structures of inequality might change. These pathways—some related to policy, some to social protest, and some to growth dynamics—provide pointers for public action, suggesting ways in which different social actors might tackle these traps and push societies toward enhanced equity.

Our third purpose is to introduce the chapters of the book through a brief description of the content and argument of each chapter. We do not analyze all the information presented in each chapter; rather, we prefer to let the text speak for itself. However, we do briefly compare the chapters by the types of inequalities they address, the ways in which they see these inequalities as being important for development, and the ways in which they suggest these inequalities might be broken. This comparison serves as a road map for the readers as they work through the book. A final section outlines the policy implications.

Inequity and Inequality: Why They Matter

There are both intrinsic (normative) and instrumental (positive) reasons for worrying about inequality. The normative argument leaves many development organizations and academics uncomfortable, though the instrumental arguments have gained more attention—especially in agencies and among economists. We would maintain that each type of argument is valid, but for different reasons.

Normative arguments against inequality do not (necessarily) aver that full equality in the distribution of assets or of other outcomes, such as income or educational level, is the most desirable way in which society should be arranged. They do, however, claim that inequality can reach extremes that are innately abhorrent and that underlying relationships in society can be so patently unfair (inequitable) as to be unacceptable. In their more general form, these positions argue that certain distributions of income and opportunities are morally unacceptable, as are inequalities in the abilities of citizens to be citizens; to exercise voice; to participate politically; and to access a range of political, social, and economic institutions. One of the most ardent voices for a normative case is Amartya Sen (1999), who argues that development is nothing if it is not about enhancing freedoms and that central to these freedoms is the ability of all people to be citizens on an equal footing and to fulfill their inborn potentials to an equal degree. These are beliefs rather than facts, though ones that find representation in a variety of world traditions, as well as in ideas underlying liberal democracy. That said, different countries and cultures attribute different values to—and often emphasize different aspects of—inequality. Most notably, North American values emphasize inequalities in opportunities or socioeconomic mobility, whereas continental European values tend to privilege inequalities in public entitlements and seem to be concerned more with inequalities in outcomes (for example, well-being).

The adverse, instrumental effects of distributional inequalities and institutional inequities receive more attention from development agencies. From this perspective, as illustrated in the limited attention to inequalities in the Millennium Development Goals, the inherent valuation of inequality is of less interest than its implications for other collectively accepted indicators of development—such as aggregate or per capita growth, educational attainment, infant mortality rates, and democratic practice. Evidence of the instrumental value of equity comes from several sources. Here, we sketch them briefly for the case of three domains: political participation and democracy, poverty reduction, and growth.[4]

Prevailing relationships of power work to the disadvantage of those at the bottom of the hierarchy. Put simply, some groups benefit from inequality and from the perpetuation of those sets of inequitable political relationships that give more voice to them than to others, thereby allowing them to exercise privileged influence over the structure of society through a range of political, social, and symbolic practices.[5] These inequalities in the control of assets and institutions create unequal relationships of power, which the more powerful use to sustain their positions of advantage. Meanwhile, those whom one would expect to value equity more highly possess less voice, with the knock-on effect that normative arguments against inequality tend to be underrepresented in public debate and policy formation. This lack of representation can happen for many reasons. Voter registration programs (or constitutions) may have excluded the disadvantaged from exercising the right to vote,[6] poor or no access to education may mean they lack the human capital that gives them greater capacity to formulate and express their voice,[7] and a variety of disadvantages (and possibly political repression) may block the emergence or reduce the effectiveness of mass and political organizations through which these concerns might otherwise have been represented.

This situation, of course, leads to an apparent dilemma in which existing relationships of inequity must be addressed for the social valuation of equity to be more accurately reflected in policy and institutional arrangements. Put more simply, to deal with inequality, societies must deal with relationships of inequality—yet the scope for doing so is restricted *because* of the relationships of inequality. Thus, questions of agency are important, a point to which we return later.

Second—and returning to the poverty-inequality nexus—is the argument that the poverty-reducing effects of economic growth fall off when inequality is greater. This observation might be so because these distributions reduce the trickle-down effects of growth or simply because much more growth must occur to bring those at the tail of the distribution out of poverty. More generally, there are many interactions between inequality traps and social welfare, and greater inequality is statistically associated with greater crime and violence (see Demombynes and Özler 2005 for South Africa), which often affect the poor relatively more than the wealthy.

Third, inequalities in asset distributions may have negative effects on economic growth. This argument perhaps gains the most attention among hardheaded scholars and policy makers for whom growth is a sine qua non of development. Where a society's wealth is concentrated in a small segment and large parts of the population lack assets, an old argument is that domestic consumer markets remain limited, thereby reducing the scope for business creation and growth (though more recent arguments have suggested that export markets can offset that effect). Meanwhile, those controlling most of societies' income frequently consume imported rather than domestically produced goods. Unequal distribution of wealth can also be accompanied by economic inefficiencies. One example here is credit distribution under conditions of asset inequality. When economic institutions lead to the exclusion of poorer groups from credit or insurance markets, this scenario necessarily curtails investment and hurts growth. If a credit market evolves in ways that deny small and medium firms access to credit from the banking system—or force them to borrow from more expensive informal sources—their level of investment will be lower, adversely affecting their viability and employment benefits. Such markets can occur both because financial market actors lack information on poorer producers and so underinvest and because powerful actors distort credit markets. A relevant example here would be Mexico, where a history of unequal influence of banking and industrial elites has led to a highly restricted level of financial intermediation and the formation of a concentrated, exclusive banking system. Such conditions lead to biases in the supply of credit against those at the bottom of the distribution. Yet microeconomic analysis of returns on investment finds very high returns among such small-scale firms, whereas returns fall steadily for medium and large firms (McKenzie and Woodruff 2003). A deeper—and more equitable—financial system would intermediate these differences with important effects on growth. Indeed, work on the wide dispersion of productivity across firms within countries suggests distortions at a micro-level can be sources of major differences at the aggregate level.

The recent literature on institutions and economic development has also argued that economic inequalities interact with other inequalities, resulting in pernicious consequences for growth. Economic dynamics and innovation depend on competitive processes of entry that are stifled by unequal economic institutions.[8] However, historical analysis of differences in long-run economic performance supports the view that political inequalities are often accompanied by predatory, extractive economic institutions that are associated with poor long-term economic performance, especially for industrialization (Acemoglu, Johnson, and Robinson 2001; Engerman and

Sokoloff 2002). A complementary argument derives from Peter Lindert's (2003, 2004) historical analysis of growth and social expenditure in Europe and the United States. One of Lindert's central conclusions is that greater equity in political institutions (in the ability to express voice) is good for growth because it is associated with broader and better-quality public provision of education—particularly primary education.[9] Better education, in turn, translates into a better-performing workforce. Thus, while Acemoglu, Johnson, and Robinson argue that political inequalities can translate into predatory economic institutions, Lindert argues that greater political equity translates into institutions that are more likely to encourage the types of investment that foster growth. The question, of course, is how equitable institutions emerge. Once again, this problem suggests the importance of agency, though Lindert also emphasizes the important effects of education itself, which helps produce a citizenry that can both exert and demand greater voice.

A final argument approaches these relationships from a different angle, contending that inequalities and inequities can themselves generate forms of collective behavior that impede growth. The essence to this line of reasoning is that inequalities can lead to social protest, as well as to institutional forms that make it difficult for opposing interests to negotiate this protest. The propensity for this protest to spill over into violence is thus greater. Several of the book's chapters comment on such cases, though these relationships are most clearly addressed by Michael Ross in chapter 7.[10] Such violence and unrest can create uncertainties about the enforceability of contracts; increase transaction and operational costs for businesses, which must guard against violence; reduce the extent to which actors in the global economy want to invest in such environments; and require the diversion of public spending toward controlling violence and away from social investment. Even when social tensions do not result in violence, perceptions of inequitable effects from policy reform can increase resistance and undermine a government's ability to introduce the very reforms needed for economic growth. (Coudouel, Dani, and Paternostro 2006).

Institutionalizing Inequality: Cross-Disciplinary Perspectives on Traps

A central concern of this book is to analyze why relationships of inequality are so apparently resistant to change. The general argument is that inequalities become embodied in and sustained by a range of formal and informal institutions that together create what has been called *inequality traps*. In the *World Development Report 2006* (World Bank 2006), a central thesis is that inequality traps are pervasive in societies, that they are inconsistent with an intrinsic concern with equity as equality of opportunity, and that in many cases they are associated with static or dynamic efficiencies that lower average incomes or social welfare (Bourguignon, Ferreira, and Walton 2007). Although in this chapter we likewise adopt the term and these arguments, the language of *inequality traps* is rarely used in the empirical and substantive chapters of the book. Rather, each chapter is concerned with the institutions—formal and informal—that sustain inequalities. Some (such as chapter 2 by Sabates-Wheeler and chapter 3 by Moncrieffe) pursue this concern quite explicitly, whereas others (such as chapter 6 by Barrientos and chapter 7 by Ross) take the existence of such institutions as more or less a given and focus on exploring their effects on particular development processes. All the chapters, however, make clear that certain types of institutionalized social relationship are central to maintaining inequality over time, analyzing the effects of these relationships on particular dimensions of development, and considering the conditions under which they may change.

With this antecedent in mind, we do three things in this section. First, we provide a general account of the concept of an inequality trap in a way that is sufficiently general to encompass its use in various disciplines. Second, we discuss the potential links to considerations of efficiency and social welfare. These links constitute an important argument why development policy should care about inequality traps. Third, we provide a general sketch of how a transition from an inequality trap can occur.

Rao (2006) coined the term *inequality trap*, defining it as "describ[ing] situations where the entire distribution is stable because the various dimensions of inequality (in wealth, power, and social status) interact to protect the rich from downward mobility, and to prevent the poor from being upwardly mobile" (Rao 2006: 11). This statement captures three important features of an inequality trap. First, it involves the persistence in the ranking of different groups in a distribution. Second, this ranking typically involves different "dimensions" of concern that confer an advantage for the individuals in the upper parts of this ranking.[11] Third, there is a causal relationship between the *existence* and the *persistence* of differences among individuals and groups—or, put more colloquially, inequalities tend to reproduce themselves. We amplify on each of these points.

The persistence in rankings in a distribution is central to the notion of an inequality trap. This concept can be stated in terms of whether the dynamics of change for different individuals or groups lead to the maintenance of rankings over time.[12] For economists, it is useful to define this outcome by the *limiting distribution*—that is, the point at which the distribution has completed its transition to a steady-state process. Other disciplines may consider a society to be in an inequality trap when the process of change in rankings is slow. India's caste system has been changing over time, for instance, but most people would still consider it to have been sufficiently persistent to qualify as an inequality trap.

It is important to note the difference between an inequality trap and the related concept of poverty trap (a concept that has been common in recent poverty analysis; see, for example, Christiaensen and Dercon 2007). A *poverty trap* refers to a situation in which a household or a society stays poor because it is poor,[13] just as Sachs (2005) has suggested that countries stay poor because they are poor (an argument criticized by others; see Kraay and Raddatz 2005). A household may lack a minimum level of human or physical capital so that it barely produces enough for subsistence and, therefore, never has the capacity to invest in human and physical capital accumulation. A country may be so poor that it cannot save enough to invest beyond what is minimally necessary. An inequality trap differs from a poverty trap in two respects. First, it involves persistence, not in an absolute level of advantage, but in a ranking. An inequality trap can, for example, still allow growth in absolute incomes at all points in the distribution. Second, an inequality trap is a product of interactions across the distribution, not just of the characteristics of the poor. In a simplified characterization, the poor stay (relatively) poor because the rich are richer. Inequality traps are thus a manifestation of "the historically generated patterns of relationships imbued and shaped by operations of power" that Eyben (2005: 1) highlights. In both poverty traps and inequality traps, different dimensions of deprivation interact to maintain the status quo.

The coexistence of multiple dimensions of advantage relates to another theme underlying the notion of inequality trap that runs through this book: namely, that economic, political, and sociocultural factors[14] are all relevant to processes of societal change and are, moreover, interrelated and causally linked. Although commentators have differing views on the relative importance of economic power or social difference—views that are often correlated with academic disciplines—we prefer the view that causation runs along each of these channels even if any one of these dimensions may have particular salience at a point in time. The core idea here is that the very structure of inequality is a source of its own persistence—in some cases through sociopolitical mechanisms and in some cases because of the causal influence of some dimensions of inequality on efficiency and growth, as previously outlined. Social science disciplines have differing—and complementary—diagnoses to offer on this problem of persistence.

In economics, an important strand of work emphasizes the interaction between "market failures" and distributions of advantage—already referred to earlier in relation to the potential influence of inequality on efficiency and growth. For example, where credit markets do not work perfectly, owing to lenders' lack of information on investment opportunities and the inability to contract for every eventuality with a borrower, access to credit can be skewed to those who have the wealth to put up collateral or those who have tighter social connections with lenders. This situation can allow the wealthy and groups with high social status to systematically accumulate physical and human capital more rapidly than less advantaged groups, hence leading to the persistence of difference.[15] Similar stories can be told with respect to market failures in insurance markets, land, education, and health.[16]

Beyond any systematic vulnerability of economic institutions to different types of failure, they themselves are also products of historically shaped conflicts and struggles—that is, they reflect the structure of power in a society. Thus, such historical processes influence the extent to which a financial system as a whole is biased toward the rich and influential. As an example, the U.S. financial system evolved in the 19th century in ways that allowed far more competition—and thus access to finance by outsiders—than did Mexico's, which remained an oligopolistic club that served the interests of a narrow economic elite (Haber 2004). This difference in the orientation and structure of financial systems can, in turn, be linked to the greater equality of political influence that existed in the United States in comparison with Mexico.

Another example from political economy is that richer groups may have access to better quality of education than do poorer groups, and the structure of power may be such that the state does not expand quality, affordable education to all.[17] More extreme examples of institutions designed to sustain difference are slavery, apartheid, and, more generally, colonialism. On this latter topic—and its continuing resonance—Mamdani's (2005) analysis of African law demonstrates how political and legal institutions can interact in ways that perpetuate inequality, in this instance by separating people into races and tribes and by establishing different legal regimes to govern these two broad categories of people. People who were not native to Africa were classified in racial terms, while those of African origin were classified in tribal terms, with different rights for members of these two broad classifications:

> Races were governed by a regime that claimed to be civic; its rule was mediated through civil law. Tribes, in contrast, were governed by a customary regime, one that claimed to administer customary law.... The civic regime spoke a language of rights. Its claim to legitimacy was that it observed rights of the governed by setting limits on exercise of state power.... The customary regime spoke a different language and ... as an enforcer of custom, it did not set limits on state power.... The civic regime was organized on the basis of *differentiation* of power: the executive, the legislature, the judiciary, and the administrative apparatus differentiated between different moments of power. In contrast, the customary regime was based on a *fusion* of power (Mamdani 2005).[18]

Mamdani goes on to argue that when such cultural differences are written into law and become the basis of a legally enforced discrimination, they lend themselves to the perpetuation and institutionalization of inequalities in how different peoples are governed, in their access to legal support, and in their subjection to repression. They also foster the politicization of culture and a certain proneness to violence around axes of socially constructed inequalities.

These insights suggest ways in which sociocultural processes are integral to the reproduction of inequality. Intrinsic to these processes are intergroup relationships in which differences are sustained not only by institutions of the sorts Mamdani describes but also through social interactions associated with underlying differences in power. Such interactions are reflected in the daily practices that shape intergroup relations and that also influence longer-term economic processes of capital accumulation and the perpetuation of social differences. Such differences can be internalized in the often tacit behaviors, outlooks, and plans of different groups, in what Appadurai (2004) describes as unequal "terms of recognition."[19] These routinized practices are partly responsible for producing what Tilly (1998) refers to as "durable inequalities." Among the different mechanisms that sustain these inequalities, Tilly notes relations of exploitation between dominant and subordinate groups, the maintenance of institutions and practices that support these relationships, and the hoarding—or protection—of opportunities by relatively advantaged groups.

Inequality traps are, then, institutionalized arrangements that become fixed with time and are reproduced through everyday practices. Institutions can be understood as bundles of rules that grow out of structural relationships and serve to organize action while being reproduced through those actions.[20] In such a framework, action, institution, and structure are each simultaneously producer and produced. Deep social structures produce institutions that reflect those structural arrangements, but it is the ongoing respect for those institutions that serves to reproduce the structures. Feudal structures, for instance, produced a series of institutions around land, property, and labor that—as long as they were respected—served to reproduce a broadly feudal system. Likewise, institutions help organize action, but their reproduction depends on their embodiment in action. Language, for instance, is a bundle of conventions (institutions) around grammar, syntax, and meaning that depend on everyday speech and interaction for their reproduction.

This joint status as produced and producer also means not only that are action, institution, and structure each part of a system that tends toward reproduction, but also that they are potentially unstable, their instability deriving from their dependence on other parts of the same system. Thus, to continue with our two illustrations, language conventions have changed over time because acts of speech have also changed—be that because of migrations, everyday resistance, or simple sloppiness, each of which ultimately creates new rules. Feudalism unraveled in part because of protest from actors who were disadvantaged by feudal arrangements and in part because of the emergence of new groups with power. These groups began to calculate that their interests would be better served by institutional arrangements based on private property and the unencumbered sale of labor. Similarly, slavery was abolished by a combination of protests by slaves, of efforts by reform-minded groups among the better off, and of (contested) economic arguments about the costs and efficiency of slavery. Understanding inequality traps as institutions is helpful for thinking about the different pathways through which change might occur—which we turn to next.

Pathways out of Institutionalized Inequalities

In this section, we discuss, in bare-bones form, some of the processes through which the institutions that underlie inequality both become consolidated and unravel. There are various reasons for interest in such processes.

Perhaps the most obvious are the normative reasons. If the existence of such self-reproducing institutions violates any ethical notion of equity as equality of opportunity—with those lower in the distribution having systematically lower opportunities than those higher in the distribution for reasons unrelated to their voluntary choice of effort—then there is a clear normative case for understanding how such institutions can be dismantled.

However, analytical and instrumental reasons also exist for being interested in how such institutions change. If the institutionalized relationships that form inequality traps are not the only possible outcome—that is, if other sets of economic, political, and sociocultural relationships in which the trap does not exist are possible[21]—then it is *analytically* interesting and important to ask how and why such an outcome occurred and under what conditions it might not occur. If such traps are associated with lower levels of growth and aggregate welfare because they are grounded in mechanisms that curtail opportunities for the poor, then there is an *instrumental* reason for being interested in how these traps change, because unraveling inequality traps would be an important part of the strategies for increasing growth and welfare.

The literature in general and the chapters in this book suggest various potential pathways out of inequality traps. First, economic development can alter the underlying social structure in ways that create new possibilities for change. A classic example is the influence of processes of urbanization and industrialization that led to concentrations of poorer groups in urban areas and that provided the organizational base for unions. This influence was central to the transitions to more egalitarian political, economic, and social arrangements that occurred in now-rich societies. Institutional change can also derive from tensions within the very structures that help mold these institutions. For example, at some point, the possibilities for economic growth may become constrained by institutionalized inequalities. For instance, arrangements allowing particularly egregious forms of labor exploitation and discrimination can ultimately obstruct the emergence of new trading possibilities. As a contemporary example, one of the sticking points in Peru's negotiation of a free trade treaty with the United States[22] related to Peru's inability to demonstrate convincing arrangements for the protection of labor. Similar arguments have been made in the literature about the social policy of the Organisation for Economic Co-operation and Development (OECD): social expenditure in the OECD has been shown to be positively correlated with openness to trade (Gough 2005). Carles Boix's chapter on Spain (chapter 8) shows how domestic institutions were reworked as something of a prerequisite to Spain's becoming more deeply embedded in the European Union (EU). The influences of globalization (for example, through entrance to the World Trade Organization) likewise contribute to significant institutional changes, even in powerful economies like China's.

In much of the political economy literature, everything is determined, or "endogenous," leaving little scope for change, absent some exogenous shock. Yet, this account is too limited. Conscious choice can be exercised, at many levels, and change can come through acts of human agency that begin systematically to break the rules (that is, to contest the institutional arrangements) that sustain inequities. This agency might come as much from oppressed groups as from groups among the relatively privileged and powerful who begin to conclude that the perpetuation of these traps no longer meets their interests nor satisfies their views of the world. Indeed, it may well be that many transitions out of inequality traps are a result of the combined agency of groups among both the disadvantaged and societal elites. Indeed, it is rare that social movements themselves *deliver* transitions toward equity. They *demand* them, but they do not design them. They also often lack the political and social networks that would allow them to bring their demands to fruition and—more importantly—consolidate them in new institutional and organizational arrangements. Furthermore, in the absence of some degree of support—overt or covert—from subgroups within societal elites, the likelihood that such mobilization will be repressed by force is also greater.

The experience of land reform in Latin America is illustrative here, because in many respects it constituted a (partial) transition out of long-standing inequality traps. This transition became possible because of convergences and synergies between the agency of groups within new emerging elites and the agency of the rural poor. On the one hand, the 1950s and 1960s began to see increasing levels of organized rural protest, with land invasions and occupations becoming increasingly common in some countries. These protests contested two interlocking dimensions of inequity that had institutionalized inequality for centuries. The first was the concentration of land in large estates; the second was the prominence of labor relationships that involved varying levels of exploitation, from bonded labor to the payment of infrasubsistence wages. At the same time, the slow modernization of Latin American economies had begun to change the sources of actual and potential wealth in society, opening up some scope for industrialization and reducing the relative power of land and landowners. These changes fostered the emergence of new subgroups, whose wealth and status depended less on landholdings and whose accumulation strategies were themselves constrained by the continued existence of rural estates based on feudal labor relations. Political economic change thus began to pitch elite groups against one another, and emerging urban and industrial elites began to see the case for land reform, both as a means of weakening the power base of other parts of the elite and as a vehicle for producing more rural entrepreneurs and better-paid rural laborers, who, in turn, increased the domestic capacity to consume (Lehmann 1978). Finally, a strong intellectual and policy argument circulated among international and some national technocratic elites that—drawing on the writings of the United Nations Economic Commission for Latin America—saw existing agrarian institutions as a severe block to national economic growth (Grindle 2007; Kay 1989).

The surge of land reforms in the 1960s and early 1970s in Latin America can be explained by the coexistence of these three broad currents, each constituting bodies of thought embedded in different types of social agencies: mass protest, elite subgroup maneuvering, and technocratic policy arguments. Mass social protest created a certain political space for institutional reforms, parts of the elite maneuvered in favor of these same reforms, and technocrats were able to provide the basic intellectual arguments and policy frameworks to sustain these reforms and carry them forward. Experiences of land reform elsewhere suggest similar convergences. In China and Vietnam, for example, land reforms were implemented by Communist parties to break powers of traditional village elites, to redistribute wealth, and to enhance political support. In India and postapartheid South Africa, land reforms were envisaged as part of the new democratic governments' efforts to modernize economies while rebalancing political power and strengthening newly emerging social contracts.[23] In all such cases, demands from landless and poor people needed the support of proactive leaders to challenge inequitable structures (albeit with varying success). As suggested by comparisons among states in India, where landownership usually overlaps with caste structure, to the extent that land reforms succeeded, they may have not only (partially) relieved inequality traps but also influenced economic development by encouraging modernizing elites to explore opportunities outside traditional forms of agrarian production.

That said, if elite agency is often a prerequisite for transition, it can also put a brake on this same transition. That is, elites typically favor transitions *up to a certain point*, and then begin to close down the scope for further change. Land reform in Latin America is, again, a case in point. If land reform became possible because a modernizing part of the elite began to see the advantage of freer markets in land and labor, as well as for more productively efficient agriculture, their view rarely stretched as far as wanting reforms that would call into question the more general status of private property in society (Lehmann 1978). Thus, in many cases, land reforms progressed far enough to put an end to bonded labor and massive and inefficient haciendas, but then they stopped. In those few cases where reforms progressed further, after a few years elites organized counterrevolutions (as in the case of Chile in 1973) or countermovements that ultimately undermined any further processes of asset redistribution or further redefinition of institutions governing the control and use of land (as in Peru after 1975 or parts of India today—notably in Bihar—where landed elites continue to resist effective economic control and social emancipation by the landless).

Subgroups among the relatively advantaged and the elites thus have important, determining roles as political agents in these transitions. In some of these roles, they play social actors; at other times, they play representatives of the state. Indeed, in the domain of policy choice, states are typically heterogeneous, and individuals or groups have at least some scope for discretion: the "reformer" is not a figment of the imagination, even if the potential for maneuver is shaped by deeper social and political forces. The role of such reformers can be critical in opening up space for new policies to become possible, just as their role as designers is important in creating both the big ideas and the nuts and bolts of institutional and policy change. Such designs are the linchpin of the relative orderliness and viability of transition. Just as one example, in Mexico, the famous program called PROGRESA (now Oportunidades), which provides transfers to poor people, conditional on school and health center attendance, was an instrument that could help break some dimensions of institutionalized inequalities. It was essentially designed by technocrats using the political space created by the reaction against the corruption and clientelism that characterized the regime of President Carlos Salinas.

The discussion so far has focused on pathways out of institutionalized inequalities that derive primarily from forces within society. But transitions can also be elicited by external forces. The clearest case of this among the chapters is the role of the EU in encouraging Spain's transitions toward equity—particularly in relation to political participation—as a prerequisite to becoming an active member (see chapter 8).[24] In more specific instances, the World Bank is noted for insisting that the government of

Chad earmark oil revenues for more equitable use on priority poverty-reducing expenditures (see chapter 7), though subsequently the government began diverting some of these resources for military expenditure. Indeed, the World Bank ultimately agreed to modify the original agreement to give more resources and discretion to the Chadian government, albeit while still according some priority for poverty-related spending. The implication here is that transitions that depend on external forces can become vulnerable when there is insufficient ownership and political commitment among national or external stakeholders. The more general point is that exogenous, large-scale, or multilateral actors can create incentives for significant institutional change in particular countries—and when the costs of such changes are tied to significant carrots (such as access to new markets or loans), these changes may become more palatable and, thus, more likely.

Of course, externally facilitated shocks need not only foster transitions toward equity; they can just as likely pull in other directions. The military coup in Chile in 1973 received external support and led to the establishment of institutions that reduced equity in political participation and in the distribution of assets and income. Rapid rises in hydrocarbon or mineral prices can also have ambiguous effects. In some cases—Norway, for instance, and contemporary Chile—they can feed into financial mechanisms that favor social investments that enhance equity. In other cases, they can further consolidate the power of authoritarian governments based in inequitable relations of political participation (exhibited in varying degrees in Angola, Nigeria, and Sudan). The lesson, perhaps, is that external shocks can influence transitions, but the ways in which they do so depend greatly on how they interact with internal political and economic processes.

It is important to close this section with a caveat. The fact that transitions toward equity *can* happen does not mean that they *will* happen. Formal institutions (rules and regulations) have a range of organizations whose role is to sustain them, as well as a range of interest groups that want to see them sustained. In those instances, only large-scale social protest—revolution—seems likely to change such institutions in the short term, and even then there is no guarantee that subsequent arrangements will be any more equitable in the medium and long terms. Transition processes are also likely to be accompanied by resistance to change and not infrequently by violence—and it is no accident that violence is part of the stories recounted in this book (chapters 5, 7, and 8). In the face of such resistance, slower, longer-term transitions out of inequality traps seem possible only through sustained building of the organizations and discourses of mass social movements and alliances that stand for different ways of organizing society. As José Antonio Lucero shows in chapter 5, for the case of indigenous peoples in Bolivia and Ecuador, this process can last four to five decades, and the transitions toward greater equity are still far from consolidated or complete.

Furthermore, inequities and inequality traps need not always elicit social protest. Indeed, more often than not, where inequality traps exist, organized protest tends to be either absent or weak. In chapter 4 on Orissa, for instance, Arjan de Haan describes a case in which resistance has remained limited to sporadic protests (and met by hostility from the Indian government). Apparently the interest of certain elites does not lie in the emancipation of the Adivasis, whose social protest, therefore, remains marginalized and ineffective. This example illustrates the importance of understanding why protest emerges in some instances and not others and—perhaps more important still—why, when protest emerges, it assumes the form that it does. Much social protest ultimately appears in ways that are explosive but lack strategy, proposal, or articulation. Chapter 5 is important on this point because Tony Lucero asks specifically why Ecuador's indigenous movement emerged in a way that reflected an important convergence of discourses and interests—and thus a greater ability to channel protest and to effect change. He contrasts the situation in Ecuador with that in Bolivia, where there has arguably been more outright protest against inequality traps of various types, yet this protest has been more dispersed and less creative and has thus had less effect on national institutions (at least until the 2006 election of Evo Morales as president, the institutional effects of which are still too early to assess). In short, inequity does not per se elicit protest, much less protest that is effective.

One reason that protest so often does not emerge may have to do with the very ways in which inequitable institutions are embodied in people's everyday lives as *habitus* (Bourdieu 1977). Such embodied institutions are especially resistant to change, and dissipate any propensity toward exercising political voice about inequities. In chapter 3, Joy Moncrieffe is particularly eloquent on this point. She shows how—and explains why—much of the everyday practice of the Batwa in Uganda serves to reproduce their relative exclusion and the inequitable relationships between them and other social and ethnic groups in that country. The arrangements and taken-for-granted assumptions that sustain their relationship of disadvantage have been so embodied in their ways of being since colonial times that they reproduce them unconsciously and in some sense willingly—a key aspect of an inequality trap. In chapter 4, de Haan notes something similar in India, notwithstanding the existence of explicit government policies to address tribal, caste, and other discrimination. In such circumstances, only intensive and sustained interventions in popular education and psychological support seem to stand any chance of fostering transitions out of these embodied inequality traps. It is no accident, perhaps, that precisely this sort of pedagogical and psychological work accompanied the early stages of Ecuador's indigenous movement.

Introduction to the Chapters

Following this overview, the chapters are organized into two sections. The first section brings together essays that deal, primarily, with pathways through which institutionalized forms of inequality emerge. The essays in the second section focus mainly on real-world paths through which these institutions have been transformed in particular societies and development contexts. Although seven chapters can give only a partial view, the essays in this collection have particular strengths. First, they throw considerable empirical and theoretical detail on the different ways in which inequality traps emerge and change. Second, they demonstrate the distinct and complementary insights that different disciplinary and theoretical perspectives can shed on the nature and emergence of the formal and informal institutions that underlie and sustain these inequalities. Third, they demonstrate the quite distinct ways in which these institutions might begin to unravel—paths that, in some cases, are largely endogenous to particular forms of growth and, in other cases, are clearly forged by particular social actors, be they social movements or policy technocrats.

The chapters in the first section bring together perspectives from an economist (Rachel Sabates-Wheeler), an ethnographically inclined social and political scientist (Joy Moncrieffe), and a sociologist-historian working for a development agency (Arjan de Haan). Together they demonstrate the contributions of these different analytical and disciplinary lenses for understanding how inequalities emerge.

In an essay that is largely theoretically oriented (chapter 2), Sabates-Wheeler addresses the relationship between asset inequality and agricultural growth. She argues that inequality in the distribution of assets—particularly in conditions of market failure—puts a significant brake on agricultural growth. Her larger interest, however, is in the ways in which these inequalities in distribution are themselves produced and sustained by particular sets of institutionalized social relationships. Although her particular interest is in the ways in which gender relationships sustain asset inequalities, her more general argument is that unequal relationships of power, often embodied in particular ideologies (such as patriarchy), produce a range of formal and informal institutions that serve to sustain these inequalities. The less powerful not only have fewer assets but also are disadvantaged in their access to economic and political institutions. As a result, policy tends to be biased, and imperfect markets are made to work to the benefit of the more powerful. The implications for inequality, poverty, and growth are all negative.

Working from institutional economics, Sabates-Wheeler makes claims that have considerable resonance with the arguments made by sociologist Bourdieu (1977, 1984) about the ways in which forms of social and cultural capital are related to and help sustain inequalities in the distribution and control of economic capital. Bourdieu linked these arguments to a theory of social practice in which he argued that many inequalities become embodied in taken-for-granted rules that, consciously or unconsciously, influence forms of behavior.

Although Sabates-Wheeler's arguments appear to have been arrived at independently of Bourdieu, Moncrieffe, reflecting her own disciplinary background, explicitly invokes Bourdieu in her analysis of the ways in which a particular ethnic group, the Batwa, has become systematically disadvantaged in Ugandan society and appears to act in ways that only further consolidate these disadvantages (see chapter 3). Moncrieffe emphasizes the importance of colonial policies and categorizations in the constitution of relationships between social groups (echoing Mamdani 1996), but goes several steps further in exploring how this history is embodied in contemporary practices. Central to her (and Bourdieu's) analysis is the notion of power: "[P]ower relations may become so ingrained that people either accept a condition that they know is unequal or fail to recognize the domination that exists," says Moncrieffe.[25] Put another way, these unequal relationships of power become deposited within peoples, become embodied in them "in the form of lasting dispositions, or trained capacities and structured propensities to think, feel, and act in determinate ways, which then guide them in their creative responses to the constraints and solicitations of their extant milieu" (Wacquant 2005, as cited by Moncrieffe). As Moncrieffe notes, if the relationships and ideologies (the social and cultural capital) that sustain inequality become embodied in how people act and how they think about themselves, addressing inequality is a deeply psychological challenge. Merely redistributing assets or changing rules governing formal institutions will not be enough.

The message from Moncrieffe and Sabates-Wheeler is that tackling inequalities requires more than simply tweaking policy (because relationships of power are themselves embodied in policy and the institutions that govern policy making) or providing training or capacity building (because relationships of power are deeply sedimented in how people think of themselves in relation to others). In his study of Orissa, now India's poorest state, de Haan delivers a similarly less than sanguine message. In chapter 4, he argues that addressing spatial inequalities will require much more than transferring resources to disadvantaged regions: regional disadvantage is produced in relationship to other regions (compare with Massey 1984, 2001). As long as the institutions underlying this relationship are left untouched, not much will change, particularly given that regional inequalities overlap with other social disparities. De Haan highlights the disparities between coastal and other parts of Orissa, disparities that have deep historical roots and that continue to be reinforced through the interplay of economic, political, and sociocultural factors. His analysis highlights the role of policies and institutions related to land and forest access, each of which is crucial to the livelihoods of Adivasis in Orissa. Despite formal institutional reforms, patterns of exploitation have continued to persist, suggesting that human development policies have a limited effect in reducing these broader disparities. Regional and social inequalities overlap and simultaneously permeate the political and administrative realm, ensuring that policy formation does little to address inequality (compare with Sabates-Wheeler's chapter also). In such a context, he argues, policy change (even if it were to happen) would be little more than a paper exercise in the absence of social mobilization demanding pro-equity change.

De Haan's thoughts on social mobilization segue into the second section, where the theme of social mobilization is directly and indirectly present in several of the pathways toward equity charted by the chapters gathered there. The essays in this section explore cases where there is compelling evidence of how enduring relationships of inequality have been broken. In some cases, such changes were a consequence of macrosocietal tendencies themselves related to economic change. In others, the changes have been fought for and won by social movements. In yet others, they have been designed by policy-making technocrats, themselves often taking advantage of windows opened by the reality (or threat) of social protest.

As in the first section, the chapters are written from differing disciplinary perspectives: political science (Michael Ross), political economy (Carles Boix), economics (Armando Barrientos), and ethnographically oriented political studies (Tony Lucero). Again, this combination of perspective demonstrates how different lenses help identify and understand different pathways out of inequality.

The first chapter in this section (chapter 5), Lucero interprets the emergence of the politically important indigenous movements in Bolivia and Ecuador. The literature on these movements has grown over the past decade and a half (Andolina 2003; Bebbington and others 1992; Perreault, Roper, and Wilson 2003; Yashar 1998). In the same tradition, Lucero explicitly explores the extent to which the acquisition of greater political voices for indigenous peoples as manifest in these movements has translated into equity. The chapter is important because, although he is clearly aligned with the metapolitical interests reflected through these movements, Lucero argues that the extent to which movement translates into voice, which then translates into enhanced political equity, depends much on the internal dynamics of movements, as well as on the political opportunity structure created by the context in which these movements emerge and operate. The comparison between Ecuador and Bolivia is useful here, as Lucero suggests that this opportunity structure has led to a relatively more unified movement in Ecuador, as opposed to a movement in Bolivia that is less united, while also displaying elements that are far more contentious and radical. Lucero suggests that, because it is more united, the Ecuadorian movement has been able to gain greater political presence and leverage than the Bolivian movement. The caveat, of course, has to be the recent election of a president in Bolivia whose origins are in a syndicalist wing of the national indigenous movement. It might be argued that this very victory will induce greater unity and convergence within the movement, though only time will tell. Whatever the case, Lucero is clear—as are his two country cases—that the more unified a process of mobilization, the more likely it will translate into institutional changes that foster greater equity in political recognition. However, he is equally clear (following Hall and Patrinos 2005) that this process has not translated into greater economic equity. Poverty continues to be concentrated and persistent among indigenous populations, and two decades of mobilization have seen no change in the overall distribution of economic wealth.

If social mobilization is central to Lucero's analysis of how inequalities based in deeply entrenched racisms are being addressed in the Andes, it also plays more than a cameo role in Armando Barrientos's discussion of the emergence and equity effects of noncontributory pension schemes in Bangladesh, Brazil, and South Africa (see chapter 6). Of all the essays, Barrientos's says the least about how inequalities emerge and become institutionalized, but it says the most about the types of policy instruments that might reduce the poverty-deepening effects of intergenerational inequalities. Noncontributory pension programs are cash transfers made to people on the basis of their age and poverty, rather than on the basis of their contributions to these programs over their life course. Barrientos argues that these programs have made an important contribution to reducing inequality across generations, primarily by offsetting the depth of income poverty (and vulnerability) experienced in old age. A particularly novel contribution of his chapter is that it also traces the emergence of these programs. The most consolidated of these programs have roots in political responses to social mobilization—rural social movements in Brazil and race-based movements in apartheid South Africa. These mobilizations do not explain the forms that these programs have subsequently taken, but they help explain the political conditions that made it possible for reformist technocrats to imagine such programs. Barrientos also lays considerable weight on the steady emergence of broad-based public support as being important in helping technocrats and politicians take these programs to scale. He notes that "natural reservoirs of political support and social contract renewals can explain the expansion of noncontributory pension programs in South Africa and Brazil in the 1990s."

The final two chapters, by Michael Ross and Carles Boix, likewise suggest that mobilization—real or threatened—can play a role in destabilizing inequality traps. However, they also lay considerable weight on the role of policy designers in creating instruments that offset such traps. In rather different ways, each author also suggests that certain aspects of regional and global integration *can* play an important role in this process, and Boix also argues persuasively that the internal dynamics of national economic change can break down the institutions that previously had served to fix relations of inequality.

In chapter 7, Ross deals with the relationships between mineral wealth, equity, and conflict and works from the premise—which he establishes empirically—that countries with significant mineral wealth (as a percentage of national wealth) are particularly prone to conflict. This conflict often emerges because of the ways in which geographies of mineral extraction and of the distribution of its benefits interact with other geographies of inequality and exclusion, which are based on remoteness, inaccessibility, racial difference, and poverty. Also, the propensity for conflict is not only because of inequities in the distribution of mineral wealth, but also it can be because certain minerals, particularly gems, are easier to divert toward the financing of rebel groups. However, given the threat and historical experience of conflict, Ross argues, companies and governments have good reason to pay special attention to ensuring that the distribution of mineral wealth lends itself to the reduction of inequalities and that the processes through which such distribution is governed lend themselves to the reduction of inequities in who participates in defining and monitoring governance processes. In this scenario, questions of policy and institutional design are critical. Design, here, has various dimensions. One dimension—the simplest and perhaps the least important in offsetting conflict, says Ross—is the design of fiscal and other institutional mechanisms to return part of the wealth generated to the areas from which minerals were extracted. Second and far more important is the design of mechanisms that allow ongoing adaptation of these mechanisms such that new local stakeholders (for example, youth becoming adults) can also participate in these governance arrangements and not be excluded from the benefits of mineral extraction, even if they were only infants when the initial accords were established. Third and also vital is the design of mechanisms that ensure that these policies for fostering equity are sustained over time. Here, Ross appears to suggest that international organizations can play an important role, though presumably only in those cases where the mineral development has involved loans from these organizations.

If Ross's analysis is sector specific and ultimately concerned with subnational units, the final empirical chapter is, fittingly, macro in orientation, dealing with processes of national economic and political change over a 70-year period. In chapter 8, Boix analyzes the transitions that have occurred in Spain from the 1930s to the present day—transitions that have been accompanied by significant reductions in inequality. Somewhat in contradistinction to the other essays (except, perhaps, that of Sabates-Wheeler), his focus is less on agency as a source of change (be this the agency of movements or of technocrats) and much more on overall economic exigencies. In essence, he argues that Spain's growth path over time—and particularly in the context of an increasingly solid and integrated EU—simply could not tolerate the continued existence of the institutions that sustained inequality. His analysis begins with the violence and social dislocation of the 1930s in Spain. This protest reflected, he argues, the inability of national institutions to handle and resolve conflicts deriving from disparities in asset (especially land) distribution. These conflicts, together with international political influences, ultimately led to the military coup of 1935 to 1936 and to severe restrictions on participation and social mobilization. This period of authoritarian rule lasted four decades, but over time it also generated seeds of its own transition. National economic growth and increasing investment in education fostered the steady rise of a middle class that came to demand more accountability in society. The presence of the EU also pushed Spain toward increased voice and accountability as it served both as an incentive to change (in order to join the EU) and a certain guarantor against Spain's slipping back into authoritarian rule following Francisco Franco's death in 1975. The subsequent democratic period has seen significant public investment in human development and social insurance programs, as well as generally equitable patterns of growth consistent with broader patterns that have been identified in the relationships between public participation, education, and growth (Lindert 2004).

Boix's chapter is, therefore, a structural and historical analysis more than a discussion of agency. However, agency is not wholly absent in his account. The emerging professionalized middle class, both produced and needed by the new economy, demanded greater equity in access to public institutions and fairness in the distribution of public spending. Just as important in Boix's analysis is the agency of policy technocrats. On the one hand, they are a privileged part of this same middle class, themselves wanting greater voice and equity in society; on the other hand, they had the competency to craft policies that would help deepen the democratizing and redistributive tendencies within the emerging economy of the 1970s and 1980s. Although policies require political economic contexts that favor their emergence, these contexts are not sufficient to design good policy: for this, the agency of competent technocrats is essential.

Boix's chapter serves as a fitting conclusion to the book, because it brings together many themes raised in the preceding chapters: the interactions between social structure and human agency and between political economy and policy; the ways in which inequality traps become fixed; and, finally, the ways in which such traps are reworked and overcome. Its particularly important message is that the emergence and nature of inequalities must be understood in their macro and historical contexts. These contexts go a long way in defining the possibility of transitions out of inequality but do not close out all options—neither for social mobilization (however timid and reformist) nor for policy.

Table 1.1 summarizes points of comparison among the chapters in four domains:

- The types of inequality on which each chapter focuses
- The ways in which each chapter views these inequalities as being important for development
- The mechanisms through which the inequalities are sustained
- The pathways through which these mechanisms and their effects on development have been broken.

The final column notes the essays' primary points of geographic reference. The simple filter of table 1.1 allows the reader to move through the chapters alert to the messages that each conveys on the nature of inequalities, their importance in structuring development trajectories, and the processes through which they have been, and might be, redressed.

As the table makes clear, the essays come from diverse geographic settings and address a range of inequalities. Among them, the essays identify poverty-aggravating, growth-dampening, and democracy-weakening effects of these inequalities. Some explore in more detail the ways in which particular types of inequality—particular those grounded in derogatory categories and prejudicial stereotyping—undermine human dignity and self-confidence. The extent to which these relationships of inequality are resistant to change seems to vary somewhat among the chapters. This variation reflects the type of inequality at stake (age-based inequalities seem less resilient than do, for instance, inequalities grounded in ethnic prejudices) and the political economic context within which the inequalities exist (inequalities seem less subject to change within contexts of authoritarian and repressive rule).

None of the essay's suggests that the inequalities they address are set in stone. Each traces out, to greater or lesser extent, pathways through which they have been, or could be, changed. However, collectively, the chapters convey a clear sense that some inequalities are far more embedded and institutionalized than are others. Those that are less institutionalized (for instance, inequalities between companies and communities or inequalities that disadvantage the elderly) appear more subject to change by well-designed policies and programs. Conversely, inequalities that are embedded in long histories of domination of some social groups by others appear to change under two main scenarios. The first—elaborated most clearly

Table 1.1. Inequalities and Development through the Lenses of the Case Study Chapters

Author	Nature of inequality explored	Why inequalities matter	How inequalities are institutionalized	How inequalities or their effects might be reduced	Primary geographic area of emphasis
Sabates-Wheeler (chapter 2)	Inequalities among social groups—in particular gender groups—that lead such groups to have differential access to productive assets and to social and political institutions	Inequalities in asset distribution can impede rates of agricultural growth. The combination of asset inequality, market failure, and unequal access to resources and institutions not only reproduces patterns of inequality but also can cause persistent poverty. Gendered and ascribed forms of inequality lead to unequal access to resources and also underlie unequal access to political institutions.	Through local relationships of power among land users, in particular through gendered power relations Through ideologies that sustain and naturalize unequal power relationships Through political institutions that exclude the voice of the disadvantaged	Policies can be implemented to deal with market failures (thus improving access to complementary factors of production) and to change the asset distribution. The inefficiency of extreme inequality cannot be cured simply by remedying market failures; other types of public action are required.	Africa and South Asia
Moncrieffe (chapter 3)	Inequalities among ethnic and racial groups based on their ethnic identities and markers	Inequalities that are inherent in the ways in which different groups are categorized lead to systematic imposition of disadvantages on some groups. These inequalities also lead those who are adversely categorized to internalize the same sense of low worth and to act in ways that perpetuate their own inequalities.	Through the exercise of power Through ethnic relationships and colonial and postcolonial institutions and policies that apportioned labels, values, and prejudices to particular ethnic and racial groups and that formalized particular relations of ethnic inequality Through processes of internalization among the poor	Addressing inequality is a deeply psychological challenge. It also implies addressing power relations through education, human rights, and reduction of discrimination. Merely redistributing assets or changing rules governing formal institutions will not be enough. Policy makers should rigorously probe the classifications and labels they adopt, should question assumptions of communities and groups, and should investigate the differing experiences of inequality and poverty that classifications tend to mask and even enforce. Without this disaggregated approach, policies may profit some and exclude others.	Uganda

de Haan (chapter 4)	Regional and spatial inequalities within a country	Regional inequalities constrain the growth potential of disadvantaged regions and contribute to the reproduction of their poverty. Spatial inequalities have particularly negative effects for the poorest of most excluded social groups.	Through other social inequalities in which regional inequalities are grounded and that are particularly resistant to changes Through state and other institutions that the social inequalities have structured and whose workings therefore contribute to the reproduction of these inequalities	Human development policies are insufficient—and perhaps even ineffective—in offsetting spatial inequalities. Social mobilization is essential if institutionalized inequalities are to be offset.	India
Lucero (chapter 5)	Inequalities among ethnic and racial groups based on their ethnic identities and markers	Inequalities that are inherent in the ways in which different groups are categorized lead to systematic exclusion of some groups and thus to unequal access to land, natural resources, services, assets, and political institutions. These same inequalities lead to uneven distribution of wealth and of economic opportunities.	Through interethnic relationships and the everyday practices of racism Through public and other agencies, because identity-based inequalities are built into the ways in which these agencies operate, so that the actions of these agencies go a long way in institutionalizing inequalities in broader sets of relationships	Inequalities can be addressed through the progressive social and political organization of ethnic and race-based groups, through the quality of leadership in these organizations, and through organizational strategies that are well crafted in relation to the existing political opportunity structure. Such mobilization and protest have reduced political inequalities but have not yet reduced economic inequalities.	Bolivia and Ecuador

(*Continued*)

Table 1.1. Inequalities and Development through the Lenses of the Case Study Chapters *(Continued)*

Author	Nature of inequality explored	Why inequalities matter	How inequalities are institutionalized	How inequalities or their effects might be reduced	Primary geographic area of emphasis
Barrientos (chapter 6)	Inequalities among age groups, in particular those inequalities that lead the elderly to have reduced access to income and opportunity	Age-based inequalities contribute to reduced access of old people to services and economic opportunities and thus contribute directly to their poverty proneness and vulnerability. The poverty status of the elderly can affect the poverty status and asset portfolios of the households of which they are a part.	Through categories associated with age and through political institutions in which the elderly and poor lack voice	Noncontributory pension programs can address effects of inequality experienced by the poor and elderly. Social mobilization precedes emergence of such noncontributory programs. Changes in public opinion in favor of such programs provide important support for the emergence of these programs.	Bangladesh, Brazil, and South Africa
Ross (chapter 7)	Inequalities between extractive industry companies and social groups in areas affected by mining that lead some social groups to enjoy reduced access to the fruits of mining Geographic, ethnic, and racial inequalities among social groups within countries	Inequalities of power can lead to uneven access to information about mining and the revenues generated by it. These inequalities can deepen tendencies toward social and political violence. In extreme instances, they can elicit, or strengthen the cause of, militarized and separatist movements.	Through the cultures and practices of national political and mineral development institutions, which cause these institutions to fail to address or foresee such problems Through company cultures, which institutionalize practices that sustain inequalities in access to information and resources	Well-designed programs of information provision, participatory monitoring of mining and revenue transfer programs, and periodic adaptation of program design can reduce inequalities and especially reduce the potential for them to lead to violence. Fiscal transfers to offset some of the economic inequalities fostered by extractive industries are insufficient.	Multiple regions

			Through community-extractive industry conflicts, which are also embedded in broader social inequalities that can further institutionalize local inequalities		
Boix (chapter 8)	Inequalities in access to land, economic opportunity, and political participation	Inequalities in access to land and other assets can fuel civil unrest. Inequalities in political participation can limit the ability of a country to participate in multilateral institutions that would otherwise facilitate economic growth.	Through political and social institutions that are backed up and sustained by practices of authoritarian and military rule and that sustain inequalities in political participation and economic opportunity	International demands are needed for reduced (political) inequality as a precondition for membership of multilateral organizations. Policy technocrats with some room to maneuver can introduce design changes in institutions. Organized middle-class demands for increased access to economic opportunity can elicit change.	Spain

Source: Authors.

by Boix—occurs when large-scale structural changes in economy and society, such as those characterizing Spain in the past three to four decades, provide the basis for institutional transition, including transition in political and decision-making institutions. The second—articulated most clearly by Lucero—occurs when institutionalized inequalities change in the face of organized forms of social mobilization and protest. This scenario, in turn, begs the question of how such protest might emerge among groups so dominated and disadvantaged. However, some of the chapters do shed light on this theme, suggesting that in the early stages such mobilizations typically involve external actors as well as members of the disadvantaged groups themselves. There is an interesting resonance here with a recent collection exploring the conditions under which capability-enhancing development policies emerge and stand the test of time even in the face of opposition (Bebbington and McCourt 2007). That collection also identified the joint importance of social mobilization, insightful and politically canny policy technocrats, and some degree of elite support in fostering "development success," albeit in varying measure depending on the political economic context.

Lessons and Implications

By now, the reader has received some flavor of the content of the subsequent chapters. As summarized in the previous sections, the analytical and policy lessons from the cases in this book indicate the following:

- Beyond any normative commitments, there is often a positive case for being concerned with inequalities: namely, that they can reduce economic growth and obstruct poverty reduction and political participation.
- There is also often evidence of persistent inequality traps, in the sense of both persistent differences across groups over time and self-reinforcing mechanisms for sustaining these differences.
- In some cases, we see a variety of ways in which societies transition, at least partially, out of inequality traps.

The book provides a set of specific examples across sectors and countries to illustrate the importance of understanding the structures and institutionalized behaviors that perpetuate inequality specific to particular settings. Although inequality traps are not inevitable, they are often important, and we need in-depth analysis of the processes involved.

Does the fact that some societies transition out of situations of embedded inequality invalidate the idea of an inequality trap? We suggest not, for two reasons:

- Slow movement out of inequality (not a full trap, but a deep hole, so to speak) should also be a source of real preoccupation.
- Even where an initial position is a self-reinforcing equilibrium, either exogenous influences or internal processes can change the parameters of the equilibrium over time.

In that sense, an equilibrium can be self-reinforcing over the medium term, but over the long term it is *self-undermining* to use the terminology of Greif and Laitin (2004). For example, as Boix's chapter argues, Spain, in the first half of the 20th century, was plausibly in a form of an inequality trap, but there was enough internal dynamism to induce structural transformations in class composition and urban structure to produce different social and political preconditions.

The approach of this book leads to several implications for the design of policy or of concerted institutional change, whether for internal actors (government agencies or social actors) or external actors (development agencies or international civil society groups). We close this introduction with a brief reflection on these implications.

Let us begin with a simple characterization of two polar positions in policy that are common in either explicit or implicit thinking on development and change. At one pole, we find the *disembodied technocrat approach*. Here, policy is designed by well-intentioned leader-technocrats, who seek the optimal approach to pursue some aggregate social welfare function (for example, a distributionally weighted pursuit of a multidimensional set of outcomes, such as pursuit of equal opportunity and avoidance of extreme deprivation). At the other pole is what might be termed the *deep political economy approach*. In this version, policies and institutions are understood as fully endogenous—fully determined by the structure of interests and power—meaning that disinterested observers either do not exist or, at best, can do no more than describe how policies are determined.

The studies in this book take us to a different place from either of these positions. They construct real-world scenarios in which the behavior of all actors is shaped by historically formed inequalities that are crystallized in formal and informal institutions. As sketched in the introduction, these inequalities can have economic, political, and sociocultural features that are typically interlocking. However, at any point in time and setting, there is likely to be some "agency" of actors and some leverage for change in the system. This potential leverage goes beyond the influence of exogenous factors or the provision of more information—the traditional sources of potential change for economists working in this area. These sources are indeed important, but—as the chapters show—other sources of change also exist. The chapters also suggest that it is not possible to generalize as to *what* really matters for change to occur, nor as to *where* points for leverage will exist. Those factors will vary according to each context and need to be assessed by the actors involved. For example, as sketched in table 1.1, in the case of Uganda, any potential transition out of inequality will require changes in the cultural terms of recognition of subordinate groups, as well as associated sociopsychological changes among both subordinate and dominant groups. In post-Franco Spain, sources of leverage were quite distinct: one involved opening up economic competition and reducing the economic market power and consequential political leverage of different banking and industrial interests, and another hinged on the greater legal room for maneuver of unions and the possibilities for intergroup negotiation in a new democratic polity.

Let us, then, suppose that there is an actor with an interest in fostering transition toward a more equitable and more efficient situation (or in the language of an inequality trap model, in fostering a shift to a new, better equilibrium). Such an actor could be a technocrat, a minister, the World Bank, or an internal or external civil society group. What would an analytically coherent approach to policy design be, within the framework of this book?

First, the diagnostic challenge has shifted. Interest in attaining the socially optimal and in showing the costs of the existing situation still remains with regard to economic inefficiency and inequity (including in political participation), but this challenge needs to be integrated with characterization of the causal forces sustaining the existing situation. This characterization would involve analyzing how the current economic, political, and sociocultural equilibrium is determined, where it is self-reinforcing, where potential points of leverage exist, and which conditions can lead to a new and better equilibrium. We are not proposing such characterization as a new form of politically and socially informed general equilibrium analysis. It is rather a prism for approaching complex real-world problems. It is likely to require a mix of diagnostic tools, and interpretations from different disciplines will be useful, depending on the case. Sometimes a game theoretic analysis will be most useful, sometimes a political institutional treatment, and at others a sociocultural treatment.

Second, policy change needs to be designed and implemented in ways that will shift—or initiate shifts in—the political equilibrium. For external agents (such as the World Bank, a foundation, or a international civil society organization), such change also requires (a) attention to why an external "intervention" could make a difference, given the initial equilibrium, and (b) sensitivity to the possibility that the intervention might also be captured, leading to new distortions, a reconstitution of the equilibrium, and so forth.

We can envisage a variety of policy approaches—technocratic and political, top-down and bottom-up. For example:

- Under some political conditions, an actor (internal or external) can support policy choices designed by internal technocratic groups that are explicitly seeking to break inequality traps. Support for conditional cash transfers in many Latin American countries and pro-poor budgeting processes in many poor countries are possible illustrations.[26]
- Processes also exist that can change the political equilibrium, either by supporting social mobilization or reworking the rules governing political participation. An example might be the contrast between the changes in equilibrium that derived from long-term social mobilization in Ecuador and an initially top-down change in local political rules with the Law of Popular Participation (*Participación Popular*) in Bolivia.
- Finally, information itself can, indeed, play a role, and some internal and external actors have agency in this regard. A range of options is available: (a) providing information to disadvantaged groups on what is possible, (b) using information to increase accountability and reduce patronage in those contexts in which an external assessment can influence domestic debates, or (c) sharing knowledge with technocratic and professional groups on experiences of policy change elsewhere.

Where does this leave the debate over conditionality? It needs to be subsumed within the broader diagnostic frame suggested here. Telling countries what to do typically fails or makes things worse, but under some conditions, external incentives or reference groups can make a difference (consider both the incentive and reference effects of Europe on Spain). External agents may be able to support internal change agents, and shifting the external contract can potentially, at the margin, shift the internal social contract in good as well as bad ways.

Finally, even for powerful development actors, some humility is in order. The contexts described in this book are inherently complex, and it will be hard to predict dynamic effects of change at points in a stable (or indeed an unstable) unequal equilibrium. This uncertainty is another reason for an approach based on experimentation and continued adjustment. We hope that the essays collected here will contribute to policy-relevant debates and real experimentation to discover ways of reducing inequality that also support the expansion of the welfare of all groups in societies.

Notes

1. Although global inequalities—and the arguments over whether they are growing or declining—are, of course, important, an analysis of their causes and dynamics would be a different project focusing more on the implications for global development policy and multilateral arrangements. On global inequalities, see, for instance, Milanovic (2005), UNDP (2005), and World Bank (2006).
2. It may be the case, however, that some or all of the chapter authors hold this opinion.
3. This notion is captured in the idea of *Durable Inequality* (Tilly 1998), which we discuss later in this chapter.
4. See the *World Development Report 2006* for a far more exhaustive exploration of this line of argument (World Bank 2006).
5. See Bourdieu (1977, 1984). Different social sciences tend to apply different definitions of inequality. Sociologists and anthropologists often pay more attention to interpersonal relations and the ways in which inequality is perceived; other social scientists tend to approach inequality as a phenomenon defined through its measurement. See Eyben and Lovett (2004) and chapter 3 in this volume.
6. This reality is present even in the United States, as Alex Keyssar's (2000) study of the history and present of voting so vividly shows.
7. See Sen (1997). Research in India has shown that poor people in remote regions (for example, Orissa) do participate in elections, but their knowledge and access to media can be severely restricted. This arguably reduces the likelihood of effective exercise of voice (Kumar 2001). See also chapter 4 of this volume.
8. Rajan and Zingales (2003) argue that capitalism needs to be "saved from the capitalists" and highlight the importance of financial systems that support entry of new firms.
9. More generally, Lindert notes that the political transitions associated with democratization in rich countries had a substantial causative influence on

the decisions by the polity to expand a range of social programs (not only education, but also pensions, health and social insurance, and so forth), thereby addressing underlying problems of market failure in a way that reduced inequities.

10. The reaction of the Chinese government to rising inequalities and its goal of establishing a "harmonious society" highlight a conscious response to such challenge.
11. Roemer (1998: 25) refers to "a certain kind of success or advantage" as a general description of dimensions that we may be concerned with. Note that these dimensions may be of intrinsic value, may have an instrumental influence on welfare, or both, to use Sen's terminology.
12. See Bourguignon, Ferreira, and Walton (2007) for a discussion of the formal definition; the treatment here draws on their article.
13. Stephen Smith (2005) describes 12 kinds of poverty traps. See http://www.theglobalist.com/storyid.aspx?StoryId=5032.
14. The phrase "economic, political, and sociocultural" is, of course, itself a shorthand for the many processes at work, but it is often a convenient way of categorizing.
15. This discussion is a simple account of Galor and Zeira (1993), an early contribution to the variety of theoretical discussions in economics on links between inequality and the growth process.
16. World Bank (2006: chapter 6) provides a survey of these different causal chains.
17. This simple idea is formally analyzed in Bénabou (2000) and Ferreira (2001).
18. On the legal and political distinction between tribes and races, see Mamdani (2001). Appadurai (2006) also illustrates how social difference can give rise to conflict.
19. A similar theme was central to the classic—and much debated—anthropological notion of a "culture" or "cycle" of poverty (Lewis 1959) and more recently in debates about the effect of welfare states and notions of an underclass (Murray 1984).
20. This conception builds both from Bourdieu's (1977, 1984) notion of *habitus* as mediating structure and practice (see also chapter 3 of this volume) and from Giddens's (1979) concept of structuration.
21. Indeed, Bourguignon, Ferreira, and Walton (2007) demonstrate formally how an inequality trap is but one of various possible equilibriums, including others in which the trap does not exist.
22. Peru had to concede on this point.
23. Unlike India, where land reform did weaken the power of the rural elites in many states, in South Africa, the goal of redistributing 30 percent of land owned by white farmers by 2015 is still far from accomplished, although a start has been made.

24. A similar phenomenon appears to be at work in more recent EU accession countries, which were required to realign their laws, policies, and institutions along lines prescribed by the EU. Johannsen and Pedersen (2008) describe the effect of Europeanization on the development of participatory values and dense networks between the state and civil society in transitional countries.
25. The argument echoes Kuran's (2004) idea of "preference falsification," in which groups with less voice further suppress their own voice and sense of their own preferences in the process of conforming with dominant power relationships that work to their disadvantage.
26. With respect to conditional cash transfers—which are now strongly supported by the World Bank—it is perhaps noteworthy that both Bolsa Escola in Brazil and PROGRESA in Mexico were initially designed as entirely domestic initiatives.

References

Acemoglu, D., S. Johnson, and J. Robinson. 2001. "The Colonial Origins of Comparative Development: An Empirical Investigation." *American Economic Review* 91 (5): 1369–401.

Andolina, R. 2003. "The Sovereign and Its Shadow: Constituent Assembly and Indigenous Movement in Ecuador." *Journal of Latin American Studies* 35 (4): 721–50.

Appadurai, A. 2004. "The Capacity to Aspire: Culture and the Terms of Recognition." In *Culture and Public Action*, ed. V. Rao and M. Walton, 59–84. Stanford: CA: Stanford University Press.

———. 2006. *Fear of Small Numbers: An Essay on the Geography of Anger*. Durham, NC: Duke University Press.

Bebbington A., H. Carrasco, L. Peralvo, G. Ramón, V. H. Torres, and J. Trujillo. 1992. *Los actores de una decada ganada: tribus, comunas y campesinos en la modernidad*. Quito: Comunidec/Abya-Yala.

Bebbington, A., and W. McCourt, eds. 2007. *Development Success: Statecraft in the South*. London: Palgrave Macmillan.

Bénabou, R. 2000. "Unequal Societies: Income Distribution and the Social Contract." *American Economic Review* 90 (1): 96–129.

Bourdieu, P. 1977. *Outline of a Theory of Practice*. Cambridge, U.K.: Cambridge University Press.

———. 1984. *Distinction: A Social Critique of the Judgement of Taste*. Cambridge, MA: Harvard University Press.

Bourguignon, F., F. Ferreira, and M. Walton. 2007. "Equity, Efficiency, and Inequality Traps: A Research Agenda?" *Journal of Economic Inequality* 5 (2): 235–56.

Christiaensen, L., and S. Dercon. 2007. "Consumption Risk, Technology Adoption, and Poverty Traps: Evidence from Ethiopia," Policy Research Working Paper 4257, World Bank, Washington, DC.

Coudouel, A., A. Dani, and S. Paternostro, eds. 2006. *Poverty and Social Impact Analysis of Reforms: Lessons and Examples from Implementation*. Washington, DC: World Bank.

Demombynes, G., and B. Özler. 2005. "Crime and Local Inequality in South Africa." *Journal of Development Economics* 76 (2): 265–92.

Engerman, S. L., and K. Sokoloff. 2002. "Factor Endowments, Inequality, and Paths of Development among New World Economies." *Economia* 3 (1): 41–88.

Eyben, R. 2005. "World Development Report 2006: Equity and Development—Response." Institute of Development Studies, University of Sussex, Brighton, U.K. http://www.ids.ac.uk/ids/news/Archive2005/EybenWDRresponse.pdf.

Eyben, R., and J. Lovett. 2004. *Political and Social Inequality: A Review*. Brighton, U.K.: Institute for Development Studies, University of Sussex. http://www.ids.ac.uk/ids/bookshop/db/db20.pdf.

Ferreira, F. H. G. 2001. "Education for the Masses? The Interaction between Wealth, Educational, and Political Inequalities." *Economics of Transition* 9 (2): 533–52.

Galor, O., and J. Zeira. 1993. "Income Distribution and Macroeconomics." *Review of Economic Studies* 60 (1): 35–52.

Giddens, A. 1979. *Central Problems in Social Theory*. London: Macmillan.

Gough, I. 2005. "European Welfare States: Explanations and Lessons for Developing Countries." Paper presented at the conference on New Frontiers of Social Policy, Arusha, Tanzania, December 12–15. http://www.worldbank.org/socialpolicy.

Greif, A., and D. Laitin. 2004. "A Theory of Endogenous Institutional Change." *American Political Science Review* 98 (4): 633–52.

Grindle, M. 2007. "When Good Policies Go Bad, Then What? Dislodging Exhausted Industrial and Education Policies in Latin America." In *Development Success: Statecraft in the South*, ed. A. Bebbington and W. McCourt, 79–104. London: Palgrave Macmillan.

Haber, S. 2004. "Political Institutions and Economic Development: Evidence from the Banking Systems of the United States and Mexico." Paper presented at the conference on Economics, Political Institutions, and Financial Markets II: Institutional Theory and Evidence from Europe, the United States, and Latin America, Palo Alto, CA, February 5.

Hall, G., and H. Patrinos. 2005. *Indigenous Peoples, Poverty, and Human Development in Latin America*. New York: Palgrave Macmillan.

Johannsen, L., and K. H. Pedersen. 2008. "The Responsive State: Openness and Inclusion in the Policy Process." In *Inclusive States: Social Policy and Structural Inequalities*, ed. A. Dani and A. de Haan. Washington, DC: World Bank.

Kay, C. 1989. *Latin American Theories of Underdevelopment*. London: Macmillan.

Keyssar, A. 2000. *The Right to Vote: The Contested History of Democracy in the United States*. New York: Basic Books.

Kraay, A., and C. E. Raddatz. 2005. "Poverty Traps, Aid, and Growth." Policy Research Working Paper 3631, World Bank, Washington, DC.

Kumar, S. 2001. "Study of Political Systems and Voting Behaviour of the Poor in Orissa." Report prepared for the U.K. Department of International Development, New Delhi.

Kuran, T. 2004. "Cultural Obstacles to Economic Development: Not Necessarily Real, Often Transitory." In *Culture and Public Action*, ed. V. Rao and M. Walton, 115–37. Stanford, CA: Stanford University Press.

Lehmann, D. 1978. "The Death of Land Reform: A Polemic." *World Development* 6 (3): 339–45.

Lewis, O. 1959. *Five Families: Mexican Case Studies in the Culture of Poverty*. New York: Basic Books.

Lindert, P. H. 2003. "Voice and Growth: Was Churchill Right?" *Journal of Economic History* 63 (2): 315–50.

———. 2004. *Growing Public: Social Spending and Economics Growth since the Eighteenth Century*. Cambridge, U.K.: Cambridge University Press.

Mamdani, M. 1996. *Citizen and Subject: Contemporary Africa and the Legacy of Late Colonialism*. Princeton, NJ: Princeton University Press.

———. 2001. *When Victims Become Killers: Colonialism, Nativism, and Genocide in Rwanda*. Princeton, NJ: Princeton University Press.

———. 2005. "Political Identity, Citizenship, and Ethnicity in Post-Colonial Africa." Paper presented at the Conference on New Frontiers of Social Policy, Arusha, Tanzania, December 12–15. http://siteresources.worldbank.org/INTRANETSOCIALDEVELOPMENT/Resources/revisedMamdani.pdf.

Massey, D. 1984. *Spatial Divisions of Labor: Social Structures and the Geography of Production*. New York: Methuen.

———. 2001. "The Progress in Human Geography Lecture, Geography on the Agenda." *Progress in Human Geography* 25 (1): 5–17.

McKenzie, D., and C. Woodruff. 2003. "Do Entry Costs Provide an Empirical Basis for Poverty Traps? Evidence from Mexican Microenterprises." BREAD Working Paper 20, Bureau for Research in Economic Analysis of Development, Harvard University, Cambridge, MA. http://www.cid.harvard.edu/bread/papers/working/020.pdf.

Milanovic, B. 2005. *Worlds Apart: Measuring International and Global Inequality*. Princeton, NJ: Princeton University Press.

Murray, C. 1984. *Losing Ground: American Social Policy, 1950–1980*. New York: Basic Books.

Perreault, T., M. Roper, and P. Wilson. 2003. "Introduction: Indigenous Transformational Movements in Contemporary Latin America." *Latin American Perspectives* 30 (1): 5–22.

Rajan, R. G., and L. Zingales. 2003. *Saving Capitalism from the Capitalists: Unleashing the Power of Financial Markets to Create Wealth and Spread Opportunity*. New York: Crown Business.

Rao, V. 2006. "On 'Inequality Traps' and Development Policy." *Development Outreach* 8 (1). http://www1.worldbank.org/devoutreach/february06/article.asp?id=350.

Roemer, J. E. 1998. *Equality of Opportunity*. Cambridge, MA: Harvard University Press.

Sachs, J. D. 2005. *The End of Poverty: Economic Possibilities for Our Time*. New York: Penguin Press.

Sen, A. 1997. *On Economic Inequality*. Oxford, U.K.: Clarendon Press.

———. 1999. *Development as Freedom*. New York: Anchor Books.

Smith, S. 2005. *Ending Global Poverty: A Guide to What Works*. New York: Palgrave Macmillan.

Tilly, C. 1998. *Durable Inequality*. Berkeley: University of California Press.

UNDP (United Nations Development Programme). 2005. *Human Development Report 2005*. New York: Oxford University Press.

Wacquant, L. 2005. "Habitus." In *International Encyclopedia of Economic Sociology*, ed. J. Becket and M. Zafiovski, 315–19. London: Routledge.

World Bank. 2006. *Equity and Development: World Development Report 2006*. Washington, DC: World Bank.

Yashar, D. 1998. "Contesting Citizenship in Latin America: Indigenous Movements and Democracy in Latin America." *Comparative Politics* 31 (1): 23–42.

PART II

INEQUALITY TRAPS AND INSTITUTIONALIZED INEQUITIES

CHAPTER 2

Asset Inequality and Agricultural Growth: How Are Patterns of Asset Inequality Established and Reproduced?

Rachel Sabates-Wheeler

How does differential access to productive assets in the agricultural sector, at various levels (regional, community, and household), affect inequalities in agricultural outcomes in terms of productivity and poverty? Reflecting the interdisciplinary orientation of this volume, this chapter's approach is to draw on diverse literatures that rarely talk to one another in order to develop a more complete understanding of how different types of inequality reinforce each other, thereby creating long-term structural inequality traps that affect equity and undermine growth.

This chapter's guiding framework is a series of challenging questions that Kanbur (2004) posed to the "inequality and growth" research community. He highlights that most discussion on policy levers for responding to inequality is removed from academic research on inequality.[1] That is, in the economic analysis of growth and inequality, little or no attention is afforded to the following question: what policies and institutions are causally related to equitable growth? Kanbur argues that the intersection of analytical and policy debates fails to answer that question. He also notes that researchers have relied too much on outcome variables, such as changes in per capita income and inequality, to the neglect of policy variables that enable such output factors to be causally related. Although this chapter will not attempt to fully answer Kanbur's question, it will explore relationships between outcome indicators (such as land and livestock distribution, gendered rights to assets, locational inequalities, and agricultural productivity) and policies, processes, and institutions.

The dominant discourse on agricultural productivity and distribution has been largely technocratic, focusing on input-output relationships, which are defined and measured with a yardstick specific to the discipline of economics. The chapter reviews certain strands of this literature. It then complements this mainstream literature with a less well-known body of work that emphasizes the social and political constructions and reproductions of a variety of inequalities to offer a more complete understanding of the interactions between technical and structural inequalities. The chapter first reviews the international literature on inequality and agricultural productivity.[2] One strand focuses on the technical relationships between asset distribution and agricultural growth (for instance, the large bodies of literature on the inverse relationship of farm-size productivity, economies of scale, and land tenure reform), and the chapter offers a brief summary of the literature's main conclusions. The policy implications coming from this literature emphasize a redistributive role for the state. Other research focuses less on distributional outcomes and more on asset accumulation and wealth differentials. In the literature, an increasing number of econometric and dynamic simulation studies aim to explore the links between risk, wealth accumulation, market failures, and production. This work shows that a combination of asset inequality and market failures has a negative effect on growth rather than asset inequality per se. The chapter reviews this work and the implications that the results have for policy.

Within the economics literature, agricultural productivity is typically equated with production efficiency, and inequality is defined in terms of wealth differentials (outcomes), where *wealth* can refer to income or a range of different assets.[3] Less well cited, at least in relation to agricultural productivity, is research that steps outside conventional understandings of inequality. The second part of this chapter reviews that research. The literature differentiates among inequalities in ownership and control, access, and empowerment. It necessarily investigates the processes and institutions through which inequality is established and reproduced and the impacts that this inequality has on production. Importantly, this work shows that it is not simply market failures that lead to unproductive outcomes, but also structural inequalities that frustrate different groups' ability to access institutions. This lack of access has implications for growth as well as equality. When policy makers focus their attention on equity (defined as fairness) of opportunities in agriculture, they necessarily confront a political question of the tradeoff between equity and efficiency outcomes with respect to agricultural growth.

By drawing on diverse literatures and discourses on inequality, this chapter reaches these conclusions:

- There are multiple pathways by which inequalities in asset holdings can lead to forgone agricultural productivity.
- When the pathways involve missing markets, the likelihood and magnitude of asset inequality generating forgone productivity is increased, although context is key.
- Structural inequalities (gender, ethnicity, and stigma) matter substantially in generating asset inequality.
- The difficulty of changing structural inequalities through conventional policy or private collective action means that poverty supported by those types of inequalities tends to be more persistent unless new forms of public action can be introduced.

Inequality and Growth at the Macrolevel: What Do We Know?

As is standard practice in economics, inequality (as well as poverty and growth) is defined through income, or the monetary value of consumption. The distribution of "real" income across individuals allows economists to calculate mean incomes and changes in mean incomes over time, and these calculations provide measurements of income growth and income poverty. This distribution also enables economists to establish measurements of dispersion within the distribution, which provides the basis for measurements of inequality, such as the Gini coefficient or the Wolfson index (a measure of polarization). In this vein, Kanbur (2004: 3) outlines some mechanical relationships between growth, inequality, and poverty:

> First, holding inequality constant, an increase in per capita income (growth) reduces poverty. Second, holding per capita income constant, an increase in inequality increases poverty. If the objective is to reduce poverty, then obviously growth is a plus for poverty reduction and inequality is a minus.

However, if growth is not viewed in isolation and is accompanied by increased inequality, then the net effect on poverty is ambiguous because it will depend on the relative magnitude of the two opposing forces. Although David Dollar and Aart Kraay (2002) claim to refute this issue, they show only that the expected growth of the mean income of a country's poorest quintile is best predicted by the growth of its mean income overall. This result does not hold much weight because of the wide consensus that there is no empirical relationship between growth and inequality (using countries as the unit of observation). The famous Kuznets curve was refuted more than a decade ago, and there is growing evidence that this relationship does not hold (Deininger and Squire 1996). These studies imply that there is no feedback from growth to equality in early economic development, although there is some evidence of the positive feedback from equality to growth (Aghion 1998; Alesina and Rodrik 1994).[4]

It is important to distinguish between the effect of income inequality on growth and the effect of asset inequality on growth. Evidence indicates that the empirical link between asset inequality and growth is strong and negative. For instance, there is wide consensus that, with equality of access to education, initial land distribution feeds back to growth and to operated farmland (Birdsall and Londoño 1997; Birdsall, Ross, and Sabot 1995; Deininger and Squire 1998).

Birdsall and Londoño (1997) suggest that the effect of income inequality on growth reflects differences in an element of economic structure, namely, the access of different groups to productive assets. Notably, their econometric work shows that any region-specific effect of income inequality disappears once asset inequality is accounted for (this result is in relation to Latin America and the Caribbean). Overall, their findings show that an unequal distribution of assets—especially human capital and land—affects growth overall and the income growth of the poor disproportionately. A more equal distribution of assets increases the income of the poor, raises aggregate growth, and reduces poverty—but as this evidence suggests, better income distribution, without asset redistribution, will not accelerate income growth.

Recent ways of thinking about inequality in the microeconomics literature, especially in agricultural economics, complement the macroeconomic studies. The literature focuses on inequality in terms of wealth differentials, where *wealth* can refer to income or to a range of different assets (such as land, labor, livestock, and capital). Those microstudies will be discussed in greater detail later in this chapter. The implications of a focus on asset rather than income distribution necessarily broadens how policy responds to those inequalities, such that we need to address more explicitly the institutional factors that inhibit equitable outcomes. The studies suggest that land and property rights reform, enhanced access to legal systems and credit, and fair competition are each crucial to unlocking opportunities for the poor and to eliminating hidden privileges.

Complementarities between Asset Inequality and Productivity

Given the cross-country regression results, this chapter focuses on asset (rather than income) inequality in the agricultural sector, with a particular focus on land and other natural assets, such as livestock, and on financial assets, such as credit. Although disciplines other than economics contribute to our understanding of inequality, this chapter will, for clarity, reserve the term *inequality* for distributional outcomes that reflect processes of asset acquisition or accumulation.[5] The ways in which people acquire, maintain, or accumulate assets are discussed in terms of equity (access, control, and empowerment). That is, considerations of equity determine the production of distributional outcomes.

In an extensive discussion of the empirical evidence on farm size and transaction costs, Eastwood, Lipton, and Newell (forthcoming) ask these two questions: what patterns can be discerned in the distribution of farm sizes across countries and across time, and how do factors such as development, environment and behavior interact to affect farm size? One of their conclusions is that factor-specific transaction costs will play a part in determining the efficient distribution of land. For instance, in a labor-intensive, capital-scarce environment, small and relatively equal farm sizes are rational for farm production (controlling for land quality and farm size), owing to the high labor-monitoring costs associated with hired labor. As capital becomes less scarce and the relative price of labor to capital increases, larger farms become more efficient. The prices of capital and labor are important in determining efficient farm-size distributions. The efficient size of the family farm will also depend on available technology. In general then, transaction costs associated with labor are lower on small farms, and transaction costs associated with capital are lower on large farms. So highly labor-intensive agriculture leads to big transaction cost advantages in small farms, and highly capital-intensive agriculture leads to big transaction cost advantages on large farms. Therefore, factor-specific transaction costs lead to a switch in optimal farm size, which has implications for inequality. In capital-intensive agriculture, larger holdings are necessary on pure productivity grounds because of transaction costs in capital markets. This cost, of course, may have negative poverty implications, because people who leave the land may not be able to find employment in nonfarm sectors. Smaller farmers could theoretically achieve this change through land pooling, cooperation, or rental markets (Sabates-Wheeler 2002, forthcoming). Of course, those results are tempered by history, and actual farm size can be frozen or influenced by colonization or land reform.

Country-specific farm-size distributions confirm this analysis, with the United Kingdom and North America being characterized by large, capital-intensive farms and with South and East Asia and much of Sub-Saharan Africa being characterized by small, labor-intensive farms. Exceptions to this general observation, such as land distributions in Latin America and southern (and some of eastern) Africa, provide interesting accounts of how past policy choices or land tenure changes create distortions in the efficient use of labor and capital. Evidence indicates that land reform in some of those countries, if the distribution is made less unequal, will have positive outcomes on equity and efficiency. Further complicating that analysis, the efficiency with which agents can use assets will depend on access to other inputs, markets, and factors (for instance, access to infrastructure and inputs, access to agricultural research, and the way in which property rights and water are distributed and accessed).

The work by Eastwood, Lipton, and Newell (forthcoming) suggests that the relationship between farm-size distribution and productivity is mediated by factors such as the history of policy choices, geographic and land quality, factor-specific transaction costs, and factor prices. To assume that there is an instrumental relationship between inequality and productivity presupposes that inequality is affected by an exogenous change in the productivity level. However, evidence shows that inequality is not, in general, pushed one way or the other by such a change. Institutions are imbued with power relations that reproduce inequalities. This sense of path dependency and asset inequality is discussed in the following section. A hypothesis linking distribution to productivity also ignores questions about why certain patterns of inequality exist, as well as how and why these patterns are sustained. It is relatively straightforward to show through the example of land and farm size that inequalities in asset holdings do not necessarily reflect efficiency or productivity differentials but rather show constraints to access and opportunities embodied in institutions and history (Binswanger, Deininger, and Feder 1995; Eastwood, Kirsten, and Lipton 2006). The next section will continue to review the economics literature to show empirically the dynamic and path-dependent effects of asset inequality on agricultural growth.

Asset and Endowment Dependency and Enduring Inequality

An increasing number of econometric and dynamic simulation studies aim to explore the links between risk, wealth accumulation, and production under multiple market failures. The common hypothesis is that when informational asymmetries constrain financial markets and when labor markets are weak and labor effort is unobservable, productivity can be affected by the distribution of endowments. As Carter and Zimmerman (2000) point out, the idea that an economy may exhibit endowment sensitivity has roots in the writings of Chayanov (1925 [1966]), who argued "that farm households with different endowments of productive resources would use those resources in different proportions, with different productivities" (Carter and Zimmerman 2000: 266). Irrespective of distortions in the market, the family farming theory predicts some variation in equilibrium farm size (for given prices, technology, and household reservation utility) arising from variations in household size and agroecological factors. However, it can be shown that beyond household size and land quality factors, enduring heterogeneity can exist across households because of the endowment of working capital, which will generate a corresponding heterogeneity in farm size and dynamics, which depend, in that case, on the pattern of capital accumulation. Eswaran and Kotwal's (1986) well-known research illustrates how the combination of assets and transaction costs helps to explain the differential income strategy that each class of household follows, and the research also predicts patterns of social and behavioral differentiation. Eswaran and Kotwal (1986)—as well as other researchers, such as Bardhan (1984)—show that when labor effort is not contractible and access to capital required for financing a production process is wealth dependent, behavioral differentiation emerges along an endowment continuum. Eswaran and Kotwal (1986) also show that in a situation of multiple-market failures, the economy in equilibrium is endowment-sensitive. Under this scenario, output and efficiency can be enhanced by egalitarian redistributions of land. However, more recent work by Bardhan, Bowles, and Gintis (1998) shows that over a certain range, economic efficiency and productivity decrease as the distribution of wealth and productive assets become less equal.

The single-period models described here have much to say about static relationships between asset access, wealth-dependent behavior, and efficiency, but they say little about the persistence of inequality over time or its productivity implications. A growing body of literature addresses those dynamic concerns (Banerjee and Newman 1993; Barham, Takasaki, and Coomes 2000; Carter and Zimmerman 2000; Dercon 1998; Zimmerman and Carter 2003). As Barham, Takasaki, and Coomes (2000) observe, this research leads to two hypotheses concerning inequality and persistent poverty. The first hypothesis, known as the *static asset dependency hypothesis*, states that, in a context of market failures, agents make production and investment decisions in accordance with the assets they hold. For example, under credit or information constraints, poorer landowners are limited in their capacity to make productive, wealth-enhancing investments to their land, which restricts their ability to accumulate assets at the same rate as wealthier landowners. The second hypothesis is an *endowment dependency hypothesis*, which posits that asset accumulation primarily depends on initial endowments; hence, poorer agents cannot attain the accumulation paths of richer agents. For instance, constraints in capital or insurance markets over time interact with poorer landholders' inability to accumulate assets, which leads to poverty traps and livelihood vulnerability. In other words, movements out of poverty appear to be largely determined by the fate of initial endowments.

Dercon (1998) uses survey data from rural Tanzania to look at wealth accumulation in the form of cattle in an agropastoral farming environment. Cattle ownership is very unequal in the survey site, with only one-third of poorer households owning any cattle, compared with 58 percent in the richer tercile (Dercon 1998: 8). The data indicate that (a) differences in welfare levels appear correlated to differences in cattle holdings; (b) despite high returns to cattle, only half the sample owned cattle; and (c) those who did not own cattle specialized relatively more often in off-farm activities and relatively less often in low-return, low-risk crops. Using a model of activity choice and asset accumulation to explain this phenomenon, Dercon illustrates that the theory of comparative advantage cannot be used to explain the latter point. The explanation instead is that missing markets prevent some households from taking up certain activities. Credit constraints combined with risk mean that low-endowment households find it difficult to accumulate enough assets to build up their cattle stocks. In keeping with Eswaran and Kotwal (1986), Dercon points out that if investments are needed to enter certain activities (such as cattle farming), then credit constraints may mean that poorer people are unable to engage in the activity, while richer households can—a difference that leads to increasing inequality over time. Furthermore, this situation has a negative effect on aggregate agricultural productivity because households are unable to specialize in those activities in which they have a comparative advantage. In other words, asset inequalities are likely to reflect imperfect markets, not inherent differences in productivity. People who do not own cattle would find it profitable to enter into cattle rearing, but they face binding constraints on entry into the activity. This persistent inequality is likely to be exacerbated over time as the comparative advantage farmers may have had at one time is lost because they lose their skills, their assets are stripped, or they move into off-farm activities.

Dercon (1998) explains that, given the Tanzanian context, land and labor constraints are unlikely to be important barriers to cattle farming; rather credit constraints pose the largest problem. Only richer households can enter the asset accumulation paths. Over time, this involvement exacerbates the inequality between rich and poor. Poorer households, which typically face more risk and income volatility, are less likely to invest in "high-risk" cattle. Furthermore, they will deplete cattle to cope with income shortfalls. Instead, poorer households will enter into low-risk, low-return activities, such as low-return crops, smaller livestock, and off-farm activities. Dercon (1998: 15) writes, "Households with a limited asset buffer for consumption therefore have an incentive to allocate relatively more labor to these activities, even if the result means lower income [and lower productivity]." Over time, a divergence in total earnings between rich and poor will occur. Dercon's work suggests that, in an intertemporal framework, assets may perform a similar role to credit, such that higher initial asset holdings at t_1 imply that households will allocate more labor to risky activities (because higher assets provide a buffer to negative consumption shocks) than households with low asset holdings. Dercon (1998: 25) concludes, "Therefore, household income is determined by initial endowments of land and labor and accumulated asset holdings in the form of cattle."

The evidence presented by Dercon suggests that the differentials in asset (cattle) holdings and activities between rich and poor households do not reflect individual productivity differentials. Entry into cattle farming was mainly explained by endowments in the form of male labor and land, which probably reflect the earning capacity of the household. Because the wealth differentials observed are not explained by comparative advantage, they are likely to have a negative effect on agricultural productivity and growth in the aggregate.

Barham, Takasaki, and Coomes (2000) test the endowment dependency hypothesis through an empirical study of multiple asset accumulation and activity choice among peasant households. Considering more than one asset activity, they explore possible cross-effects arising across different assets (that is, households could use one asset to advance their activities in another). Furthermore, they are interested in distinguishing the effects of endowment from those of time or life cycle. They ask, is time a dominant constraint to asset accumulation such that in the longer term poorer agents cannot move to the asset mix obtained by richer ones? If yes, then endowment dependency is only a short- to medium-term phenomenon. However, endowment dependency may dominate in the long run and, thus, will have different implications for the processes of moving toward more egalitarian asset distributions and efficiency.

Takasaki, Barham, and Coomes (2001) use data from an Amazonian tropical rain forest environment, where high biodiversity sustains a wide range of livelihood options. They have chosen seven villages for the study: five mainly agricultural villages and two mainly fishing villages. Their analysis focuses on two major activities (agriculture and fishing) and their associated physical assets (agricultural land and fishing capital—specifically, fishing nets). The two activities provide different labor opportunities for asset-poor households, mainly because land is scarce and fishing capital is reproducible. The econometric results indicate that life-cycle factors play an important role in asset accumulation. Takasaki, Barham, and Coomes (2001)

> highlight the distinctive asset accumulation dynamics existing among peasant households, contingent on asset types and local environmental endowments. They find that land accumulation in agricultural villages is mainly determined by endowments, whereas in fishing villages land accumulation for land is associated with both endowment and life-cycle factors. Capital accumulation in agricultural villages depends on life-cycle factors; however, in fishing villages the accumulation of capital does not depend on endowment or life-cycle factors.

Importantly, this work shows that different asset types can offset initial endowment differentials by influencing the "fate" of poor households. In other words, persistent inequality depends very much on the nature of different assets, a household's asset portfolio, and other economic and labor opportunities. In fishing villages, however, capital-poor fishers work with richer fishers and, thus, improve their incomes and assets. They have the opportunity to do so because of the nature of the activity and the reproducibility of the asset.

A crucial lesson from Takasaki, Barham, and Coomes's work is that any policy addressing the links between inequality, persistent poverty, and agriculture must pay careful consideration to various asset portfolios of both households and communities and must consider the nature of the asset activity itself.

Work by Greenwald and Stiglitz (1986, as cited in Dercon 2003) suggests that market failures (uncertainty, externalities, and so forth) imply that interventions can be made that will make many people better off without making others worse off. This implication is particularly relevant for asset-poor groups, because market failures reduce the efficiency with which they can use their assets. Interventions focused on these groups would, therefore, lead to efficiency outcomes for them and could increase overall efficiency. If so, the efficiency-equity tradeoff that is predicted by the standard welfare theorems of economics would not occur. As revealed in the farm-size literature, the extent and scale of an efficiency-equity tradeoff at the aggregate level is contingent on factor-specific transaction costs and factor prices. However, if one is interested primarily in equity and agricultural productivity, increasing equality in access to and control of assets will have a positive effect on the productivity of those groups that are most affected by the market failure.

An important caveat to that last point is that, political constraints aside, "in densely populated areas such as Ethiopia or Bangladesh, redistribution or related policies such as tenure security is unlikely to achieve much more than a dent in poverty levels" (Dercon 2003: 7). In Ethiopia, technological complements to land use are clearly needed to make much progress. In Bangladesh, initial land inequality is rather small, so fewer output gains are to be expected from moving toward some optimum size in between very big and very small. Furthermore, redistributing land and other assets more equally in regions that have a very low resource base and are densely populated is unlikely to have a significant effect on productivity and poverty reduction. Dercon (2003: 9) makes this point in relation to externalities related to the specific local context (for example, low local endowments in terms of public goods, common property resources, and private asset holdings): "[I]f growth requires a certain threshold of local endowments to take off, then poorly endowed areas may well find it hard to escape poverty." Evidence from China in the 1980s indicates that community characteristics affect the living standards of otherwise identical households. Geographic poverty traps result from initial community characteristics. Unlocking the growth potential of asset-poor areas or regions is likely to be related to a variety of policy responses, such as irrigation provision or health and education provision. Clearly, any program of asset redistribution or distribution will depend on the context. It is not always straightforward to change asset distributions because of political constraints and so forth. Furthermore, dealing with market failures turns out to be very complicated.

The literature shows that the combination of asset inequality and market failures (credit, information, missing markets, and so on) has a negative impact on growth, because agents (especially poor people) are unable to act efficiently under the circumstances. The policy implications from this literature are either to deal with the market failures (thereby improving access to complementary factors of production) or to change the asset distribution. However, it is important to remember that, even in the absence of market failures, constraints to opportunities may exist that would lead to inequalities. For instance, in very unequal societies, big farmers may enjoy privileged access to capital because of law, custom, or prejudice. There may be thresholds below which the poor do not or cannot enter certain key markets, even if those markets work perfectly. If so, the inefficiency of extreme inequality cannot be cured simply by remedying market failures. So inequality that creates extreme poverty excludes the poor from competing in certain markets, sometimes with no market failure.

Incorporation of the Social and Political: Insights from Gendered Analysis of Inequality

The theoretical frameworks and empirical studies reviewed earlier represent the dominant academic and policy discourse around (a) agricultural growth and productivity and (b) inequality. Technical relationships between farm size, land reform, and inequality are often discussed with respect to national policy levers and the existence of markets. Studies looking at asset and endowment accumulation are typically microeconomic studies that focus on household behavior and draw implications for persistent poverty and structural changes in the economy. Other studies move inside the household to discuss the implications of individuals' differential access to inputs and assets and the implications of these differences for productivity.[6]

For instance, the influential findings of Udry and others (1995) on the production effects of intrahousehold gender relations coalesce with those of Smith and Chavas (1999) and Wold (1997) to emphasize the importance of the distribution of resources within the household, rather than between households, and the implications of this distribution for efficiency outcomes. As Whitehead (2001: 13) notes,

> [T]he argument is that allocative inefficiency and depressed production arise in African agriculture because the separation of resource streams implies individual, not shared, incentives with respect to crop outputs. Women's low level of inputs on smaller parcels of land can be seen as a measure of their weak bargaining position, while men act to protect and maximize "their own" production.[7]

In the studies, the central factor affecting outcomes is a division of labor by gender in production and reproduction, which typically results in crops and farming tasks that are largely men's or women's work. The gendered division of labor is fed through the separate and gendered resource streams of households to give a different structure of incentives (and constraints) to men and women. The various studies consider specific features of the intrahousehold relations that might affect men's and women's response to price signals, using existing datasets to explore the implications of those aspects of gender relations for agricultural production. The aspects thus fall into the category of gender-specific constraints as outlined by Kabeer and Subrahmanian (1997). Gender-specific constraints on household livelihood activities apply to either women or men by virtue of their gender. As far as women are concerned, some of those constraints reflect their biological role in reproduction and their social role in caring for children and the family.

Although such studies move the mainstream literature into the household and, thus, draw attention to structural inequalities that are otherwise ignored within household-level studies, they are similar to mainstream economic work in that they still say little or nothing about the social and political institutions that reproduce differential outcomes. Furthermore, the literature remains largely focused on outcomes, in the sense that it is interested in demonstrating the difference in productivity outcomes and in supply response for men and women. Moreover, such studies focus on a limited set of gender-specific constraints (biological roles in reproduction and social roles in caring). Other gender-specific constraints reflect differences in the norms, values, and customs that make up local constructions of masculinity and femininity. Those constraints include restrictions on women's movement in the public domain and taboos against women using certain forms of technology (such as the plow, weaving loom, or potter's wheel). Men too face social constraints that militate against their taking up certain "feminine" occupations or undertaking certain feminine tasks. As Whitehead (2001: 11) points out,

> In Sub-Saharan Africa, gender-specific constraints include not only the respective roles of men and women in reproduction and domestic work, but also in the division of labor in agriculture—assigning men and women to specific crops or specific tasks.[8]

In the conclusions of the study by Udry and others (1995), brief mention is made of the "extra-environmental parameters" that affect the bargaining process—and, thus, the resource distribution—within the household. Those parameters include demographic, legal, and other macroeconomic conditions external to the household, such as "sex ratios in marriage markets, laws and conventions regarding divorce, the ability of women to return to their natal homes, and prohibitions on women working outside the home" (Udry and others 1995: 419). Furthermore, Udry and others (1995: 420) move on to make the point that "the credibility of guaranteed access [to resources] is the heart of the matter."[9] In other words, unless people have credible access to resources, policy intervention or changes in resource provision will stimulate a limited supply response. Although this analysis is very useful, especially as a critique of mainstream economic models, it only scratches the surface of the nature of inequality and the processes by which various individuals and groups are able to equitably access institutions or to obtain sufficient trust in institutions to lead to a productivity response. For instance, what determines credible access to resources, and how do people get this access?

Bina Agarwal's (1997) work addresses many of the gaps identified in the earlier studies. She views access to resources such as land as both subject to and determining the bargaining power of individuals in the household. She argues that bargaining by individuals, though often unspoken, accounts for the allocation of resources and tasks within the household. The power of this bargaining, in turn, depends on control of resources—most often arable land—and access to common resources. The inequities in landholdings and other resources, along with social perceptions and norms against women (including inheritance rights) and women's self-perceptions, are important factors behind the low bargaining power of women, thereby leading to greater inequities in resource and task distributions within the household. Agarwal argues for strengthening women's fallback positions to increase their voice in the home, which can, in turn, lead to increased land rights and to fewer inequities in landholdings within the household. Agarwal (2000) also stresses that women's participation is essential to gender equitable distributional outcomes. That participation depends on rules, norms, perceptions, and personal endowments, as well as household endowments and attributes. Those rules, norms, perceptions, and endowments determine the extent to which women are included or excluded from decision-making bodies. Furthermore, the extent to which there is gender equity in cost sharing (such as share of work and responsibilities) depends on social norms governing the gendered division of labor, while equity in benefits sharing is contingent on rules and norms, perceptions about deservedness, and—more important—personal and household attributes and endowments. A reduction in the gender bias embedded in those factors would depend on women's bargaining power within the state, the community, and the family.

Less well cited with respect to agricultural productivity is research that steps outside conventional understandings of inequality (Whitehead 2001; Whitehead with Kabeer 2001). This literature, much of which has been inspired by a feminist critique of mainstream microeconomic studies, differentiates between inequalities in ownership and control, inequalities in access, and inequalities in empowerment. The studies necessarily investigate the processes and institutions whereby inequality (or equity) is established and reproduced, and they examine the impacts that inequality has on production through changing production relationships. Recent work moves away from visualizing inequality in terms of outcomes and segmented spheres (that is, rural and urban, male and female, landed and landless). Rather, it focuses on how institutions mediate access to resources (land, capital, and credit) and the effect that mediation has on agricultural productivity. The great advantage of this work over other studies is that it enables an investigation into the interaction of inequalities with policy choices and the implementation of policy choices. Findings from these studies highlight the importance of institutions for managing equity for growth and inequality. The richness of much of this literature allows us to see how the interaction of inequality and policy perpetuate different modes or paths of development.

Rather than focus on inequality in outcomes (the primary concern of microeconomic writing), sociological approaches emphasize inequities in processes and opportunities. Eyben and Lovett (2004: vii), for instance, understand inequality as "the condition, process, and experience of unequal power relations that constrain individuals, communities, and even wider groups, such as nation states, from the same freedoms that are enjoyed by those with whom they are in a position of subordinate relationship." Such a conceptualization enables us to focus on the social and political issues in the creation and recreation of inequality and to explore the ways in which categories of class, gender, and race lead to differences in access to resources, in processes of exclusion and inclusion, and in processes of oppression and domination. This concern for process would, for instance, make evident the importance of institutions in the formation and functioning of markets and in any explanation of the segmented nature of market organizations and their rules and norms.[10] It would also demonstrate how gender-based constraints on output lie not only in intrahousehold relations but also in the inadequacies of public policy, especially those relating to "the terms and conditions on which women have access to, and control over, land and how well served they are by markets" (Eyben and Lovett 2004: 1343). Thus, strengthening marketing structures to ease women's access and to improve the terms of women's participation is critical for sustaining a supply response from women-managed crops (Sida 1996; UWONET 1995; Wold 1997).

More important for this chapter's particular concern with gendered inequalities, an emphasis on institutions takes analysis beyond the notion of "gender-specific" constraints. Indeed, authors such as Kabeer and Subramanian (1997) refer instead to gender-intensified constraints that reflect gender inequalities in opportunities and resources. Such constraints are gender intensified because, while inequalities in opportunities and resources may reflect factors such as class, poverty, ethnicity, and location, they tend to be exacerbated by gender. Gender-intensified constraints reflect the asymmetrical distribution of material resources between women and men within the household. Such asymmetries sometimes reflect the ascribed norms of the community (for instance, customary laws governing inheritance or access to common property resources). However, even when they result from decisions made at the household level, such decisions often reflect responses to ascribed forms of disadvantage rather than expressions of individual discrimination. As a result, regions where women are denied economic opportunities often tend to be characterized by gender-biased investments in the well-being, health, and education of members (Kabeer and Subrahmanian 1997; Whitehead 2001).

The notions of gender-specific and gender-intensified constraints can be equally well applied to other categories of people or groups that face structural disadvantages, such as the extreme poor, various ethnic groups, and geographically remote groups. Inequalities in resource access for various groups represent ascribed forms of disadvantage and are exacerbated and reproduced because of a variety of cultural, political, and economic factors. In chapter 3, Joy Moncrieffe elaborates in much more detail on this theme of ascribed forms of disadvantage.

Other forms of disadvantage reflect biases, preconceptions, and misinformation on the part of those who are external to the household and community and have the power to allocate resources in ways that counter or exacerbate custom-based forms of discrimination. These biases are imposed forms of disadvantage because they generally reflect the informal reconstitution of cultural norms and beliefs within the institutions, as well as the personal prejudices and misconceptions of individual actors, rather than an aspect of their formalized rules. Kabeer and Subrahmanian (1997) include a whole range of disadvantages that are the effect of public policy, such as credit, agricultural extension, and land tenure reform.

The more process-based, institutional accounts of inequality not only go beyond microeconomic approaches, but also attack them directly. For example—continuing with gender—Whitehead (see Whitehead 2001; Whitehead with Kabeer 2001; Whitehead with Tsikata 2003) has discredited many of the commonly held simplistic assumptions about separate gendered spheres of activity within agriculture, such as those of Udry and others (1995). Notably, Whitehead's work moves away from analysis of intrahousehold models to study how institutions mediate gendered access to resources (land, capital, and credit) and how that arbitration has an effect on agricultural productivity. Responding to the claim by Winters (2000) that it is difficult to build gender into trade and poverty models, Whitehead (2001) provides a gendered account of the effects of trade liberalization on poverty in African countries. She concentrates on economies dominated by low-productivity agriculture in which personally produced food is an important output, and she seeks to understand the structural issues that lie behind gender disadvantages in economic well-being:

> I go beyond a focus on the structure and dynamics of household relations as the main locus where economic processes affect men and women differently. Two particular economic institutions—the markets for agricultural

> inputs and outputs and rural labor markets—are examined closely for the extent to which, as bearers of gender themselves, they intensify or impose unequal gender relations and gender differences. (Whitehead 2001: 3)[11]

Whitehead agrees with Gita Sen (1999), who asserts that we "need to move beyond the critical assumption that gender power relations at the local level are embedded in conjugal intra-household relations alone. The structures of power that women confront at the local level operate not only within the home, but also in the terrain of communities, local markets, and local government officials" (G. Sen 1999, as quoted in Whitehead 2001: 8). Like Grown, Elson, and Cagatay (2000), Whitehead understands gender as "a category of social and economic differentiation that influences the division of labor and the distribution of work income, wealth, productivity of inputs, and economic behavior of agents" (Grown, Elson, and Cagatay 2000: 1148).

Inequality in Access to Institutions and Poverty

In a major research study on inequality in Latin America and the Caribbean, de Ferranti and others (2004) argue that, to counteract long traditions of inequality, societies need to, among other things, undertake deep reforms of political, social, and economic institutions. De Ferranti and others focus on the historical roots of inequality and the processes by which inequality gets reproduced—what they refer to as the "burden of history." That is, observed distributional outcomes (wages, labor supply, and access to services) are the reflection of a history that shows a "lifelong process of accumulation of experiences, human capital, preferences, and constraints" (de Ferranti and others 2004: 86). Although the economic literature presented in this chapter certainly acknowledges the importance of history and path dependency in the reproduction of inequality and in the institutional failures reflected in market failures and transaction costs, little attention is paid to the actual processes that perpetuate and exacerbate the institutional rigidities and market failures. Furthermore, the economic literature is unable to convincingly account for the establishment and persistence of inequalities when markets are working relatively well (for instance, ascribed inequalities because of gender or ethnicity). Yet, as de Ferranti and others (2004) note, regardless of market structure, political power in any society is unequally distributed, and this inequality of empowerment (or agency) is closely intertwined with economic distributional outcomes and institutional forms.

Institutions play a particularly important role in establishing and reproducing inequalities. As Grown, Elson, and Cagatay (2000: 1148) state, "They embody social norms which shape the behavior of individuals about what it is appropriate to want and to do." Goetz and Jenkins (2005) argue that the inequities and deprivations endured by the poor may be exacerbated by failures in the "institutions designed to [ensure] public probity and regulate economic activity." Those "accountability failures" can play out in four spheres, affecting equity in access to the following:

- Livelihood opportunities, particularly land and fair wages
- Capability enhancing services, particularly education and health care
- Decent environment (clean air and unpolluted water)
- Physical security, particularly freedom from abuse.

Such accountability failures arise from corruption, but also through reproduction of elite biases (Goetz and Jenkins 2005). The absence of mechanisms to listen to the needs of the poor, combined with a failure to account for their performance by erecting unintended obstacles to those who might demand answers, help to maintain the cycle of inequities as perpetuated through institutions. In addition, "biases embedded in the formal remits, operating procedures, and informal practices of accountability institutions can be racist and sexist as well as anti-poor" (Goetz and Jenkins 2005: chapter 3). Also, political capture of oversight bodies, the judiciary, and the police often make matters worse for the poor.

Those accountability failures have a disproportionately negative effect on the poor, primarily because the poor have fewer options for alternative services than do wealthier groups, they have lower capacities to raise their voices against corruption, and any payments that they make illicitly represent a greater proportion out of their meager incomes. Institutions often have access barriers, which can discriminate between and exclude certain categories of poor people, such as ethnic minorities and women. Furthermore, the different effects of programs, such as dams, on men and women are often overlooked, thereby creating further gender inequities.

The insights from this work are relevant in understanding equity of opportunities to assets and services in the agricultural sector. Provision of land access and ownership alone will not enhance output if access to complementary factor markets is denied or exclusionary. Without complementary addressing of multiple rural factor markets, market forces will be biased toward larger farms and wealthier agents. In other words, policy needs to focus on a range of markets simultaneously. Lack of access to one asset will affect access rights to other assets and services. For instance, Evers and Walters (2000) show that the lack of property rights to land in Sub-Saharan Africa affects women's access to other resources, such as credit, water rights, and grazing rights. Also, because ownership of land is linked to labor relations, "control over land also confers on men property rights over women's labor" (Evers and Walters 2000: 1342).[12]

Policy Levers and Inequality

This chapter has reviewed and sought points of contact among many bodies of literature that help to throw light on the relationships between inequality and agricultural growth. The literature on farm size and agricultural growth indicates that transaction costs, factor scarcities, and factor prices are crucial in explaining various distributions of landholdings and, thus, have implications for inequalities in farm-size distributions in different contexts. Whether the results of unequal farm-size distributions are growth enhancing, growth neutral, or growth reducing depends significantly on context-specific factors, the history of policy choices, and institutions. The literature on asset and endowment dependency highlights the ways in which economic inequality reproduces itself over time and can lead to poverty traps and asset thresholds that need to be reached if poor people are to move out of poverty. Asset redistribution and market failure correction are the main policy implications emerging from this work.

The feminist literature and gendered analysis of inequality lends itself well to thinking about inequalities among all types of groups, including groups based on ethnicity, age, labor relations, and landownership. Importantly, it complements the recent critique by Kanbur (2004) of the growth and inequality literature. This critique highlights the need to focus on policy variables that enable output factors (such as income equality and more equal access to resources) to be causally related. Although this body of feminist literature dealing with growth and inequality is relatively small, it can broaden our understanding of the processes and institutions that link inequality and productivity. Rather than unidirectional causalities, it points to a complex system in which inequality affects growth, which, in turn, reinforces processes that exacerbate and reproduce inequalities.

The crucial point concerning the relationship between asset inequality and agricultural growth is that it is mediated by the causes of inequality and poverty as they relate to access to assets and a range of institutions that govern agriculture (land markets, labor markets, credit, extension, water, and so on) and opportunities that complement productive use of assets and institutions. This access and opportunity is obviously moderated by the history of policy choices and interventions specific to each context.

A lesson that emerges from all those studies is that agricultural productivity is related to access to resources: land, labor, capital, and increasingly water. The majority of studies (both economic and other) acknowledge that asset distributions in most countries do not reflect comparative advantages or true relative productivity between individuals and groups. Therefore, agricultural productivity is compromised. The difference between the bodies of literature reviewed in this chapter is the level of attention that they give to how those distributions are created and reproduced. As a result, the policy implications of the studies turn out to be divergent. Some studies are interested primarily in establishing whether there is a link between productivity and inequality, whereas others are more interested in the processes that determine this link.

Four main conclusions emerge from this literature review:

- *Inequality does not necessarily reduce productivity or growth.* Relationships between asset inequality and productivity must be understood in the context of constrained markets, factor prices, and factor scarcities. The components imply that simple, general links between asset inequality and productivity are not useful. Efficient distribution of assets in any context will depend largely on an understanding of the issues and complementary factor markets for any one asset being investigated. It will also depend on how equality is measured. In the case of land, is it equality of land per capita, per family worker, or per household? Is it equality of land in efficiency units? Or is it some other unit of measurement? Similar questions apply to labor, machinery, and other assets.
- *Inequality reproduces inequality because of economic reasons.* Asset and endowment dependency are phenomena related to transaction costs and market failures. They lead to path-dependent, inefficient distributions of assets and to poverty traps. These cycles of asset and

endowment dependency can be remedied in part by redistributing assets or eliminating constraints in markets.
- *The causes of inequality are also political and social.* Inequality is not just a result of market imperfections and economic factors. Its causes are political and social by nature, thus reflecting a combination of historical choices, unequal opportunities and access, inequalities in empowerment, unequal power relations, exclusion, oppression, and domination. Those types of structural inequalities highlight the endogenous nature of inequality. Thus, inequality breeds inequality not just because of economic reasons, but also because of exclusionary practices, differential access to institutions, and the reproduction of power relations in society.
- *The combination of asset inequality, market failure, and unequal access to resources and institutions not only reproduces patterns of inequality, but also can cause persistent poverty.* This result occurs because the combination of those factors leads to differential productivity between the asset rich and the asset poor. Although the implication for increasing asset inequality over time has ambiguous implications for absolute poverty, it is likely that relative poverty and subjective poverty will increase over time.

There are multiple pathways by which inequalities in asset holdings can lead to forgone agricultural productivity. When those pathways involve missing markets, the likelihood and magnitude of asset inequality generating forgone productivity is increased, although context is key. Furthermore, structural inequalities (gender, ethnicity, and stigma) matter substantially in generating asset inequality. To make matters worse, the difficulty of changing structural inequalities through conventional policy or private collective action means that poverty supported by those types of inequalities tends to be more persistent, unless new forms of public action can be introduced.

Notes

1. This observation is true in general, but the discussion of the impact of different land policies seems to be an exception. For example, Hayami and Rutten (1985) show that tenancy reform without land reform, while designed to reduce inequality, is normally incompatible with incentives and cannot provide a lever to do so. They note that landlords instead expel tenants and resume

direct cultivation, thereby raising farm size and, hence, for transaction cost reasons, replacing labor by capital and cutting employment.

2. This chapter will not address productivity and efficiency measurements directly because of the paucity of studies that link productivity (in allocative and technical efficiency terms) to inequality. Instead, it will review studies that link agricultural growth to inequality.
3. Efficiency can be allocative or technical, where farm productivity is defined by a range of physical factors of production, such as land, machinery, labor, irrigation, and livestock.
4. Inequality is seen to contribute to social inequality and political unrest, and, in turn, it affects people's capacity to contribute to sustained economic growth.
5. Although economists tend to view the terms *equality* and *equity* as definitionally distinct (the latter term being reserved for the realm of welfare economics and public finance theory), once one begins to think of the causes of inequality as more than simply distributions, but also as the processes that create distributions, then conceptualizations of *inequality* and *equity* become less demarcated.
6. These studies have been reviewed by Whitehead (2001) from which this account is drawn.
7. This quotation has been taken with permission from Whitehead (2001).
8. This quotation has been taken with permission from Whitehead (2001).
9. This observation relates to Amartya Sen's (1990) points about exit options for the wife (partly cooperative games).
10. See Goetz (1995) and Harris-White (1998) for a discussion of this example in relation to gender.
11. This quotation has been taken with permission from Whitehead (2001).
12. Warner and Campbell (2000) make this point: "One of the most oppressive economic institutions in Africa is male centered inheritance/control of land" (Beneria 1982: 11).

References

Agarwal, B. 1997. "Bargaining and Gender Relations: Within and Beyond the Household." Discussion Paper 27, International Food Policy Research Institute, Washington, DC.

———. 2000. "Group Functioning and Community Forestry in South Asia: A Gender Analysis and Conceptual Framework." Working Paper 172, World Institute for Development Economics Research, Helsinki.

Aghion, P. 1998. "Inequality and Economic Growth." In *Growth, Inequality, and Globalisation: Theory, History, and Policy*, ed. P. Aghion and J. G. Williamson. Cambridge, U.K.: Cambridge University Press.

Alesina, A., and D. Rodrik. 1994. "Distributive Politics and Economic Growth." *Quarterly Journal of Economics* 109 (2): 465–90.

Banerjee, D., and N. Newman. 1993. "Occupational Choice and the Process of Development." *Journal of Political Economy* 101 (2): 274–98.

Bardhan, P. K. 1984. *Land, Labor, and Rural Poverty: Essays in Development Economics*. New York: Columbia University Press.

Bardhan, P. K., S. Bowles, and H. Gintis. 1998. "Wealth Inequality, Wealth Constraints, and Economic Performance." In *Handbook of Income Distribution*, ed. A. Atkinson and F. Bourguignon. Amsterdam: North-Holland.

Barham, B. L., Y. Takasaki, and O. T. Coomes. 2000. "Are Endowments Fate? An Econometric Analysis of Multiple Asset Accumulation in a Biodiverse Environment." Research paper presented at the Second Annual Global Development Network Conference, Tokyo, Japan, December 10–13.

Beneria, L. 1982. *Women in Development: The Sexual Division of Labour in Rural Societies*. New York: Praeger.

Binswanger, H. P., K. Deininger, and G. Feder. 1995. "Power, Distortions, Revolt, and Reform in Agricultural Land Relations." In *Handbook of Development Economics*, vol. 3, ed. J. Behrman and T. N. Srinavasan. Amsterdam: Elsevier Science Publishers.

Birdsall, N., and J. L. Londoño. 1997. "Asset Inequality Matters: An Assessment of the World Bank's Approach to Poverty Reduction." *American Economic Review* 87 (2): 32–37.

Birdsall, N., D. Ross, and R. Sabot. 1995. "Inequality and Growth Reconsidered: Lessons from East Asia." *World Bank Economic Review* 9 (3): 477–508.

Carter, M. R., and F. J. Zimmerman. 2000. "The Dynamic Cost and Persistence of Asset Inequality in an Agrarian Economy." *Journal of Development Economics* 63 (2): 265–302.

Chayanov, A. V. 1925 [1966]. *The Theory of Peasant Farm Organization*. Homewood, IL: Irwin.

de Ferranti, D., G. Perry, F. Ferreira, and M. Walton. 2004. *Inequality in Latin America: Breaking with History?* Washington, DC: World Bank.

Deininger, K., and L. Squire. 1996. "Measuring Income Inequality: A New Data-Base." *World Bank Economic Review* 10 (3): 565–91.

———. 1998. "New Ways of Looking at Old Issues: Inequality and Growth." *Journal of Development Economics* 57 (2): 259–87.

Dercon, S. 1998. "Wealth, Risk, and Activity Choice: Cattle in Western Tanzania." *Journal of Development Economics* 55 (1): 1–42.

———. 2003. "The Microeconomics of Poverty and Inequality: The Equity-Efficiency Trade-off Revisited." *Poverty, Inequality, and Growth: Proceedings of the AFD-EUDN Conference, 2003*. Paris: Agence Française de Développement.

Dollar, D. and A. Kraay. 2002. "Growth Is Good for the Poor." *Journal of Economic Growth* 7 (3): 195–225.

Eastwood, R., J. Kirsten, and M. Lipton. 2006. "Premature Deagriculturalisation? Land Inequality and Rural Dependency in Limpopo Province, South Africa." *Journal of Development Studies* 42 (8): 1325–49.

Eastwood, R., M. Lipton, and A. Newell. Forthcoming. "Farm Size." In *Handbook of Agricultural Economics, Vol. 4: Agricultural Development—Farm Policies and Regional Development*, ed. R. Evenson and P. Pingali, chapter 5. Amsterdam: North-Holland.

Eswaran, M., and A. Kotwal. 1986. "Access to Capital and Agrarian Production Organisation." *Economic Journal* 96 (382): 482–98.

Evers, B., and B. Walters. 2000. "Extra-Household Factors and Women Farmers' Supply Response in Sub-Saharan Africa." *World Development* 28 (7): 1341–45.

Eyben, R., and J. Lovett. 2004. *Political and Social Inequality: A Review*. Brighton, U.K.: Institute of Development Studies, University of Sussex. http://www.ids.ac.uk/ids/bookshop/db/db20.pdf.

Goetz, A. M. 1995. "Macro-Meso-Micro Linkages: Understanding Gendered Institutional Structures and Practices." Paper prepared for the SAGA (Structural Adjustment and Gender in Africa) workshop on Gender and Economic Reform in Africa, Ottawa, October 1–3.

Goetz, A. M., and Jenkins, R. 2005. *Reinventing Accountability: Making Democracy Work for Human Development*. London: Palgrave

Greenwald, B. and J. Stiglitz. 1986. "Externalities in Economies with Imperfect Information and Incomplete Markets." *Quarterly Journal of Economics* 101 (2): 229–64.

Grown, C., D. Elson, and N. Cagatay. 2000. "Introduction to Special Issue on Growth, Trade, Finance, and Gender Inequality." *World Development* 28 (7): 1145–56.

Harris-White, B. 1998. "Female and Male Grain Marketing Systems: Analytical and Policy Issues for West Africa and India." In *Feminist Visions of Development: Gender Analysis and Policy*, ed. C. Jackson and R. Pearson, 189–213. London and New York: Routledge.

Hayami, Y., and V. W. Rutten. 1985. *Agricultural Development and International Perspective*. 2nd ed. Baltimore, MD: Johns Hopkins Press.

Kabeer, N., and R. Subrahmanian. 1997. *Institutions, Relations, and Outcomes: Methodologies for Planning and Case Studies from the Indian Context*. Delhi: Kali for Women Publishers.

Kanbur, R. 2004. "Growth, Inequality, and Poverty: Some Hard Questions." Paper prepared for the State of the World Conference, Princeton Institute for International and Regional Studies, Princeton University, Princeton, NJ, February 13–14.

Sabates-Wheeler, R. 2002. "Farm Strategy, Self-Selection, and Productivity: Can Small Farming Groups Offer Production Benefits to Farmers in Contemporary Post-socialist Romania?" *World Development* 30 (10): 1737–53.

———. Forthcoming. "Safety in Small Numbers: Local Strategies for Survival and Growth in Romania and the Kyrgyz Republic." *Journal of Development Studies* 43 (8).

Sen, A. 1990. "Gender and Cooperative Conflicts." In *Persistent Inequalities: Women and World Development*, ed. I. Tinker. New York: Oxford University Press.

Sen, G. 1999. "Engendering Poverty Alleviation: Challenges and Opportunities." *Development and Change* 30 (3): 685–92.

Sida (Swedish International Development Cooperation Authority). 1996. *Uganda: Country Gender Profile*. Stockholm: Department for East and West Africa and Department for Policy and Legal Issues.

Smith, L. C., and J.-P. Chavas. 1999. "Supply Response of West African Agricultural Households: Implications of Intrahousehold Preference Heterogeneity." FCND Discussion Paper 69, International Food Policy Research Institute, Washington, DC.

Takasaki, Y., B. L. Barham, and O. T. Coomes. 2001. "Amazonian Peasants, Rain Forest Use, and Income Generation: The Role of Wealth and Geographical Factors." *Society and Natural Resources* 14 (4): 291–308.

Udry, C., J. Hoddinott, H. Alderman, and L. Haddad. 1995. "Gender Differentials in Farm Productivity: Implications for Household Efficiency and Agricultural Policy." *Food Policy* 20 (5): 407–23.

UWONET (Uganda Women's Network). 1995. *Women and Structural Adjustment: A Case Study of Arua District, Uganda*. Kampala: UWONET.

Warner, J. M., and D. A. Campbell. 2000. "Supply Response in an Agrarian Economy with Non-symmetric Gender Relations." *World Development* 28 (7): 1327–40.

Whitehead, A. 2001. "Trade, Trade Liberalisation, and Rural Poverty in Low-Income Africa: A Gendered Account." Background paper for *Least Developed Countries Report 2000*, United Nations Conference on Trade and Development, Geneva.

Whitehead, A. with N. Kabeer. 2001. "From Uncertainty to Risk: Poverty, Growth, and Gender in the Rural African Context." Working Paper 134, Institute of Development Studies, Brighton, U.K.

Whitehead, A. with Dzodzi Tsikata. 2003. "Policy Discourses on Women's Land Rights in Sub-Saharan Africa: The Implications of the Return to the Customary." *Journal of Agrarian Change* 3 (1–2): 67–112.

Winters, L. A. 2000. "Trade, Trade Policy, and Poverty: What Are the Links?" Background study for *World Development Report* 2000/01, World Bank, Washington, DC.

Wold, B. K. 1997. "Supply Response in a Gender-Perspective: The Case of Structural Adjustment in Zambia." Statistics Norway, Oslo.

Zimmerman, F. J., and M. R. Carter. 2003. "Asset Smoothing, Consumption Smoothing, and the Reproduction of Inequality under Risk and Subsistence Constraints." *Journal of Development Economics* 71 (2): 233–60.

Suggested Readings

Barham, B. L., S. Boucher, and M. R. Carter. 1996. "Credit Constraints, Credit Unions, and Small-Scale Producers in Guatemala." *World Development* 24 (5): 793–806.

Berry, R. A., and W. R. Cline. 1979. *Agrarian Structure and Productivity in Developing Countries*. Baltimore, MD: Johns Hopkins University Press.

Binswanger H., and J. McIntyre. 1987. "Behavioral and Material Determinants of Production Relations in Land Abundant Tropical Agriculture." *Economic Development and Cultural Change* 36 (1): 75–99

Carter, M. R. 1984. "Identification of the Inverse Relationship between Farm Size and Productivity: An Empirical Analysis of Peasant Agricultural Production." *Oxford Economic Papers* 36 (1): 131–45.

———. 1987. "Risk Sharing and Incentives in the Decollectivization of Agriculture." *Oxford Economic Papers* 39 (3): 577–95.

Carter, M. R., and F. J. Zimmerman. 2000. "Can Time and Markets Eliminate Costly Land Ownership Inequality?" Paper prepared for the Annual World Bank Conference on Development Economics, Washington, DC, April 18–20.

Cornia, G. A., ed. 2004. *Inequality, Growth, and Poverty in an Era of Liberalisation and Globalisation*. Oxford, U.K.: Oxford University Press.

Darity, W. 1995. "The Formal Structure of a Gender-Segregated Low Income Economy." *World Development* 23 (11): 1963–68.

Deininger, K. 1999. "Making Negotiated Land Reform Work: Initial Experience from Colombia, Brazil, and South Africa." *World Development* 27 (4): 651–72.

Deininger, K., and H. Binswanger. 1995. "Rent Seeking and the Development of Large-Scale Agriculture in Kenya, South Africa, and Zimbabwe." *Economic Development and Cultural Change* 43 (3): 493–522.

Deininger, K., and P. Olinto. 2000. *Why Liberalization Alone Has Not Improved Agricultural Productivity in Zambia: The Role of Asset Ownership and Working Capital Constraints*. Washington, DC: World Bank.

Dercon, S. 1996. "Risk, Crop Choice, and Savings: Evidence from Tanzania." *Economic Development and Cultural Change* 44 (3): 485–514.

———. 1999. "Income Risks, Coping Strategies, and Safety Nets." Centre for the Study of African Economics Working Paper Series, Oxford University, Oxford, U.K.

Dercon, S., and P. Krishnan. 1996. "Income Portfolios in Rural Ethiopia and Tanzania: Choices and Constraints." *Journal of Development Studies* 32 (6): 850–75.

Eastwood, R., and M. Lipton. 1999. "The Impact of Changes in Human Fertility on Poverty." *Journal of Development Studies* 36 (1): 1–30.

———. 2000. "Rural-Urban Dimensions of Inequality Change." Working Paper 200, United Nations University/World Institute for Development Economics Research, Helsinki.

Elson, D. 1999. "Labor Markets as Gendered Institutions: Equality, Efficiency, and Empowerment Issues." *World Development* 27 (3): 611–27.

Elson, D., and B. Evers. 1997. *Gender Aware Country Economic Reports: Uganda.* Manchester, U.K.: University of Manchester Graduate School of Social Sciences, Genecon Unit.

Harris-White, B. 1996. "The Gendering of Rural Market Systems: Analytical and Policy Issues." University of Oxford, Oxford, U.K.

Kabeer, N., and T.-T. V. Anh. 2000. "Leaving the Rice Fields but Not the Countryside: Gender Livelihood Diversification and Pro-Poor Growth in Rural Vietnam." Occasional Paper 13, United Nations Research Institute for Social Development, Geneva.

Kevane, M. 1996. "Agrarian Structure and Agricultural Practice: Typology and Application to Western Sudan." *American Journal of Agricultural Economics* 78 (1): 236–45.

Quisumbing, A. 1996. "Male-Female Differences in Agricultural Productivity: Methodological Issues and Empirical Evidence." *World Development* 24 (10): 1579–95.

Reardon, T. 1997. "Using Evidence of Household Income Diversification to Inform Study of the Rural Nonfarm Labor Market in Africa." *World Development* 25 (5): 735–47.

Rosenzweig, M. R., and H. Binswanger. 1993. "Wealth, Weather Risk, and the Composition and Profitability of Agricultural Investments." *Economic Journal* 103 (416): 56–78.

Sadoulet, E., A. de Janvry, and C. Benjamin. 1998. "Household Behavior with Imperfect Labor Markets." *Journal of Industrial Relations* 37 (l): 85–108.

Vierich, H. 1986. "Agricultural Production, Social Status, and Intra-Compound Relationships." In *Understanding Africa's Rural Households and Farming Systems*, ed. J. L. Moock. Boulder, CO: Westview.

Walters, B. 1995. "Engendering Macroeconomics: A Reconsideration of Growth Theory." *World Development* 23 (11): 1869–80.

CHAPTER 3

Beneath the Categories: Power Relations and Inequalities in Uganda

Joy M. Moncrieffe

Mainstream views on the relationships among inequality, growth, and poverty have been changing since the 1930s. First, many economists now refute the Kuznetsian position that inequality has an invariably positive role and assert, instead, that high levels of inequality can curtail the potential poverty-reducing effect of growth. Conversely, where there is low or falling inequality, lower-income groups will have a larger share of any increase in national income (Naschold 2002). Second, following Sen (1992, 1999) and other researchers, it is now fairly well accepted that individuals have differing levels of advantage. In addition to income, these levels of advantage could be understood as their capability and freedom to make choices and to convert their incomes into well-being by establishing personal goals and having realistic means of attaining them. Thus, poverty is commonly conceptualized as deprivation in income and consumption, as well as in capabilities, such as health, education, and civil liberties. Third, as Stewart's (2002) "horizontal inequality" thesis gains in popularity, some analysts are moving beyond their original preoccupation with inequality among individuals and are also examining how poverty and inequality affect different categories of people,[1] recognizing that disparities—perceived and real—are among the fundamental causes of conflict, which often culminates in low growth. Fourth, there is renewed emphasis on facilitating political "agency"—that is, promoting the actions and interventions that are directed at making effective claims on the state (Fox 1996).

How adequate are these shifts in thinking? Do they allow for a sufficiently broad analysis of the dynamics of poverty and inequality? Although this chapter does not refute the importance of assets and opportunities, of group inequalities, or of political agency, it encourages more explicit consideration of the relationships that often underpin inequalities and poverty, because these relationships can have substantial influence on when and how assets and opportunities work. The chapter emphasizes that inequality and poverty can result from the exercise of power: people can become and remain poor because of the deliberate actions and inaction of others. Accordingly, the chapter focuses on the processes and power relations that produce and sustain poverty and inequality, including those within defined categories.

Explicit attention to relationships and power can expose issues that are often overlooked but that are highly consequential for analyses of poverty and inequality:

1. *People, in their roles as social actors, might accept and uphold conditions that perpetuate their own inequality.* People are social creatures and actors. As interdependent social agents, they expect mutual accountability—which involves mutual susceptibility—and, accordingly, they develop standards and processes for approval and disapproval. It may, therefore, be sensible and judicious—that is, perfectly rational—for people to act in ways that uphold shared ways of living and agreed understandings, even if these actions do not serve individual interests (see Barnes 2000, chapter 5). These relations might sustain a status quo, even an unequal status quo, but those whom outsiders regard as disadvantaged might place great value in the norms that hold these "inequalities" in place.
2. *Power relations—coercive and noncoercive, visible and hidden, agreed and imposed—can cause poverty and help sustain inequalities.* Therefore, a realistic approach to promoting political action must seriously consider the multiple ways in which power can constrain people's choices and capacity for action.
3. *Relational considerations have important implications for political agency.* As Fox (1996: 1090–91) outlines, political agency and the collective action that supports it depend on available opportunities. "Associational life does not unfold in a vacuum: state or external societal actors can provide either positive or negative sanctions for collective action." Further—citing Tarrow (1994)—Fox (1996: 1090–91) points out that collective action emerges largely in response to changes in opportunities that lower the costs of association, "reveal

potential allies and show where elites and authorities are vulnerable." In ideal circumstances, reformist officials will not only provide positive incentives, but also block negative societal and state sanctions. Political agency reflects ideas and motivations, both those historically formed and those that are influenced or shaped by leaders and other actors. The action-oriented approach to collective action prioritizes those ideas and motivations that lead people—and particularly leaders—to persist despite the odds.

4. *Finally, scaling up is important.* The most effectively represented claims are those that transcend the village level and gain higher levels of expression, particularly at the regional level. Regional representation is considered instrumental in representing the interests of "dispersed and oppressed" people because it can "overcome locally confined solidarities, provide representative bargaining power and access to information" Fox (1996: 1090–91).

Points 1 and 2 will be discussed in detail in the chapter. Point 1 suggests an important qualification: even where it appears to matter most, people, for a variety of reasons, may not act in the rational ways expected. Point 2 suggests that political agency through collective action may help change institutions and policies in important ways; however, it is risky to assume that these changes will necessarily produce equitable benefits for all the people that associations claim to represent. Stratifications occur even among people who appear to share the same disadvantages. As Nussbaum (2003: 5–14) explains:

> a. Groups [can] contain hierarchies of power: thus giving legal privileges to a group is usually tantamount to giving more power to those already in power within the group.
>
> b. Groups have unclear and changing boundaries of membership; group rights often reify the current definition of a group and militate against change.
>
> c. There are "dispersed groups" that may be very important in people's identity but that do not figure in the usual discussions of group ethnocultural rights.... Such groups are unlikely to win legal privileges but then, giving legal privileges to [recognized or mainstream] groups makes them more salient by contrast with the "dispersed groups."

This observation raises important political questions: In what ways and to what extent should we recognize groups? Whose identities does recognition celebrate and with what consequences? Whose does it deny?

In what ways can or does the focus on groups produce unintended social consequences, and what are the implications for equity?

The case study that follows uses historical data and current qualitative research findings to underscore selected dimensions (the discussion is certainly not exhaustive) of the processes and power relations that produce and sustain poverty and inequality.

It is divided into three sections. The first section summarizes key features of the development of identities and inequalities in Uganda, starting with the precolonial period. History is often underestimated or even explicitly ignored in policy formulation and analysis; however, it is critical not only for understanding institutional legacies or more tangible factors, such as asset distribution, but also for appreciating the relationships, norms, values, and expectations that can have long-standing influence on people's behaviors. The section traces some of these existing behaviors to their origin in the precolonial and colonial periods and assesses their implications for poverty, inequality, and policy.

The second section is subdivided into two parts, which comment on some of the relationships of power that underpin interethnic and gender inequalities. The section pays special attention to the key themes raised earlier: (a) as social actors, people might accept and uphold conditions that perpetuate their own inequality; (b) power relations—coercive and noncoercive, visible and hidden, agreed and imposed—can cause poverty and help to sustain inequalities; and (c) stratifications occur even among people who appear to share the same disadvantages, which has significant implications for group-based policies. The final section concludes the case study.

It is not a comprehensive study. It does not attempt to present detailed historical analyses or a thorough account of the relational dimension of inequality. Furthermore, it does not reiterate prevailing views on the relationship between inequality, growth, and poverty—though it does not discount them—but concentrates on establishing that relationships of power underpin inequalities and poverty and that these relationships can have substantial influence on when and how assets and opportunities work.

Relationships and Inequalities in Uganda

This section discusses how relationships of inequality were built during the precolonial and colonial periods in Uganda.

The Precolonial Period

At the end of the 15th century and beginning of the 16th century, Nilotic Luo speakers (from the southern areas of Sudan) migrated into northwestern Uganda and subsequently moved southward. In the northern regions, they colonized Sudanic-speaking areas, spreading the Luo language, particularly in Acholi, Lango, and West Nile. In the south, they joined and attempted to conquer Bantu-speaking peoples (who had started to occupy the area from around 500 BC), establishing the Babito dynasty in Bunyoro and, subsequently, the kingdoms of Ankole and Buganda before proceeding to found other societies in northwestern (mainland) Tanzania (Karugire 1980). During the same period, another group of people—from among the Ateker—moved from their base in Karamoja and spread from the northeast to the southwest. The Ateker and Luo peoples intermingled at various points; there was a fusion of cultures and the creation of new ethnic communities, particularly the Langi and Kumam (Karugire 1980). Also, as a consequence of these movements, other communities—such as the Jo Abwor—became bilingual and adopted some new customs.

Across the north, the Luo, Sudanic, and Ateker speakers established basic forms of government, which gave precedence to the clan. Clans managed their own affairs independently, apart from occasions when it was necessary to collaborate with others, such as during wars or cultural festivities. Within the clans, the main social distinction was between elders and nonelders. Elders were elected to serve on community councils but were not entitled to special tributes or other privileges. They were responsible for selecting clan leaders, who, in turn, chaired the councils. Clan leaders were responsible to the council and could not make war or peace without consensus. Similarly, elders had joint responsibility for resolving disputes (Kanyeihamba 2002; Kasozi 1999). These nonstratified social systems existed in much of northern and eastern Uganda and in some parts of the south (Kasozi 1999).

Around 1680, Luo-speaking peoples (the Palwo) from northern Bunyoro migrated through Acholi and Karamoja and then to Bukedi and western Kenya. The Palwo brought new methods of government, including the institution of kingship (with the attending regalia—stools, royal spears, and royal drums) and more centralized political administration. However, these new institutions did not change fundamental Luo principles: "the belief and practice that all important decisions affecting the community could only be arrived at, not by a single person, but by the consensus of the elders representing the different clans constituting the community."

Therefore, these new kings effectively "reigned rather than ruled," acting as spokespeople for the clan elders (Karugire 1980, 9–11).

Across southern kingdoms, there were better environmental conditions, higher concentrations of people, and greater opportunity for sedentary occupations; thus, more bureaucratic forms of government emerged. Yet, even in these societies, the clan was extremely important. Hence, members defended the interests and integrity of the whole group and accepted the consequences when one or a few of their kin caused offense. As in the north,

> some individuals were more wealthy than others just as some were poorer than others. The wealthy never lost sight of their obligations to the kinship group just as the poor members of such a group were never slow in claiming their due from them. The point is that nobody could become wealthy without reference to his kinship group for this must have helped him in numerous ways, although his personal merits may contribute towards his success. In such societies, there had never been room for individualism or impersonal governorships requiring equally impersonal regulations to service them. (Karugire 1980: 13)

Principles of mutual accountability and susceptibility were at the core of clan relations in precolonial Uganda, and despite evident societal changes, they still have important roles in many contemporary communities. People tend to dismiss such group and kin behavior as regressive, patrimonial, or both. However, such easy categorizations overlook the weight and value of social and family mores, including the part they may play in sustaining visible inequalities and, conversely, the avenues they might provide for redressing them. As noted earlier, such norms can be upheld through mutual agreement; however, there are also coercive and noncoercive relationships of power that attempt to hold certain structures, systems, beliefs, and practices in place and to dictate the pace and direction of change. For example, the gender inequalities that still exist—among certain groups more than others—have roots in precolonial practices and, in some contexts, deepened in the colonial period, as less hierarchical societies came into contact with more centralized and patriarchal ones.

Roscoe (1966) provides a detailed historical account of gender relations in Buganda. He notes that the Baganda deeply objected to women rulers. Consequently, even when princes were too young to rule, it was the prime minister—who was invariably male—who was appointed to rule in their stead. Generally, women were considered to be minors and men's properties. They were unable to inherit property and required a male guardian who had full authority and who had to represent them in legal proceedings (Schiller 1990). Men had to consent and provide an escort when women traveled outside the home, and women were required to kneel when saluting a man. Within the home, men enforced dominance, even regulating women's diets.

> In peasant households men, rather than women, enjoyed all of the available high protein food. Even sitting positions were gendered. Women were always required to sit with their legs placed together and folded back from the knees so that the feet were together under the hips—*okufukamira*. To sit otherwise, such as with their legs straight in front of them or apart, was considered very unbecoming. (Musisi 2001, 174–75)

The state supported violent forms of domination: "[N]o punishment was inflicted on a man who speared his wife or slave to death" (Roscoe 1966: 20). Women suspected of adultery could be tied and tortured until they confessed and were "put in the stocks when they displeased their husbands" (Roscoe 1966: 23). Men received similar treatment only if they seduced married women from the royal household (Musisi 2001: 174). Women understood that submissive behavior was good behavior, and it was reinforced through socialization of Kiganda norms and by force: the cultural construction of the good woman. In contrast, women who flouted this order were labeled bad women and met the disapproval of both men and conforming women (Musisi 2001).

Class inequalities. Long before colonialism, class inequalities had begun to develop, particularly in the south, and these helped change the nature of clan relations. Up to the 17th century, the county, or *saza*, was the prime unit of administration in Buganda, and clan heads had important political roles. However, as the kingdom expanded, the administrative system grew more complex, and the new units—the *Bitongole*—that developed at subcounty levels grew to have substantial control. As the kingdom accumulated new territories—which were not under traditional chief control—kings developed the leverage to reward their own appointed leaders at the expense of traditional chiefs. Therefore, by the time the earliest European explorers—John Speke and James Grant—arrived in 1862, Buganda had become a highly centralized and stratified society, in which "every functionary of the state held office at the king's pleasure" (Karugire 1980: 23).

New divisions and identities emerged as industries developed. Agriculture was the key to Buganda's economic development, and the chiefs' authority extended to rights and control over land. Similarly, the *Kabaka* was vested with control over all the land in his jurisdiction, which, in principle, he should administer in the people's interests. This allocation of land produced and was used to signify class divisions. From Roscoe's (1966) description, the foremost chiefs—the *Katikiro*, who served as prime minister and chief justice, and the *Kimbugwe*, who was responsible for guarding the king's umbilical cord—were granted estates throughout the country. Neither was required to provide tributes, although they ensured that district chiefs collected and returned the correct amounts. Similarly, these favored chiefs were not required to contribute laborers for the upkeep of royal buildings. Given the social distinctions, the peasants regarded the *Katikiro* and *Kimbugwe* as kings in their own right. Below these principal chiefs were the 10 district chiefs, who had responsibility for administering the country and had to account directly to the *Katikiro* and through him to the king. Chiefs had great stature within the villages, where, like local kings, they enjoyed vast enclosures, with slaves, wives, and menservants. Even their close relations treated them with the utmost respect.

In contrast, Bunyoro's major industries comprised both pastoralism and agriculture; therefore, no special priority was given to land. Eventually, pastoralism became the mainstay of the economy. Because pastoralism did not require a complex administrative structure, Bunyoro retained a fairly simple system, although its rulers insisted that all administrative agents, many of whom served as military personnel, should own cattle. Eventually, rigid social divisions developed between Bunyoro's pastoral aristocrats and agricultural serfs. Ankole, too, became a class-based society, in which the Bahima ruling class owned the cattle. However, though territorial leaders in Ankole and Bunyoro had the power to contest the kings' actions, the *Kabakas* of the more centralized Buganda had substantial authority and were known to frequently use their power over life and death.

Religion and inequalities. Religion, too, was one of the most significant causes of intragroup and intergroup divisions in Uganda. Religious tensions increased after the arrival of the first Anglican missionaries (in 1876) and the French (Roman Catholic) White Fathers (in 1879). As Pulford (1999) describes it, though both groups of missionaries had the same evangelical objectives, intense rivalries developed because they had fundamentally different interpretations of the scriptures. The Protestant-Catholic discord caused deep disunity within Buganda. Rivalries also developed among Christianity, Islam, and traditional Kiganda religions. Eventually, the Protestants and Catholics formed political parties in opposition to the Muslims and traditional groups. In 1892, Catholics and Protestants fought to control Buganda. The Protestant victory relegated Roman Catholics to a secondary position and marginalized the Muslims. Anglican Protestantism became the prominent religion and was the basis for favored access to resources, both during and after the colonial period.

The Colonial Period

Intergroup inequalities and conflicts preceded the colonial period. Groups seized and raided each other's territories, and Bunyoro and later Buganda became the wealthier and more powerful states. However, ample intergroup trade occurred, and group identities were fairly loose. In many places, outsiders could be absorbed and acculturated. Karugire (1980: 30) suggests that "even where hostile encounters occurred, the objective and, more importantly, the scale of destruction was never of such intensity or duration that they could create enduring enmity. In Uganda, there were no such phenomena as inter-ethnic total wars." However, the colonial period capitalized on old inequalities, created new ones, and attempted to "fix" group identities in a manner that has proved costly in Uganda.

First, the colonialists favored the Baganda, whom explorer Henry Stanley described as "an extraordinary people, as different from the barbarous pirates of Uvuma, and the wild, mop-headed men of Eastern Usukuma, as the British in India are from their Afridi fellow-subjects, or the white Americans of Arkansas from the semi-civilized Choctaws" (Pulford 1999: 23). It was the Baganda oligarchy that benefited most from the 1900 Uganda Agreement, which (a) stipulated the terms under which future *Kabakas* were to be selected and recognized Buganda dependent on its loyalty to the protectorate, including its administrative systems; (b) defined the boundaries of Buganda; (c) imposed hut and gun taxes and declared that the protectorate had prime rights to any minerals and sources of wealth discovered; and (d) reallocated land, such that the elite—particularly the "great chiefs" and the royal household—retained political control (Karugire 1980, 103). Peasants now became tenants of the new Baganda *mailo* (mile-owning) landlords. Sathyamurthy (1986) argues that the Uganda Agreement both legitimized the social changes that had already taken place in Buganda and triggered new tensions and conflicts within Buganda and between the Baganda and other ethnic groups. Among the Baganda, economic inequalities increased as the new landowners managed and exploited the peasantry.

Second, Baganda chiefs were instrumental in mediating British rule or, as Mamdani (1996: 18) describes, in instituting "decentralized despotism." Native administrations followed ethnic boundaries, except in areas where it was not feasible to form a district (such as West Nile, Bugisu, Bukedi, Toro, and Kigezi). Rather than use indigenous leaders, the British deployed the Baganda and its Kiganda (centralized and hierarchical) model of administration throughout Uganda. At the local level, appointed chiefs held judicial, legislative, executive, and administrative power. Under the guise of native laws, they forced labor, crops, sales, and contributions. Revolts against Baganda rule became common throughout Uganda.

Third, the British actively stratified the kingdoms. Although Ankole and Toro did not enjoy Buganda's special standing, they were also given agreement status; however, Bunyoro was treated as enemy territory. It was not until 1907 that the British adopted a more conciliatory stance, though by now the Banyoro were deeply resentful, particularly of British discourtesy and "maltreatment of the royal family" (Karugire 1980: 108). The British had little use for the northern regions. In 1906, Commissioner Hesketh Bell described the north as "a grave economic liability" and promptly downgraded its status to that of a district. Bell argued that "the communities of that region did not have any concept of institutional authority, such as was to be found in the Bantu kingdoms of the South. [Furthermore], the Kiganda model of administration would neither be understood nor accepted in northern Uganda" (Karugire 1980: 113). Subsequently, the British used the north as a reservoir for labor and to supply soldiers for its army. Lwanga-Lunyiigo (1989: 28) is clear that the colonialists used the army primarily for coercion and not for defense against external forces. Furthermore, much of Uganda, including the northerners, came to believe that only groups from the north had the right to bear arms. Lwanga-Lunyiigo emphasizes that this myth was one that both Milton Obote and Idi Amin exploited, with dire consequences.

Thus, group identities, particularly of the Baganda, became fractured and more complex, as people developed additional allegiances, such as to religion and class. These new allegiances did not mean a rejection of the clan. Karugire is quick to qualify that clan principles were still treasured. However, the new exploitative roles of some clan leaders eventually ruptured groups. In addition to these divisions, regional inequalities intensified and racial and ethnic inequalities grew under the British policies of favoritism.

Yet, despite the colonial precedent, few would have predicted Uganda's considerable postindependence decline or the violence and mayhem that accompanied it. Instead, there was an expectation that economic growth would continue, with a leading role for the Baganda elite. Up to 1986, when the National Resistance Movement (NRM)—under Yoweri Museveni's leadership—took over the government by coup, postindependence political leaders, particularly Milton Obote and Idi Amin, substantially deepened the divisions in Uganda, using religion, ethnicity, and politics to secure their regimes.

Structural Reforms and Legacies of Ethnic and Gender Identities

This section outlines some of the major structural reforms that were introduced in Uganda after the NRM took over the government in 1986. Despite these reforms, legacies of ethnic and gender identities have persisted.

Background

In 1986, the NRM committed to building democracy and eradicating poverty. To build democracy, it expanded resistance councils (RCs) to the entire country. Previously established in the areas under guerrilla control, RCs operated on the principle that decision-making power, authority, and policy-making responsibilities should also be located at the local levels and that citizens should be able to reach and influence their representatives and to hold them accountable for the quality of services. The local council (LC) system that replaced the RC system operated on the same principles. Uganda's highly decentralized LC system comprises five administrative levels, ranging from the village (LC1) through the parish (LC2), subcounty (LC3), county (LC4), and district (LC5). Representatives are directly elected at the LC1 to LC3 levels; however, one-third of all council seats are reserved for women, and the constitution allows for affirmative action for all marginalized groups. To ensure broad-based representation at the highest levels and to demarginalize select groups, the 1995 Uganda constitution provides for a unicameral parliament comprising "members directly elected to represent constituencies; one woman representative for every district; such numbers of representatives of the army, youth, workers, persons with disabilities, and other groups as Parliament may determine."

The Poverty Eradication Action Plan (PEAP) originated in 1995, with the Uganda government's recognition that economic growth was not benefiting the majority of the poor. The 2000 PEAP, which serves as Uganda's Poverty Reduction Strategy Paper, established four major objectives:

- Creating a framework for economic growth and transformation through rapid and sustainable economic growth and structural transformation
- Establishing good governance and security, focusing on transparency of public actions; respect for human rights; zero tolerance for corruption, security, and accountability
- Increasing the ability of the poor to raise their incomes through employment promotion and through improved access to services and information
- Enhancing the quality of life of the poor, thereby emphasizing health, education, housing, service delivery, and information.

In principle, Uganda's poverty policies should be guided by other pressing and complementary objectives. For example, the 1997 National Gender Policy stipulates that all development planning, resource allocation, and program implementation should be conducted from a gender perspective. Furthermore, all levels of local government should participate in the planning and budget process. Views from the village level should feed into the subcounty and then district plans. Therefore, the resulting district development plans should be a true reflection of local needs.

Until the late 1990s, there were substantial gains in poverty reduction. Lately, the Ministry of Finance, Planning, and Economic Development acknowledged that poverty levels have since increased and that inequality has deepened. Among the more frequently cited concerns are the long-standing (north–south) regional inequalities; the social inequalities, persistent gender disparities, and perceived inequalities across ethnic groups; and the deepening chronic poverty. Explanations vary for why inequality and poverty persist, particularly among some groups of people; policy recommendations tend to focus on supplying economic incentives and opportunities and on opening political space.

Some Relational Dimensions to Ethnic and Gender Inequality

It is difficult to gauge the actual inequalities across ethnic groups, because poverty data are not disaggregated in this way. Furthermore, researchers are somewhat reluctant to conduct this type of analysis, given fears of potential social and political costs. However, there are widespread perceptions of interethnic group inequality, and claims of ethnic favoritism at high levels of government are common. Participatory poverty appraisals also provide accounts of ethnic bias at local government levels, and there is evidence that, despite the formal goals and principles of decentralization, resources are, in places, diverted to ethnic associates, at the expense of other groups.

Hickey (2003: 36) argues that the government's project of "replacing ethnic politics and patrimonialism with accountable governance and citizenship has faltered if not entirely failed" because of a number of policy lapses:

- The government's inability to insulate policy-making processes from local elite pressure. One consequence is that the government has succumbed to elite demands for local autonomy and increased the number of administrative districts (from 39 to more than 56). Most of the new districts coincide with areas of high single ethnic group concentration that, Hickey (2003: 36) contends, "marks a return to the ethnic-territorial basis of governance that the Movement claimed to reform."
- The failure to reform landownership. The current system combines state, customary, and commercial landownership. Consequently, Hickey (2003: 36) notes, "[T]he local politics of citizenship in Uganda is divided between the electoral and representative system whereby the rights of participation are accorded to all residents, and the politics of belonging that surrounds local land landownership, and which remains subject to ethnic territorialism."
- The failure to develop an entrepreneurial middle class that is not dependent on the state.

Hickey provides an example of how these "policy failures" have affected social and economic inequalities across ethnic groups: in Mbale, landownership is closely associated with clan membership, which, in turn, is related directly to length of settlement in a given area. The 2002 local elections at both the LC3 and LC5 levels saw power return to the dominant landowning group. As such, the poorest groups are subject to a form of double exclusion in both the local political economy of development and the politics of governance.

Cases such as these are often used to explain how patrimonialism and corruption dispossess some groups and incur substantial economic costs.

The customary recommended course of action is to design appropriate accountability mechanisms to expose and sanction such behavior and, as Hickey maintains, to develop rules and procedures that are transparent and not susceptible to elite manipulation and capture. Furthermore, many policy makers envision a democratic environment, in which people value and celebrate their ethnic allegiances but also support and, ideally, prioritize a national Ugandan identity.

This section turns now to two issues mentioned earlier and their relevance to Uganda.

People, in their roles as social actors, might accept and uphold conditions that perpetuate their own inequality. Although claims of patrimonialism and corruption may be valid in many instances, these labels are in cases wantonly applied and, as a consequence, misinterpret and misrepresent relationships and norms that have been central to some clans since the precolonial period. Earlier, the chapter suggested that in some clans and among some ethnic groups, responsibility to kin transcended the colonial and postcolonial periods despite the substantial disruption. Such norms of kin responsibility and accountability have had an important role in checking intraclan poverty, even though they may also contribute to interclan inequalities. Although it is true that leaders can—and perhaps often do—capitalize on these norms for their own personal advantage and interests, it is important to understand that within some clans and ethnic groups, such long-held beliefs are still maintained and are considered legitimate standards for social relationships. As will be demonstrated, in the case of the Batwa, by discounting the value and role of these norms, policy makers not only misrecognize groups but can uproot a key resource for addressing intragroup poverty and inequality. The value of the relational perspective is that it demonstrates the complex relations and processes that underpin inequality and poverty and suggests that multifaceted and sensitive responses may be required.

Many examples reinforce that group recognition must entail knowledge of values and norms. The historical overview outlined the development of intraclan inequalities in Buganda and suggested that, particularly since the colonial period, these inequalities have resulted in growing disaffection among the Baganda, as people contested and breached boundaries. One prominent Muganda[2] explained her reluctance to support officials within the kingdom: "The Lukiko [Buganda parliament] has transformed the progressive dynamic interest into self-interest. People are only there to rule, to gain, and to utilize us without acknowledging the resource" (personal interview, Kampala, July 17, 2003, name of respondent withheld).

However, the Baganda elite still maintains a substantial base of support across social classes and age groups. People place tremendous value on traditional norms and expectations. Wealthy and poor Baganda are willing to sacrifice their earnings and talents for the kingdom and their *Kabaka*. During the recent debates on Federo (federalism), many Baganda demonstrated their fervent loyalty to the *Kabaka*. Federo restates the claims for self-government that Buganda has been making since 1900. Under a federal system, Buganda would handle its internal affairs, including poverty reduction programs. It would also be able to preserve itself as a unit.

The Baganda leadership was strategic in promoting Federo. First, it has garnered substantial support among the people. In response to an initial cabinet decision not to grant Federo, the *Kabaka* canceled his 10th coronation anniversary celebrations and declared that his people would be mourning, not celebrating. There were numerous pro-Federo demonstrations and study sessions, which both the young and the old widely supported. Federo was so effectively politicized that people demanded that the *Kabaka* go into exile so that they could launch another liberation struggle. People have demonstrated their loyalty to the *Kabaka* and the kingdom in ways that some Western policy makers might consider irrational. For example, in one interview, the *Katikiro* explained how people are willing to sacrifice for the purpose of the kingdom:

> When we were organizing the *Kabaka's* wedding, we did not have the resources and the kingdom cannot beg. However, we almost collapsed. People were fighting to give money. Similarly our ministers in the Lukiko are not paid. They work for free. If we do not have money to run things, they put money in (Personal interview with the *Katikiro* of Buganda, Kampala, July 15, 2003).

One commentator explained how these belief systems have undermined the goals of some early poverty reduction programs:

> When the poverty alleviation program was first implemented, it was passed by the *Kabaka* and through him to the people. The people felt bad that the *Kabaka* was giving to them and so gave the money back to the *Kabaka*. This is because there is a principle that if you get some money, you should return it to the pool (Personal interview with a minister of Buganda, Mengo, Uganda, July 15, 2003).

These examples reinforce the proposition that people, in their roles as social actors, might accept and uphold conditions that perpetuate their own inequality.

Similarly, despite institutional and structural changes and progress on gender issues, recent analyses of the links between gender and poverty indicate that pervasive inequalities still exist (Klasen 2003; Lawson 2003; Wengi and Kyasimire 1995). Successive participatory poverty appraisals (PPAs) demonstrate that beneath inequalities in assets and opportunities are substantial imbalances in power within households, in the market, and at the local government level. Other reports show the limitations to political agency at state levels. Furthermore, the second participatory poverty appraisal (PPA2), completed in 2002, shows how some women have internalized and even defend the unequal gender norms, and how this tacit acceptance helps sustain inequalities and poverty (UPPAP 2002).

PPA2 interviews conducted in the Masindi, Mubende, Ntungamo, Rakai, and Wakiso districts confirm that power imbalances within the home are among the major underlying causes of poverty among women. The reports provide various examples of how women are consistently exploited and, as a consequence, impoverished. Across all sites, for example, women have primary responsibility for domestic duties. They are also involved in agricultural work for subsistence and for commercial production, as well as in other business activities. In many rural sites, women were responsible for providing food for the family throughout the year and for other households needs, including providing school fees. Men were involved in productive activities but also spent considerable time resting or at leisure, particularly drinking alcohol. In urban communities, women generally had better opportunities for engaging in income-generating activities, though some were restricted from working outside the home and from running businesses.

According to PPA2, "Men reported that they fear their wives will become promiscuous; indulge in extra-marital affairs; and become uncontrollable, unmanageable, and unruly if they gain economic independence" (UPPAP 2002: 27). The cycle 1 reports from PPA2 provide some interesting case references. In Rwakayata, Masindi, men justify the unequal distribution of resources by asserting the importance of maintaining the status quo:

> After selling the maize, the husband may buy a dress or *lesu* for the wife. If women are allowed to own property, they will be on top of men. (Man, Rwakayata, as quoted in UPPAP 2002: 34)

Some women agreed; they provided examples of women who were allowed to own property and subsequently left their husbands. Likewise, in fishing communities, women are generally excluded from the lucrative activities: very few own boats, and most are excluded from fishing. Cultural beliefs, including among women, are at the root of this exclusion. In Kasensero and Ntoroko, for example, older women, in particular, are convinced that "if a woman were to swim in the lake, then the fish would disappear" (UPPAP, 2002: 67). The Kasensero, Rakai, site report for PPA2 notes that in this fishing community, younger women are beginning to challenge some of the norms that sustain gender inequality: "We have to rely on the men all the time because we cannot go to get the riches ourselves from the resource, the lake. Our poverty will be continuous until we are allowed to go to the lake" (young woman in focus group discussion, Kasensero, Rakai, as quoted in UPPAP 2002: 67). However, older women tend to uphold and enforce traditional norms, sanctioning those who flout the rules. Consequently, women remain marginalized from the lucrative fishing.

Such views are often attributed to a lack of education and exposure; however, some prominent people at higher policy levels also accept their inferiority, and some lack the power to resist. For example, one government official, a Muganda, explained that her husband permits her to hold her position in the government as long as she observes her customary position in the home, which entails not eating high-protein foods, sitting appropriately, and laying prostrate when greeting male visitors, as is the custom, even though, in her occupational capacity, these individuals may be her juniors. In her view, these norms are important for maintaining family, and she does not and cannot object to them:

> There are certain dishes that men take but not women: those that are very high protein. Women putting on trousers is still not accepted in villages. Women are not allowed to ride bicycles. Women are not supposed to argue or even suggest anything to their husbands. Women are not supposed to sit in chairs while their husband is sitting there. It is not accepted, especially when parents are there. Women should be kneeling down while men are sitting, especially in Buganda. All of us accept it. If the president comes to my village, I must kneel before him. Women are still inferior and still submissive. The government has brought in equality, but it is not universally applied (Personal interview, government official, Kampala, Uganda, July 14, 2003).

Unfortunately, women also accept physical violence, sometimes describing it as the just retribution for their conduct. For example, in Kigusa,

Bugiri, one woman explained a commonly accepted perception: "I was bought by the man, so my body is his asset to use as he wishes" (UPPAP 2002: 33). Correspondingly, in Katebe, Rakai, one man argued that "if you buy a cloth, do you not wash it any time you want?" (UPPAP 2002: 33). Meanwhile, "the women agreed that as men have paid cows for them, they are property in the home to be used as the man wishes" (UPPAP 2002: 33). In some other sites, women agreed that men had the "right to use violence to discipline them" (UPPAP 2002: 34).

Poverty analyses could do more to understand and plan for such social expectations and behavior. As Kabeer (1999: 440) argues in her reflections on measuring women's empowerment, there is an "intuitive plausibility to the equation between power and choice as long as what is chosen appears to contribute to the welfare of those making the choice." In contrast, analysts have much more difficulty accommodating those instances when women not only accept but also choose their inequality.

Power relations—coercive and noncoercive, visible and hidden, agreed and imposed—can cause poverty and help sustain inequalities. As the examples above suggest, there may be diverse and complex reasons for observing norms that may have outcomes that onlookers would deem disadvantageous. People may genuinely accept social norms and be willing to observe cultural principles of accountability and susceptibility. They may—as in the case of the Muganda official cited—calculate that losses in one respect may lead to gains in another. People may be systematically coerced, which limits their capacity to resist. Furthermore, power relations may become so ingrained that people either accept a condition that they know is unequal or fail to recognize the domination that exists. Bourdieu (1990) defines this situation as *habitus*. As Wacquant (2005: 316) explains, Bourdieu's conceptualization of habitus "helps us to revoke the duality between the individual and the social by capturing the 'internalization of externality and the externalization of internality'; that is, the way society becomes deposited in persons in the form of lasting dispositions, or trained capacities and structured propensities to think, feel, and act in determinate ways, which then guide them in their creative responses to the constraints and solicitations of their extant milieu." Habitus presents major challenges to empowerment and to assumptions that, given the assets and opportunities, people will act to improve their condition. People have different capacities for agency. These are not merely the outcomes of deprivations in income and material assets but of other social and psychological (not easily quantifiable) sources of poverty. The following case study of the Batwa shows how people can become trapped in circumstances and systematically conditioned to accept their inferiority.

Misrecognition of the Batwa

According to historical records and oral accounts, the Batwa were the first to inhabit the high-altitude forests in Kigezi-Bufumbira in southwestern Uganda—that is, up until the middle of the 16th century when the first Batutsi arrived in the area. The majority of these Batwa were former hunter-gatherers, although some lived in savannahs and forest lake environments. In 1912, British colonialists took over the Kigezi-Bufumbira area and initiated a policy for protecting parts of the forest as reserves. To create the Bwindi, Echuya, and Mgahinga forest reserves, the British expelled the Batwa from those areas. Forest exploitation still continued under Idi Amin's rule (1971–84), largely through non-Batwa-led commercial hunting, timber extraction, and mining.

In 1991, the World Bank provided a grant of US$4.3 million to establish the Mgahinga and Bwindi Impenetrable Forest Conservation Trust, which was intended to conserve the biodiversity of the parks. Supplementary funding provided by the U.S. Agency for International Development and the Embassy of the Netherlands increased the trust funds to approximately US$7 million (Zaninka 2003). Of those funds, 20 percent were earmarked for park management, 20 percent for research, and 60 percent to support local community projects. The Uganda National Park authorities then began to enforce the Batwa's prior exclusion from the forests. The World Bank required that the government assess the impact on indigenous peoples and follow defined compensation procedures. However, the National Park authorities have only lately admitted that "the process of evicting the Batwa did not take into account Batwa realities and left them with nothing" (Zaninka 2003: 170). The fundamental cause was that the World Bank and local policy makers presumed that the Batwa and their neighbors constituted a community. No attempt was made to understand the power relations beneath the broadly accepted categories. Zaninka (2003: 171) records a reflective interview from one local park official:

> All communities were considered as though they were a uniform group. Information was never segregated to reflect any unique characteristic and Batwa property was often included in that of their landlords. Batwa views on compensation were not sought. The valuing was flawed and the donors determined the procedure for compensation. They insisted on payment

> through the bank using cheques. Instead of giving them cash, alternative land should have been bought for them as a group. The compensation was given with the view that they would acquire alternative land on an individual basis and yet the Batwa prefer to live in groups, maintaining kinship ties.

This expulsion from the forests and persistent denial of Batwa rights to hunt and gather are one dimension of the pervasive discrimination that the Batwa encounter at all levels of society. The Batwa are subject to negative stereotypes; they are regarded as subhuman and primitive and are subject to discrimination at all society and state levels.

It is easier to understand group inequalities when they are manifested in contexts of marked disparities in assets and income. Studies of the noneconomic dimensions of inequality in communities in which the majority is poor (whether in income or assets) are still fairly rare. Kisoro District, located in southwestern Uganda, borders the Democratic Republic of Congo and Rwanda. The PPA1 report describes Kisoro as an area in which the majority are poor and the area with the highest dependent ratio in Uganda (UPPAP 2000). In Kisoro, people are concerned about shortages of food; lack of and low levels of education; inadequate opportunities; helplessness because of old age, sickness, disabilities, and widowhood; lack of land; insecurity; lack of markets; and similar problems. The three ethnic groups in the area are the Bafumbira, the Bakiga, and the Batwa; the Batwa are in the minority. The Kisoro site report (UPPAP 2000: 22) describes the Batwa's condition:

> [The Batwa] are a group of people who are despised [and] have no means of production, such as land, credit and training. They are regarded by other ethnic groups in Kisoro as a people with no rights. The Batwa are exempted from tax. However, instead of this exemption enabling them to accumulate something productive, it is interpreted by other ethnic groups as a symbol of nonrecognition by the government. One respondent reported that [the Batwa] can be beaten up and told that they have nowhere to report, because "in any case, they do not pay tax," implying that government does not recognize their existence. Researchers were told by some of the Batwa children who had not gone to school at the time of the visit to the community that at times these children absent themselves because of the unfriendly school environment. They are despised by fellow children. When one of these children was asked what [she] would like to be when [she] complete[s] school, she replied, "a cleaner." During the exercise of drawing the Resource Map in Kisoro

> Hill there was a debate about whether their village should be included on the map or not. None of the Batwa, even their chief, came to any of the meetings. They were not mobilized to come. When the researchers probed they were told that "Batwa would never come to such meetings, so there is no point in mobilizing them." Because of this attitude by other communities the Batwa are a marginalized group, which is excluded from the mainstream of development. They constitute an ideal example of a group of people who are entangled in the vicious cycle of poverty.

In one community interview, Batwa men and women summarized their experiences:

- How do you live or survive?
- *We live by working for other people in the village and in other communities, but if we had our own land, we would work for ourselves.*
- Are you paid in cash or food?
- *Sometimes in food, sometimes soap or other things.*
- When you're paid with food, is it enough?
- *It's not enough, and children cry at night. When they pay with money, we get 1,000 shillings.*
- Why do you think you get 1,000 shillings?
- *Because we are 'Twa. They say the Batwa are weak, and because we don't have our own hoes, we are paid less.*
- Do you have any way of reporting this to the authorities?
- *No, we can't report this because we are poor and have no money. Only those with money can pay to open their case.*
- How are you treated?
- *During church services, we are welcomed; we don't have any problem. But outside people say the Batwa are dirty and badly dressed. They won't share with us. For that reason, we always ask ourselves how do we solve this problem in order to develop like others?* (Focus group discussion, Kisoro, Uganda, July 2003)

Lewis (2000: 14) expands on some of the ways in which the Batwa are segregated by their neighbors:

> Despite different ideological emphases, the types of segregation practiced by the Batwa's neighbors are similar and equally extreme. Other people will not eat or drink with them, will not marry them, [and] will not allow Batwa to approach too close, to sit with them on the same bench, or touch cooking and eating implements. They must live apart from others, collect water downstream from others, remain on the margins of public spaces, and, when selling goods in markets, can only sit on the outskirts away from other sellers.

The Batwa also experience exclusion at the center of government, where some officials expect them to assimilate and express frustration at their intransigence. One government minister explained:

> I have had some interesting experiences with them. I was on a mission to promote agricultural food crops. I took hoes and seeds and distributed them. The Batwa sold all the inputs to pay for alcohol [note that the Batwa are not agriculturalists]. Also, in 1984, we built a community centre in Bundibugyo district as a settlement home. They abandoned it. Very many tourists wanted to interact with these people. They would spend nights with them and give them clothes. Next day, they would sell all these to tribes in the districts. They prefer living around a huge tree with a fire in front of them. The issue is that we have 56 tribes. Each tribe is at its own level of social advancement. Life began here in Africa, but Africa does provide a whole range of levels of civilization, from the most original to modern style of living. Batwa still live in primitive communal system.... Nothing we do for them works (Personal interview, government official, Kampala, July 2003).

These excerpts describe some of the ways in which power can be exercised to enforce inequalities. On the one hand, the examples highlight the significance of group recognition; on the other hand, they demonstrate clearly that it is important to go beyond easy categories. Policies that are directed at women's empowerment, for example, will have different consequences for Bafumbira, Bakiga, and Batwa women in Kisoro. Presumptions of "community" obscure the deep power relations and processes, which prevent a Mutwa woman[3] from taking advantage of—or even having access to—assets and opportunities. There are numerous examples of how the Batwa are denied services, including by front-line services providers who should provide for all equally. In their assessment, for example, Kabananuyke and Wily (1996) note that the Batwa "do not feel welcome" and that health workers reject the idea of visiting Batwa households: "They just want everything free; how could I help a Mutwa" (Kabananuyke and Wily 1996, as cited in Zaninka 2003: 178).

Implications for Political Agency and Collective Action

As noted in at the beginning of the chapter, the action-oriented approach prioritizes those ideas and motivations that lead people—and particularly leaders—to persist despite the odds. However, such a stance can avoid the power structures and relations that lead people to disengage, withdraw, and resign themselves to their poverty. Such power relations often underlie chronic poverty and destitution.

How have the Batwa responded? With external assistance, some have begun to form associations to represent their claims and are hopeful that they will obtain the assets that will improve their circumstances. Others have internalized the negative perceptions. Golden and Edgerton (2003) argue that playing the part or reflecting the stereotype is also a key survival strategy. By remaining docile and submissive, the Batwa evoke pity but also reaffirm the social hierarchies to which other groups have assigned them and make their marginalized status more concrete (Golden and Edgerton 2003). A further excerpt from the community interview demonstrates this:

- Do you have representation on the local committee?
- *No, we have no representative.*
- Why?
- *We don't have anyone who is educated. It's because of ignorance.*
- If you have problems, how do you resolve them?
- *We keep quiet like birds who stay in trees. There is no one who can hear us.*
- During elections, do you vote?
- *Yes.*
- If during elections, you vote, do you expect the politicians to work for you?
- *Yes, but after voting, that's the end of the story; we don't have a voice. Sometimes, we hear of assistance at subcommittee level, but when we go, we don't get it. It's distributed to relatives of the representatives.*
- Among your societies, don't you have anyone to speak on your behalf at subcommittee level?
- *In certain meetings, when we want we go, but they don't hear us.*
- Why do you think they don't hear you?
- *Maybe because they recognize us as people who don't have any value* (Focus group discussion, Kisoro, Uganda, July 2003).

Arguably, power relations are such that the Batwa are yet to effectively organize and lobby state and influential nonstate interests. Their small population is another important factor that limits collective action. Women, who have benefited from the commitment of the political directorate, have had more success, though some much more than others. As noted, local-level reforms are meant to tackle gender inequalities by providing the institutional basis for women's inclusion, participation, and empowerment. The reasoning is that with more opportunities for voice and agency, women will be able to transform their circumstances.

However, the local council system has had mixed results. Some evidence indicates that women are growing increasingly influential in some districts. There are reports that women representatives have become more confident; they can now speak in public and voice concerns. Also, various communities report that women's participation has resulted in a reduction in domestic violence and more access to land (UPPAP 2002). However, women representatives commonly feel they "lack the autonomy to pursue women's interests where they may conflict with either Movement policy and/or local male elite interests" (Hickey 2003: 11). Brock, McGee, and Gaventa (2004: 42) observe that women are often marginalized in the political process:

> The system of separate and parallel councils for women, people with disabilities, and youth ... is seen as a cure worse than the illness, at least with regards to addressing women's concerns at the local level. Being parallel and weakly linked to the LC system—where real power resides at the local level—and being imperfectly connected to the national-level women's political machinery, the local level Women Council structure effectively hives off women's concerns into a political cul-de-sac and ensures that the LCs remain dominated by men and their concerns.

Successive PPAs report that women are directly disadvantaged by the officials who should represent them. Although PPA1 (UPPAP 2000) corroborates claims that LC1 officials are held in high regard, PPA2 (UPPAP 2002) reports that women were more critical of these officials than men were. As far as many women were concerned, LC1 officials are biased against them, disregard their opinions, and ignore women representatives. Khadiagala (2001) states that one of the principal failures of popular democracy in Uganda is that although the National Resistance Movement promised that local councils would provide culturally appropriate forms of justice, which would benefit poor rural and uneducated women, local elites have used their positions to reinforce social control. Furthermore, the gap between theory and practice arises out of misconceptions about the character of local spaces, particularly the notion of community. Thus, gender discrimination continues despite structural reforms.

At the national level, most analysts accept that the NRM's policy of broad parliamentary representation has increased the visibility of women and other interest groups. Furthermore, women's organizations have had an important role in encouraging policy change, and Tripp (2001) suggests that this has much to do with their ability to resist co-optation by the NRM and to advance a far-reaching agenda. However, analysts also suggest that this increased presence and political agency have not produced the expected gains. For example, despite the recognized achievements of the women's movement in Uganda (and executive actions to promote equality), Tamale (1999) suggests that the government has obstructed women's efforts to act as an interest group. Furthermore, ingrained sexism and patriarchy undermine effective women's representation in parliament. Goetz and Hassim (2003) conclude that participation does not necessarily result in effective policy influence.

Advantages and Limitations of the Group Approach

Policies that are designed to promote women's empowerment and equality are important. However, it is dangerous to assume that the group approach will benefit all women equally. There is a marked lack of data in Uganda on how women's experiences differ across ethnic and religious communities or other social categories. Much more work is required to understand the stratifications among differing classes of women, which allow some women to capture opportunities and which marginalize others. One should not presume "community." PPA2 indicates that women's councils are not viewed favorably, even among women (UPPAP 2002). Some members insisted that women's councils had not been useful and had offered no personal benefits. One respondent claimed, "Women leaders have only empowered themselves. They have made so many investments, which they got from our money" (UPPAP 2002: 168). Some women were clearly reluctant to continue to elect representatives.

The preceding case study of the Batwa also shows how ethnic and other distinctions can pose added disadvantages to some women, as opposed to others. It demonstrates the importance of going beyond categories and of conducting the disaggregated power analysis that is necessary for responding to the special needs that some people may have and minimizing the blocks to their agency. Many of those blocks can come from members of their own "community." Stratifications occur even among people who appear to share the same disadvantages. Lewis (2000: 13) notes that the "Batwa discriminate among themselves." A Mutwa who has acquired wealth or status may renounce "the Batwa identity." He gives an example from Burundi, where communities that have acquired land are offended at being described as Batwa and insist on being called "Abaterambe," which means "people who are developing." These divergent views and responses limit organization and collective action.

Policy makers, in turn, blame this lack of collective action or failure to exercise political agency as the cause for the Batwa's poverty.

Summary: The Implications

Power relationships can sustain poverty and inequality. Therefore, policy makers should rigorously probe the classifications and labels they adopt, question assumptions of community and group, and investigate the differing experiences of inequality and poverty that classifications tend to mask and even enforce. Without this disaggregated approach, policies may profit some and exclude others. Furthermore, the more powerful can manipulate policies in ways that deepen social, political, and economic inequalities.

The essay contends that assets and opportunities alone are unlikely to solve inequalities. As the references to the Batwa and women in Uganda demonstrate, equity requires deep understanding and real recognition—meaning knowledge—of the groups, subgroups, and individuals that policy makers aim to support and, importantly, of the relations of power that hold inequalities in place. As a general principle, recognition must involve respect for people's lifestyle choices and preferences, with the important qualification that these choices and preferences should not contravene the human rights of group members—including the right to form new associations and develop new identities—and the rights of people external to the group. Such an approach might well result in more profitable engagement with groups such as the Batwa. Rather than forcing assimilation, policy makers should, instead, recognize the Batwa's livelihood choices; work with the Batwa to ensure safe use of the forests; expand the Batwa's involvement in forest-based occupations; protect the Batwa's pottery industry and introduce improved pottery techniques; help to provide markets, while teaching marketing principles and techniques; suggest new opportunities and sources of livelihood; and ensure that conditions are appropriate so that the Batwa can build their assets and expand their choices.

The case examples reinforce that, for some groups and subgroups, poverty reduction depends, critically, on addressing power relations. Key strategies include education (designed to help people recognize and observe the fundamental rights and value of others and to help those who have internalized negative perceptions to begin to view themselves and their prospects differently); revaluation (which may need to include re-presenting people's histories); discrimination containment (which should be visibly enforced at all levels, including through traditional authorities); and respect and defense of human rights. These strategies require a visible commitment at high policy levels and vigilant implementation from the center to the household. They are not short-term options and, accordingly, do not suit the time-constrained project approach to development (Appadurai 2004). Furthermore, recognition of the sort outlined requires what may be described as an anthropological insight into poverty. This anthropological approach is crucial for uncovering the relational dimensions to poverty and inequality. Understanding and addressing the adverse power relations that underpin poverty are, in turn, necessary for building capabilities and ensuring that assets and opportunities have the best prospects.

Notes

1. The act of categorization is itself an act on power (Eyben and Lovett 2004). For a more detailed treatment of the power of categorization and labeling, see Moncrieffe and Eyben (2007).
2. Muganda is the singular form of Baganda.
3. Mutwa is the singular form of Batwa.

References

Appadurai, A. 2004. "The Capacity to Aspire: Culture and the Terms of Recognition." In *Culture and Public Action*, ed. V. Rao and M. Walton, 59–84. Stanford, CA: Stanford University Press.

Barnes, B. 2000. *Understanding Agency: Social Theory and Responsible Action*. London: Sage Publications.

Bourdieu, P. 1990. *The Logic of Practice*. Stanford, CA: Stanford University Press.

Brock, K., R. McGee, and J. Gaventa. 2004. *Unpacking Policy: Knowledge, Actors, and Spaces in Poverty Reduction in Uganda and Nigeria*. Kampala: Fountain Publishers.

Eyben, R., and J. Lovett. 2004. *Political and Social Inequality: A Review*. Brighton, U.K.: Institute of Development Studies, University of Sussex. http://www.ids.ac.uk/ids/bookshop/db/db20.pdf.

Fox, J. 1996. "How Does Civil Society Thicken? The Political Construction of Social Capital in Mexico." *World Development* 24 (6): 1089–103.

Goetz, A. M., and S. Hassim. 2003. *No Short-Cuts to Power*. London: Zed Books.

Golden, T., and A. Edgerton. 2003. "Forgotten People: The Batwa Pygmy of the Great Lakes Region." Refugees International, Washington, DC.

Hickey, S. 2003. "The Politics of Staying Poor in Uganda." CPRC Working Paper 37, Chronic Poverty Research Centre, University of Manchester, Manchester, U.K.

Kabananuyke, K., and L. Wily. 1996. "Report on a Study of the Abayanda [Batwa] Pygmies of Southwest Uganda." Prepared for the Mgahinga and Bwindi Impenetrable Forest Conversation Trust, Kampala.

Kabeer, N. 1999. "Resources, Agency, Achievements: Reflections on the Measurement of Women's Empowerment." *Development and Change* 30 (3): 435–64.

Kanyeihamba, G. W. 2002. *Constitutional and Political History of Uganda.* Kampala: Centenary Publishers.

Karugire, S. R. 1980. *A Political History of Uganda.* Exeter, NH: Heinemann Educational Books.

Kasozi, A. B. K. 1999. *The Social Origins of Violence in Uganda, 1964–1985.* Kampala: Fountain Publishers.

Khadiagala, L. S. 2001. "The Failure of Popular Justice in Uganda: Local Councils and Women's Property Rights." *Development and Change* 32 (4): 93–113.

Klasen, S. 2003. "Gender and Growth in Uganda: Some Preliminary Findings and Policy Issues." Background paper, U.K. Department for International Development, Kampala.

Lawson, D. 2003. Gender Analysis of the Uganda's National Household Surveys (1992–2003). Background paper, U.K. Department for International Development, Kampala.

Lewis, J. 2000. "The Batwa Pygmies of the Great Lakes Region: The Problem of Discrimination." Minority Rights Group, London.

Lwanga-Lunyiigo, S. 1989. "The Colonial Roots of Internal Conflict." In *Conflict Resolution in Uganda*, ed. K. Rupesinghe, 24–43. Oslo: International Peace Research Institute.

Mamdani, M. 1996. *Citizen and Subject: Contemporary Africa and the Legacy of Late Colonialism.* Princeton, NJ: Princeton University Press.

Moncrieffe, J. M., and R. Eyben. 2007. *The Power of Labeling: How People are Categorised and Why It Matters.* London: Earthscan.

Musisi, N. 2001. "Taking Spaces/Making Spaces: Gender and the Cultural Construction of 'Bad Women' in the Development of Kampala-Kibuga, 1900–1962." In *"Wicked" Women and the Reconfiguration of Gender in Africa*, ed. D. Hodgson and S. McCurdy, 171–87. Portsmouth, NH: Heinemann.

Naschold, F. 2002. "Why Inequality Matters for Poverty." Inequality Briefing Paper 2, Overseas Development Institute, London.

Nussbaum, M. 2003. "The Complexity of Groups: A Comment on Jorge Valadez." *Philosophy and Social Criticism* 29 (1): 57–69.

Pulford, C. 1999. *Eating Uganda: From Christianity to Conquest.* London: Ituri Publications.

Roscoe, J. 1966. The Baganda: Their Customs and Beliefs. London: Cass.

Sathyamurthy, T. V. 1986. *The Political Development of Uganda: 1900–1986.* Aldershot, U.K.: Gower.

Schiller, L. 1990. "The Royal Women of Buganda." *International Journal of African Historical Studies* 23 (3): 455–73.

Sen, A. 1992. *Inequality Reexamined.* Oxford, U.K.: Oxford Clarendon Press.

———. 1999. *Development as Freedom.* New York: Anchor Books

Stewart, F. 2002. "Horizontal Inequalities: A Neglected Dimension of Development." CRISE Working Paper 1, Centre for Research on Inequality, Human Security, and Ethnicity, Oxford, U.K.

Tamale, S. 1999. *When Hens Begin to Crow: Gender and Parliamentary Politics in Uganda.* Boulder, CO: Westview Press.

Tarrow, S. 1994. *Power in Movement: Social Movements, Collective Action, and Politics.* Cambridge, U.K.: Cambridge University Press.

Tripp, A. M. 2001. "The Politics of Autonomy and Cooptation in Africa: The Case of the Ugandan Women's Movement." *Journal of Modern African Studies* 39 (1): 101–28.

UPPAP (Uganda Participatory Poverty Assessment Project). 2000. *Uganda Participatory Poverty Assessment Report.* Kampala: Ministry of Finance, Planning, and Economic Development.

———. 2002. *Second Participatory Poverty Assessment Report: Deepening the Understanding of Poverty.* Kampala: Ministry of Finance, Poverty, and Economic Development.

Wacquant, L. 2005. "Habitus." In *International Encyclopedia of Economic Sociology*, ed. J. Becket and M. Zafiovski, 315–19. London: Routledge.

Wengi, J. O., and E. Kyasimire. 1995. "Report of Study on Legal Constraints to the Economic Empowerment of Uganda Women." Prepared for the World Bank and the Ministry of Gender and Community Development, Kampala

Zaninka, P. 2003. "Uganda." In *Indigenous Peoples and Protected Areas in Africa*, ed. J. Nelson and L. Hossack, 165–87. Moreton-in-Marsh, U.K.: Forest People's Programme.

Suggested Readings

Brock, K. 2003. "Poverty Knowledge and Policy Processes in Uganda: Case Studies from Bushenyi, Lira, and Tororo Districts." IDS Research Report, Institute of Development Studies, Brighton, U.K.

Collier, P., and R. Reinikka. 2001. "Introduction." In *Uganda's Recovery: The Role of Farms, Firms and Government*, ed. R. Reinikka and P. Collier, 1–11. Washington, DC: World Bank.

Hossain, N. 1999. "How Do Bangladeshi Elites Understand Poverty." IDS Working Paper 83, Institute of Development Studies, Brighton, U.K.

Linz, J., A. Stepan, and Y. Yadav. 2004. "Nation State or State Nation? Conceptual Reflections and Some Spanish, Belgian, and Indian Data." Background paper for the *Human Development Report*. New York: United Nations Development Programme.

Migdal, J. S. 2004. *Boundaries and Belonging: States and Societies in the Struggle to Shape Identities and Local Practices*. Cambridge, U.K.: Cambridge University Press.

Museveni, Y. K. 1997. *Sowing the Mustard Seed*. London: Macmillan Education.

Van Acker, F. 2000. "Ethnicity and Institutional Reform: A Case of Ugandan Exceptionalism." In *Politics of Identity and Economics of Conflict in the Great Lake Region*, ed. R. Doom and J. Gorus, 149–73. Brussels: Vrije Universiteit Brussel Press.

CHAPTER 4

Inequalities within India's Poorest Regions: Why Do the Same Institutions Work Differently in Different Places?

Arjan de Haan

Inequalities exist at many levels and have many different causes and manifestations. This chapter looks at inequalities within Orissa, asking how, in India's democratic structure, such disparities have prevailed. During the 1990s, but with roots well before then, Orissa gradually became India's poorest state, with regard to the proportion of people living below the poverty line. It had much slower improvements in human development indicators than other parts of India (and even Bangladesh) and perennial reports of starvation deaths in its southern and western areas.

This chapter is the product of intermittent analysis while I was working as social development adviser in the U.K. Department for International Development (DfID) Orissa program, and I owe much to my colleagues for encouraging me to continue my research even though it was not formally part of my work program. I also owe much to Amaresh Dubey, who urged me to continue to work with him on the data analysis. He provided the quantitative analysis of poverty data and is credited with pursuing data disaggregation; data are reported more extensively in our joint paper (de Haan and Dubey 2003). Biswamoy Pati encouraged me to delve deeper into the structures of elite politics in Orissa, and I probably draw more on his writings than the notes acknowledge. Many people have given detailed comments on various drafts, and I would like to thank in particular Tony Bebbington, Anis Dani, James Manor, N. C. Saxena, Saurabh Sinha, and—in the DfID office—Aruna Bagchee, Elizabeth Burgess, Dennis Pain, Amarjeet Sinha, Sarojini Thakur, and Geeta Unnikrishnan.

Not only is Orissa poor and stretched by fiscal crisis; it also is a very unequal state, with large disparities among regions, social groups and classes, and men and women. These disparities are multidimensional and often overlap and reinforce each other, with the regional and social group internexus being particularly strong in this state in which Adivasis form 22 percent of the population, concentrated in noncoastal areas. Gender discrimination crosscuts many of the other disparities. Tribal women in remote areas are among the most deprived people on the subcontinent. There are significant sustained gender gaps in human development indicators in Orissa, though gender divisions of labor and responsibilities may have been more equal among tribal groups than among others. The female–male (under age five) ratios have also begun to decline in Orissa, primarily in the better-off areas.

The key question for this chapter is why these disparities are so stark and have prevailed over time. The empirical description of well-being indicators shows how the disparities are overdetermined, how regional disparities overlap with social disparities—particularly those related to social group identity and gender—and are closely connected to access to livelihoods or economic opportunities, and how these disparities are shaped by institutions with a legacy of the colonial period and mixed records of reforms since. The chapter will provide a better understanding of the deep roots of existing disparities and will explore why, in the country's democratic structure and relatively well-developed formal institutions, policies—including those explicitly targeting intergroup and interregional disparities—have had a limited effect in reducing the disparities. The second section summarizes the well-documented data on these disparities, but the real question for this chapter is why policies have not succeeded in reducing disparities. Hence, the chapter pushes the analysis of inequalities ever further back, highlighting the interrelated arenas of economic opportunities, institutions, and social mobilization. In particular, the chapter attempts to highlight the kinds of institutions responsible for what appears to be sustained deprivation. Conversely, it asks which institutions need strengthening and which need weakening—for reducing those disparities.[1]

The third section highlights the long, deep historical roots of many of the disparities identified earlier. In Orissa, they include the sequences and geographies of conquest and the state's short history as an administrative unit, which has limited the political and administrative responses for equitable development. Since independence, three sets of sectoral policies or institutions have played key roles: (a) forest policies that have focused on revenue generation or environmental concerns and the institutions that emerged around these past state policies still affect development, (b) "development" that has led to large-scale displacement and disproportionately affected remote regions and Adivasis, and (c) land policies that have been relatively ineffective in broadening access to livelihoods of large parts of the population. For the description of the durable inequality that affects Adivasis in particular, this chapter emphasizes the interplay between the largely coastal, state officials and representatives and their administrative history in relation to the cultural and administrative history of the tribal societies they encounter. Such histories are by no means deterministic for development outcomes, but the regional and social disparities do suggest the existence of very durable structures that continue to influence disparities in well-being.

These complex but significant and sustained disparities are remarkable in the context of well-designed government programs to enhance development and to reduce disparities between groups. The fourth section explores government programs and forms of political representation that should have played a role in reducing disparities, and it discusses why their effects in Orissa have remained limited. They include the wide range of programs for scheduled tribes,[2] the programs for women, and the special area program KBK (Kalahandi-Bolangir-Koraput), with some reference to the performance of health and education programs. The varied program performance across India illustrates the conditions under which inequalities are likely to be reduced.

An important factor in the disparities and the limited effect of progressive programs within Orissa lies, it is hypothesized, in a lack of accountability and the underlying social mobilization or transformation that are key for program implementation and institutional change to be successful. The contributing factors include continued the dominance of the traditional elite, an extremely heterogeneous population, the limited development of decentralization, the low levels of political awareness among poor people, and the role played by nongovernmental organizations (NGOs). The chapter will end with some speculative thought based on experience with budget support and sector programs in Orissa regarding ways in which outside agencies may contribute to more equitable development paths in the context of such overdetermined disparities.

Multiple Disparities: The Quantitative Picture

Data are abundantly available to describe inequalities among the Indian population: poverty data from National Statistical Survey (NSS), education data from the census, and health indicators from the National Family Health Survey (NFHS) and Sample Registration Survey (SRS). Analysis of income poverty draws on NSS data, particular its consumption survey, which is conducted every five years. There has been much debate regarding the comparability of the 1999/2000 survey, with estimates of a decline during the 1990s varying from 10 to 3 percentage points (Deaton 2003a, 2003b; Sen and Himanshu 2004; Sundaram and Tendulkar 2003).[3]

State-level income poverty data reveal that in 1999/2000, Orissa had become India's poorest state, surpassing Bihar, which was still the poorest in 1993/94, but showed a substantial decline in poverty during the late 1990s.[4] Orissa's poverty headcount stagnated around 48 to 49 percent between 1993/94 and 1999/2000, whereas the headcount for all of India declined markedly. In Andhra Pradesh, poverty was cut in half, and even Madhya Pradesh showed a decline of five percentage points. Orissa's trend of falling behind the Indian average has a longer history, but it is particularly marked during the 1990s.

The NSS income poverty data allow for regional disaggregation, as presented in table 4.1. In Orissa, the NSS divides the state into coastal, southern, and northern regions. The uncorrected data show a remarkable picture. Although rural poverty in coastal Orissa was 32 percent in 1999/2000, it was 50 percent in northern Orissa (itself very heterogeneous) and a staggering 86 percent in southern Orissa.[5]

Comparisons are sensitive to price indexes and may influence the picture of high levels of poverty in the south. However, two sets of corrections do not change the picture of disparities substantially. Analysis by Manoj Panda (2002) using an adjusted cereal price indicates that poverty in the southern region would still be two and a half times that in the coastal region. If an adjustment is made to restore comparability between the 50th and 55th rounds of surveys, Kijima and Lanjouw (2003) show slightly lower levels of poverty in rural Orissa and somewhat smaller disparities, but the divergence between the coast and the south is still evident.[6]

Understanding the high levels of poverty in particular regions requires an understanding of economic growth performance, because economic growth is one of the most important statistical determinants of rates of poverty reduction. India's economic growth has varied greatly across states

Table 4.1. Poverty in Orissa's National Statistical Survey Regions, 1983–99/2000

	Official poverty line				International poverty line (US$1/day)			
Year	Coastal (191)	South (192)	North (193)	Orissa	Coastal (191)	South (192)	North (193)	Orissa
Rural areas								
1983	57.97	80.76	75.22	68.43	47.57	75.93	68.64	60.46
1987/88	48.37	82.98	61.01	58.62	55.33	85.61	65.49	63.98
1993/94	45.33	68.84	45.82	49.80	66.71	83.85	62.51	68.40
Corrected data	38.97	63.23	39.26	43.47	n.a.	n.a.	n.a.	n.a.
1999/2000	29.30	86.16	50.98	48.13	47.85	92.70	66.98	63.44
Corrected data	34.68	67.79	36.42	41.27	n.a.	n.a.	n.a.	n.a.
Urban areas								
1983	46.15	45.48	54.35	49.66	24.84	27.84	33.55	28.84
1987/88	42.11	52.93	39.90	42.58	22.64	29.71	25.59	24.74
1993/94	47.24	41.94	32.54	40.68	29.44	35.84	16.08	25.09
Corrected data	15.13	26.72	11.06	15.19	n.a.	n.a.	n.a.	n.a.
1999/2000	41.65	43.97	45.81	43.51	25.26	30.01	24.65	25.64
Corrected data	18.83	24.45	14.28	17.94	n.a.	n.a.	n.a.	n.a.
Total								
1983	56.49	79.08	72.28	66.24	44.74	73.65	63.70	56.77
1987/88	47.67	80.29	58.16	56.75	51.67	80.62	60.10	59.42
1993/94	45.57	66.07	43.92	48.64	62.06	78.91	55.86	62.88
1999/2000	31.51	81.28	50.10	47.37	43.81	85.46	59.81	57.24

Sources: Calculations by Amaresh Dubey; corrected data for the 50th and 55th rounds from Kijima and Lanjouw (2003).
Note: n.a = not applicable. Districts follow the 1991 classification: Coastal = Baleshwar, Cuttack, Ganjam, and Puri; South = Kalahandi, Koraput, and Phulbani; North = Balangir, Dhenkanal, Kendujhar, Mayurbhanj, Sambalpur, and Sundargarh.

and districts, as well as across sectors (Datt and Ravallion 2002). Orissa's poverty trend appears closely associated with the lack of economic growth in the state, because annual per capita state domestic product grew by 2.3 percent between 1993/94 and 1999/2000—higher than in Assam and Bihar, but well below the Indian average of about 3.5 percent.[7] Agricultural growth was sluggish (less than 2 percent per year), though industrial growth performance was even worse,[8] and the growth rate of agricultural wages hardly rose above zero (Deaton and Drèze 2002). Although no data are readily available, it is likely that regional growth within Orissa has also been diverse; for example, agricultural growth has been lower in the southern areas.[9] Disaggregation of growth trends, thus, may partly explain a low growth–poverty elasticity. However, it is equally important to highlight—as was done in Currie's (2000) in-depth study on Kalahandi and Pradhan's (1993a, 1993b) analysis of the mid-1980s drought—that even the districts that witness hunger have continued to produce a food surplus (that is, showing classic cases of entitlement failures and processes of marginalization at the local level).

Income poverty is only one of the elements determining ill-being and well-being. Deprived people suffer similarly from lack of access to education, to health care, and to personal security.[10] The census provides detailed information on literacy rates at the district level and below. In 1991, 49 percent of Orissa's population was literate, and literacy increased to 64 percent in 2001. Even in 2001, however, literacy levels in the southern districts were still around 30 to 35 percent, and female literacy was below 25 percent, whereas levels in coastal districts rose to around 80 percent. Adult literacy in 2001 was 69 percent in Puri and 23 percent in Koraput. The trend over the 1990s showed a small decrease in the regional disparities in literacy. Although not as reliable and easy to disaggregate as education data, NFHS data that are available at the district level show that infant and maternal mortality rates in Orissa are well above the Indian average, but the rates still substantially declined during the past decade. Data on the percentage of women receiving skilled attention during pregnancy show very large regional inequalities, whereas the data on child immunization show somewhat more moderate inequalities.

There are well-known substantial differences in well-being across social groups in India. Scheduled castes (SCs, or Dalits) and scheduled tribes (STs, or Adivasis) are particularly disadvantaged. Through their position at the bottom of the caste hierarchy, Dalits are characterized both by cultural forms of exclusion (such as pollution) and by economic deprivation (concentrated in the worst forms of manual labor); Adivasis similarly suffer great disadvantages but are placed outside the caste hierarchy and tend to live separately from mainstream society (although, as described later, they have been included in the mainstream economy but on particularly disadvantageous terms).

Average per capita income of SCs and STs at the all-India level is about one-third lower than that of other groups. In 1999/2000, headcount poverty was 16 percent among nondeprived groups, 30 percent among minorities (Muslims), 36 percent among SCs, and 44 percent among STs. These disparities have shown few signs of being reduced. Deprived groups also have much lower literacy than other groups. NFHS data for India in 1998/99 showed that 88 percent of ST women, 73 percent of SC women, and 44 percent of women from other groups were illiterate. NSS data on neonatal, postneonatal, infant, child, and under-five mortality indicators for socially excluded groups are similar to those of other indicators (for example, the infant mortality rates for SCs and STs are about 84 percent, in contrast with 62 percent for nondeprived groups).

Within Orissa, these disparities are as large—and larger for some indicators—as disparities in India on average (see tables 4.2 and 4.3). As elsewhere in India, the poverty incidence of STs (72 percent) and SCs (55 percent) is well above that of other groups (33 percent). The differences between STs and others are larger in rural areas than in urban areas, and they are slightly larger in Orissa than in India as a whole. Because poverty, in particular, is extremely high in southern Orissa, where the concentration of STs is high, the deprivation of STs may be caused mainly by their location. However, even in southern Orissa, the incidence of poverty among STs (92 percent) is higher than among others (78 percent, which is still very high). Since 1983, poverty incidence has declined more rapidly among other groups (23 percentage points) than among STs (a mere 14 percentage points) and SCs (20 percentage points)—a trend that is unusually adverse compared with the trend in India as a whole.

Health and education also show significant group differences. In education, differences between India and Orissa are small, but though 27 percent of the nondeprived population in rural coastal areas is illiterate (17 percent in urban areas), 82 percent of the ST population in the southern areas is illiterate. According to NFHS-2 (as cited in de Haan and Dubey 2003), 88 percent of the female tribal population, 73 percent of SC women, 56 percent of other backward caste women, and 34 percent of "other women" were illiterate. Some 37 percent of ST women receive no

Table 4.2. Poverty Ratios by Social Group, Orissa and India, 1983–99/2000

	Rural				Urban				Total			
Social group	1983	1987/88	1993/94	1999/2000	1983	1987/88	1993/94	1999/2000	1983	1987/88	1993/94	1999/2000
Orissa												
ST	87.08	83.82	71.31	73.08	73.73	61.37	62.81	59.38	86.22	82.34	70.76	72.08
SC	75.99	65.75	49.79	52.30	69.53	59.52	45.46	72.03	75.38	65.35	49.39	55.08
Other	58.52	47.31	40.18	33.29	41.86	37.87	36.32	34.18	56.16	45.92	39.55	33.48
All	68.43	58.62	49.79	48.04	49.66	42.58	40.68	43.59	66.24	56.75	48.63	47.31
All India												
ST	63.89	56.31	47.05	44.35	55.30	52.26	35.67	37.42	63.27	55.93	46.29	43.67
SC	58.96	50.79	48.27	35.44	56.12	54.65	49.08	39.13	58.50	51.38	48.42	36.14
Other	40.90	33.80	31.20	21.14	39.94	36.44	28.67	20.78	40.66	34.48	30.46	21.04
All	46.51	39.36	37.28	26.50	42.32	39.16	31.70	23.98	45.57	39.31	35.95	25.87

Source: Calculated by Amaresh Dubey from official National Statistical Survey data; for details, see de Haan and Dubey (2003).
Note: In Orissa, 23 percent of the population is classified as scheduled tribe (ST) and 16 percent as scheduled caste (SC).

Table 4.3. Headcount Index in Regions of Orissa by Social Group, 1999/2000

	Rural				Urban			
Region	ST	SC	Other	All	ST	SC	Other	All
Coastal	66.63	42.18	24.32	31.74	63.47	75.74	34.26	41.84
South	92.42	88.90	77.65	87.05	72.28	85.02	24.59	43.85
North	61.69	57.22	34.67	49.81	54.44	63.11	37.77	46.06
Orissa	73.08	52.30	33.29	48.04	59.38	72.03	34.18	43.59

Source: Calculated using the official poverty line by Amaresh Dubey from official National Statistical Survey data.

prenatal checkups, compared with 15 percent of women from nondeprived groups, and rates of full immunization among ST children are about half that among children of nondeprived groups. The dropout rate at the primary education level was 42 percent for all children (similar for both boys and girls), 52 percent for SCs (substantially higher for girls), and 63 percent for STs (NCDS 2004: table 4.19).

Patterns of landownership highlight disparities between groups. Although average cultivable landholdings in Orissa are relatively small, particularly in coastal areas, SCs have average landholdings just over half that of others. STs, on average, hold more land, but these landholdings are likely to be in marginal areas and not irrigated.[11] According to a World Bank (2000: 18) analysis of NSS data, the share of those employed working as cultivators declined between 1993/94 and 1999/2000 from 45 percent to 30 percent, and small landowners began entering into casual wage labor.

Thus, Dalits and Adivasis in Orissa suffer the same disadvantages as they do elsewhere—in some cases even more so—and the gaps show little sign of being bridged. Poverty among deprived groups is higher because of lower levels of literacy and other forms of assets; hence, primary education programs will go some way in addressing the disparities. However, analysis also shows that STs and SCs tend to be poorer than other populations even if they have the same levels of education. Moreover, returns to assets are lower among deprived groups than among others. Hence, it is clear that they face discrimination. Although findings are similar throughout India, such discrimination, particularly for STs, appears higher in Orissa than in India on average (de Haan and Dubey 2003: annex 15).[12]

Separate poverty data are not available for men and women, because income and consumption surveys such as the NSS take the household as a unit of analysis. As elsewhere, evidence regarding whether female-headed households are poorer than others is mixed: NSS data (de Haan and Dubey 2003) show no significant correlation in Orissa between female-headed households and poverty, but primary data analysis by Pradeep Kumar Panda (1997) suggests that female headship is closely linked to poverty and child disadvantage.

Female education lags behind male education and varies across Orissa's regions and districts. Disparities between men and women declined only a little between 1991 and 2001. Regional disparities also decreased marginally, and improvements in enrollment show some reduction in disparities (NCDS 2004). Against the considerable efforts toward universalizing primary education over the 1990s, these gaps are significant and indicate the deep-rooted problems of underdevelopment.

Health indicators also highlight the considerable disadvantages women face. Maternal mortality is still extremely high and well above the Indian average, although it declined substantially during the 1990s. Data on women receiving skilled attention during pregnancy emphasize large disparities across the state (for example, 10 percent in Malkangiri versus more than 50 percent in some coastal districts). In poorer districts, the age of marriage is substantially younger than in better-off areas (NCDS 2004).

Census data indicate that sex ratios (number of boys to girls) in Orissa may be worsening, indicating discrimination against girls. However, female disadvantage varies across social groups: the worsening of sex ratios appears to occur first among the better off and in better-off areas, and not, for example, among many tribes—though their human development indicators fall far behind the average. Different groups have different values and social relations, and gender division of labor and responsibilities is more equitable in tribal areas than in other areas in Orissa.

Gender inequalities may be growing in these areas, however, and the character of inequality is changing. The movement of Adivasis to new areas has often led to registration of ownership in the name of male heads of households, affecting traditional land use. The assignment of individual use of land has resulted in discrimination against women, and women's traditional economic role and freedom may not always lead directly to participation in new forms of decision making. Also, a gender bias has evolved in the more traditional or mainstream education system, though residential schools are effectively combating this problem. Dowries have been emerging among ever-larger proportions of the population, indicating an undervaluation of women's contribution and, in turn, causing discrimination against female offspring. Some of the worst expressions of gender discrimination—that is, the worsening sex ratios—tend to be denied or neglected in most circles.[13]

Historical Origins of Underdevelopment: Colonial and Postcolonial Institutions

To understand the regional and social disparities, one must consider the relatively recent existence of the state of Orissa. The extension of colonial power to the area now constituting Orissa was very limited, with 26 princely or feudatory and tributary states (Garjat historical area). Only a small percentage of the area was under direct colonial control (formerly under control of the Mughal Empire). The coastal area that was under direct British control was part of the much larger Bengal Presidency and was probably a relatively neglected or underresourced area. After a short period of administrative unity with Bihar, the state of Orissa came into being in 1936. This short history, arguably, has had an effect on the kinds of policies and institutions promoted by the elite, the fluent nature of an Oriya identity (Pati 2003; Sengupta 2001), a quest for uniting Oriya-speaking areas into a single territory and the role of the Jagannath cult, the lack of knowledge among Oriyas about their own province (Pati 1993), and a strong emphasis on insider-outsider distinction, as will be discussed later.

The current area of Orissa fell under the three main administrative colonial divisions with distinct forms of land registration, administration, and taxation—which still influence and complicate land administration (Mearns 1999). Most land fell under (Bengal) Zamindari control, with various layers of intermediaries exacting land revenue. Southern Orissa fell under the Madras Presidency, with a peasant proprietor system, and a small part of cultivated area in Orissa was under the Mahalwari system. Land regimes within the former princely states varied, but they often had poorly documented land rights (which had equity implications for subsequent survey and settlement, with Adivasis often described as encroachers); had repressive regimes generally; and brought in administrators from outside the area (Bailey 1963). Bailey (1957) describes the entry of outsiders in a village in the Kondmals (only 100 miles east of Cuttack), noting that the area was incorporated within the political boundary only in the middle of the 19th century. Administrators entered from the south, and Oriya colonists came from the north, from another tributary state, over a period that may have been as long as three centuries. In 1957, while the new political reality was starting to affect the socioeconomic structure,

> the region still shows many of the characteristics of a settlers' frontier. The newcomers have taken the best land. Their religion and language are different from those of the native inhabitants. They took concubines, but rarely wives,... live in separate villages,... [and] claim superiority,... [and] the Oriyas shook off metropolitan control and retained only the loosest ties with the Hindu Rajas on the plains. (Bailey 1957: 242)

The frontier economy led to large numbers of land transfers, which were stimulated by the pressure of a growing population and were helped by, as Bailey (1957) emphasizes, the title of landholder and rights to buy and sell. The institution of private rights thus played an important role in the process, facilitated by the colonial authorities.

During the colonial period, both landownership and forest management were explicitly designed to enhance state revenues, though with different intensities in different places. Since independence, both have undergone enormous transformations and have become clearly more equitable in design. However, the effects of these changes have been mixed; in the case of Orissa, many of the old exploitative structures have remained to a large extent unchallenged.

First, land reforms have done less to broaden the economic and political power structure in Orissa than in other places. A land ceiling may have prevented concentration of landownership and may have benefited the poor, but redistribution of land has not changed greatly since independence. Tenancy reform has had varied effects across India, though it has overall, according to some analysts, led to a substantial loss of access to land by the rural poor. Bans on tenancy as in Orissa have probably done little to protect security of access, and bans on the sale of tribal land to nontribal members have been largely ineffective. Land alienation has continued, and, as shown elsewhere too, indebtedness and forced possessions of land are the major causes. The power balance in rural areas allows for rent seeking by revenue inspectors from encroachers, making it difficult for the poor to convert de facto access into de jure ownership.

The position of women is negatively affected by their lack of access to landownership, despite far-reaching legal rights to own land and recent provisions for joint land titling (with a delayed introduction in Orissa). Processes that have restricted access to common property resources can lead to a vicious cycle of at least relative and possibly also absolute deprivation, because women stand to lose more access to productive opportunities. This effect can lead to the devaluation of their contribution within the household, a move from systems of bride price to systems of dowry, and likely sex discrimination.

Second, changes in access to common property resources have been insufficiently studied, even though about 100 million people in India derive their livelihoods from forests (Saxena 2003). Some 20 percent of all land in Orissa consists of common areas (wasteland, grazing lands, forest), and Adivasi families derive about half their livelihoods from forests. Although landownership has not shown great changes at the macrolevel, access to forests or common property resources has changed enormously (Mearns 1999). Orissa has lost more than a quarter of its forests in the past 25 years. This decline appears to have continued longer than elsewhere in India, and less has been done to rehabilitate forests in Orissa.[14] Deforestation has a particularly negative effect on women, because the collection of nontimber forest products has been their primary occupation and because access to resources outside these areas is not equally secured (Agarwal 1995).

The institutions determining forest access are far from traditional (box 4.1). Under colonial authorities, firm control over forests was established, with revenue generation a key objective that still influences formal instructions for officers (Saxena 2003). The policy environment after independence is still being determined by a belief that forests are state property. Many products relevant to the livelihoods of poor people have been subject to control. Trade and processing used to be leased to a small number of traders, who donated money to political parties. From the early 1970s, regulation and nationalization were introduced, with the stated objective of protecting the poor against exploitation by private traders and intermediaries. By the mid-1980s, this policy was partially reversed, with the state of Orissa encouraging private leases. This move was widely criticized. From 2000, *Gram panchayats* (local government bodies) obtained the authority to regulate, purchase, procure, and trade most nontimber forest products, while kendu leaves, bamboo, and sal seeds remain under government monopoly (the role of gram panchayats and the process of decentralization is described in more detail in the last section).

The well-being of people in forest areas, through livelihood opportunities and access to markets, is greatly influenced by public policies and institutions and the evolution of those institutions. The outcome of progressive policies

BOX 4.1

Livelihoods and Institutions in Forest Areas

Nontimber forest products (NTFPs) provide substantial inputs to people's livelihoods, but the highly complex institutions that enable the extraction and marketing of these products are biased against primary producers in India. NTFP management is complex, products are diverse, production is uncertain, and local markets are highly imperfect. Yet no forest inventories through NTFP yield studies and regeneration surveys exist. The Forest Department lacks orientation and has so far been unable to build the capacity for local forest management.

A host of government and nongovernmental institutions are involved in local-level trade of NTFPs, including corporations such as the Tribal Development Cooperative Corporation. But these institutions have never shared profits with the primary collectors, nor have they engaged in promoting adding value to NTFPs. They are constrained by shortages of staff and capital and have ended up drawing on the services of the local traders.

It is estimated that mobile local traders may control half the NTFP trade. These traders advance small loans to tree owners and collectors, usually without interest, to prebook all the product collected by the debtor. The trade practices are far from being fair and include misconduct in measurement as well as purchase rates.

The monopoly of 68 NTFPs ended with a resolution in March 2000, which vested the *gram panchayats* (local government bodies at the village level) with the authority to regulate the purchase, procurement, and trade so that the primary gatherers receive a fair price. By empowering the gram panchayats to regulate trade, the resolution abandoned state-level price setting, thus introducing price setting at the district level, with the district collector empowered to set a minimum procurement price. However, Saxena's (2001) assessment highlighted that the markets continued to be buyers' markets:

- Prices continued to remain below the minimum.
- The Forest Department continued to control storage, transit, and processing and to harass traders.
- Unregistered traders still operated in the market.
- Unethical practices of advance trading and distress selling and unethical weighing methods continued to be used.
- The village-level, multiple-buyer system had failed to develop.
- The gram panchayats and the community were unaware of policy provisions.

Source: Saxena 2001, 2003.

depends on a wide range of factors. Commercial objectives and vested interests by public sector corporations have continued to work against the interests of the poor, even though payments to kendu leaf pickers have increased on paper (Saxena 2003). The effect of far-reaching reforms devolving responsibilities to panchayats depends on capacity at the local level—generally recognized as being absent—and the creation (as in the case of land rights) of awareness and availability of information. Moreover, Orissa's changes have done little to promote the interests of marginalized population groups. The large proportions of people who depend on policies relating to forests have done remarkably little to affect policy making—a topic that will be discussed later.

Third, in Orissa as elsewhere, development has caused—and will continue to cause—large-scale displacement, which has disproportionately affected tribals (Pandey 1998). Some 3 million to 5 million people (of which more than 50 percent are Adivasis) have been displaced in Orissa since 1950 because of various development projects (Saxena 2001). In some areas, displacement has been complicated by the settlement of Bangladeshi refugees. The record of resettlement policies has been extremely patchy (Xaxa 2001).

The socioeconomic disparities and the institutions that have affected the life of the rural population are mirrored in Orissa's political and administrative power structures.[15] The former princely states of Orissa were unsuccessful in retaining political power, and right-wing parties were influential during the first decades after independence. A Brahman-Karan middle class has dominated society and politics in Orissa, and caste associations and politicization of lower castes by and large failed to develop. Moreover, the Adivasis have not emerged as an independent force, despite numerical presence, and leaders have been largely co-opted within existing power structures.

Major change in political mobilization happened under Biju Patnaik, chief minister of Orissa, who in opposition to the Congress Party broadened the social and political base and stimulated some form of an agrarian middle class, mainly through mobilization of middle-caste Khandayats. But electoral politics have retained a strong personal character and have continued to compete from the same social base, and the political divide between the Biju Janata Dal–Bharatiya Janata Party (with Naveen Patnaik, the current chief minister of Orissa) and the Congress Party—with control changing at almost every election—is widely regarded as creating indifference to development outcomes and policy implementation. The fact that two of Orissa's chief ministers (Giridhar Gamang, a tribal leader, and Naveen Patnaik) did not speak Oriya fluently seems of major symbolic importance.

Rulers have had an exceptionally strong focus on industrialization (Manor 1998). This interest, however, has remained largely at the level of rhetoric, as displayed through both industrialization plans and power sector reform. The focus on industrialization contributed to a neglect of agriculture and of the interests of the rural population. Moreover, at least Biju Patnaik took a very relaxed attitude to the corruption of both bureaucrats and politicians. Naveen Patnaik's reputation and electoral success was to a large extent based on being clean, but he made few proactive efforts to reduce corruption. In Manor's (1998) analysis of power sector reforms, Orissa's administrative top lacks the technical sophistication and self-confidence of administrations elsewhere in India. Moreover, in debates with the central government, the Orissa administration appears to take on a position of victim (for example, claiming special status with regard to conditions for central program funding).

The first phase of land reforms and integration of the princely states into the nation and state has occurred in Orissa, as elsewhere, but the land-based middle peasants have not challenged the power structure that emerged after independence, as has happened in other states. Recent challenges to power by lower castes (as occurred recently in Uttar Pradesh and Bihar) or, indeed, to land reforms (as were organized in West Bengal by the elite through well-functioning local governance systems) did not occur in Orissa either. Personal observations suggest a much greater insider–outsider distinction in Orissa than elsewhere. Challenges to the power structures by the tribal parts of the state, which have led to bifurcation in Bihar and Madhya Pradesh, while existent in Orissa, have not been significant, even though Adivasis constitute a larger proportion of the population in Orissa than in any other major state in India.

Although analysis of the nature of Orissa's elite leads to fairly pessimistic predictions on the potential for overall development of the state, there is even less reason for optimism about the likelihood of development patterns becoming equitable regionally and across social groups. Preindependence practices of bringing outside administrators into the feudal states have continued to a great extent. Orissa is quite exceptional in its lack of local cadres of administrators. Possibly partly as a result of this absence, Orissa has a legendary problem of unfilled vacancies in remote areas. Local development projects thus still play out—according to Alan Rew (personal communication), who has followed local development trends in Keonjhar—in the context of the division between largely coastal and upper-caste officials and the tribal peoples of Garjat and in the midst of wariness, suspicion, and resistance, informed by the colonial and administrative history (even though the tribal groups have become a local political force).

The focus on the need for investment (including foreign investment[16]) in mineral resources highlights the unrepresentative nature of Orissa's power structure. To some extent, Orissa confirms the hypothesis regarding problems caused by rich mineral resources (and the argument by Michael Ross in chapter 7 regarding the key role of structured and continued consultation, which appears largely absent in Orissa)—with the unfortunate fact that these resources are located mostly in tribal areas. The opposition to such investments—on the grounds that they usually lead to displacement and a distrust of resettlement policies—has been branded as antidevelopment, and rulers have shown little compassion even when Adivasis were killed by police fire during protests.

The lack of roots of the elite has been illustrated starkly, too, in the Orissa government's reaction to news reports of starvation deaths in the western parts of the state. Often reports from outside the state (for example, from the National Human Rights Commission, the Supreme Court, or study teams from the central government), are met with skepticism from Orissa government officials; with comments about regular politicization of the issue, including through the "familiar federal handle"; and with denial that deaths were caused by starvation (box 4.2).

Studies emphasize the continued dominance of an extremely narrow elite with little base in society and of "procedural" rather than "substantive participatory democracy" (Jayal 1999: 100). They indicate that major changes in the political structures of other Indian states have bypassed Orissa—though why local and group political representatives have not had a greater effect on the policy agenda still remains to be explained. Although it is true that many individuals have shown great commitment to the welfare of deprived groups, there seems to be a clear association between the composition of the ruling elite and the overdetermination of disparities. A very small, geographically limited, and nationally marginalized elite has not—as has happened elsewhere in India—either diversified its interest (opening up space for progressive changes) or seen its power base challenged (forcing progressive, if messy, policy change). Consequently, many of the potentially progressive institutions have

BOX 4.2

Orissa's Emergency Responses to Destitution

Assembly questions related to destitution in southern Orissa tend to elicit delayed and weak responses. It is common for the state administration to deny the existence of starvation, arguing that the increased death rates were due to old age, dysentery, meningitis, consumption of mango kernels, and so forth. However, the denial of starvation does not preclude the Orissa government from claiming increased central assistance, and the official emphasis on droughts (which also attributes the problem to the will or whimsies of nature) helps the government in this plea. According to Jayal (1999: 63), the first time a state minister admitted in the Legislative Assembly that people had died because of a lack of adequate food was in October 1987, a month after Rajiv Gandhi's second visit to Kalahandi. Even in 2002, as in 1991, much of the debate, centered on whether the increased death rates were starvation related.

That questions are raised in democratic forums should not lead one to conclude that there is widespread interest in the issue. According to Jayal (1999), a mere 14 questions about Kalahandi were raised in the Lok Sabha (lower house of India's parliament) during 1985 to 1988, and most were unrelated to starvation issues. Any of the official responses appear of very poor quality and extremely defensive. A clear exception was the 1991 Mishra Commission report, which charged the administration with lax enforcement of the Land Reform Act and Money Lenders' Acts, mismanagement of resources for development, corruption, and collusion with moneylenders and village headmen, locally known as *gountias*.

This investigation and others highlight the structural nature of deprivation and emphasize reforms related to land alienation and awareness of rights and entitlements, whereas the official response has largely focused on charity and relief expenditures in reaction to events beyond the government's control. Significantly, whatever response emerged was largely not the result of pressure by the people directly affected (even nongovernmental organizations were slow to respond to calls for evidence), for whom the calamities that are highlighted in the press are probably part of their usual existence.

proved ineffective at best and exploitative at worst. Orissa's historical path of political-economic development provides clear clues regarding why disparities have not been reduced in any significant measure. As argued in the next section, the relative lack of success in implementing various programs results at least partly from this same power structure.

Policies for Reducing Disadvantages of Historically Deprived Groups: What Is the Evidence of Effect?

Orissa is not a failed state in the sense of a collapse of political and administrative structures. Political differences have been contained within the democratic structure, and bifurcation of a Kosal state (consisting of 11 western Orissa districts) appears only a remote possibility. The administrative structure is operational, and administrative data and auditor's reports are generally available.[17] Reform-minded individuals have been able to make a difference because the infrastructure is in place (even in the case of recent initiatives for self-help groups). Orissa does not do as badly as is often reported in leveraging and using central government funding. A large majority of the people own ration cards, albeit with a bias toward better-off households (Kumar 2001), and these people have recently been counted in the census as below the poverty line, a designation that is a precondition for access to a range of targeted programs.

As the health and education progress described earlier suggests, administrative and front-line services are present even in the remotest areas (even though posts are hard to fill). Primary health care and education workers have been exempted from the recruitment freeze,[18] and social sector spending has remained protected (perhaps because that expenditure is mostly for salaries, rather than public pressure for social programs) and is not notably low compared with that in other parts of India.[19] However, the quality of program implementations is very mixed. For example, access to medical facilities is well below the national average, particularly in remote areas (NCDS 2004: table 5.19). The Integrated Child Development Scheme, which provides nutrition, health, immunization, and referral services for young children, has not had uniformly bad reviews in Orissa. National data suggest the scheme is not performing poorly in Orissa compared with elsewhere in India, and a study by the Praxis Institute for Participatory Studies (2002) indicated immunization performance was fairly good. However, the same study suggested worse performances for food supplies and care to pregnant women (Centre for Youth and Social Development 2002).

Similarly, programs for primary education, including a new initiative for hot meals in schools, evidently exist throughout the state, demonstrating that much construction has occurred and enthusiastic communities have been mobilized. At the same time, though, alternative schooling—through local management and locally appointed teachers and village education committees—is constrained by the lack of implementation capacity in Orissa, and politicians at the district level and below are using these new structures for political patronage (a problem that in other states appears to have been averted [A. Sinha, personal communication]).

A key conclusion regarding many of these policies is how mixed the effect has been across sectors, programs, and districts. The rest of this section explores this conclusion for two programs that were designed to address group and regional disparities.

Deprived Groups

India has an elaborate system of programs with the explicit objective of reducing disparities between historically deprived groups and the rest of the population. These programs have sets of policies for affirmative action, economic empowerment, and protection against violence and discrimination, and they include a wide range of public bodies and commissions and rules for disaggregation of spending for deprived groups, women, Dalits, and Adivasis.

The core of these policies was designed to be temporary following independence, but the policies have survived and proliferated, perhaps because of limited success in reducing disparities, but more likely because the policies have met the vested interests of elites from deprived groups and have become the terrain of significant political struggle and mobilization (Balagopal 2000). Deprived groups have at times demanded to be included in SC and ST categories so that they can obtain state benefits, and recently there have been demands to extend job reservation to the private sector.

The effect of programs to address disparities between social groups in Orissa is unknown, and the absence of information is itself suggestive of a lack of accountability. Because disparities have not been reduced significantly does not, of course, prove that these programs have not worked. However, assessments that are fairly widely shared by researchers include the following. First, though on the one hand a great deal of emancipation has been achieved across the country, the caste structure has remained, on the other hand, much more strongly present after independence than progressive thinkers and policy makers expected. As authors such as Alam (1999a,

1999b) and Kaviraj (2000) have emphasized, emancipation has occurred mainly on the political front and not in the achievement of social equality.

The policy of job reservation has been subject to a fair amount of analysis, and conclusions have inevitably been mixed. First, it is important to highlight how much the language and policies around caste have changed the political dynamics, not only, as indicated before, by providing deprived groups access to the political arena and by allowing new claims to such access, but also by reinforcing group identities. Second, analysis of reservation in education (Weisskopf 2004) shows that (a) even though it creates a "creamy layer" among the deprived groups, this "elite" continues to suffer from disadvantages; (b) the effects of such a policy have been limited, seats often go unfilled, and students from deprived backgrounds tend to choose arts rather than the more prestigious fields of engineering and medicine; but (c) there is evidence that students of lower socioeconomic status perform better and are upwardly mobile because of these policies.[20]

Over time, these policies have added a range of special features for Adivasis.[21] Areas with high concentrations of Adivasis were characterized administratively as scheduled areas (almost half of the 300 blocks[22] in Orissa). Recently, special and potentially radical provisions for local government were included in the Panchayat Extension to Scheduled Areas (PESA), which brings far-reaching power to *gram sabha* and *pali sabha* (village councils) in tribal areas. However, in Orissa, capacity for effective local governance has remained limited, with few if any efforts to strengthen it (box 4.3). The Institute for Socio-Economic Development (2002) indicates that even awareness of PESA is very limited.

An important policy instrument has been the Tribal Sub Plan, which was adopted from the Fifth Five-Year Plan onward following observations of very low outlays for programs for Adivasis and focuses on blocks with majority tribal populations (118 blocks in Orissa). Integrated tribal development agencies implement a range of income-generating activities and infrastructure development projects. Spending for Adivasis is intended to be proportional to their percentage of the population.[23] This approach has suffered from two key problems (Mander 2004: 114). First, spending targets do not guarantee development outcomes and can—particularly in the absence of users' accountability—become goals rather than a means to an end. Second, there is much evidence of creative accounting within special component plans, with indivisible outlays (for example, for infrastructure) booked to funds earmarked for Adivasis.

BOX 4.3

Neglect in Special Programs

A visit to Ganjam and Koraput districts in December 2003 by two U.K. Department for International Development representatives highlighted many good government and nongovernmental initiatives that addressed poverty, in the context of a state's capacity crippled by debt. The trip also generated some insights (based on very short visits) into discrimination against and inadequate care of Adivasi children in residential schools.

In one village, a hostel at a government school with 4 teachers for 240 children and amalgamated classes had a metal bed, a small trunk, a mosquito net, and one blanket for each child. The government stipend for food, clothing, and health care was considered inadequate, and some boys informed the visitors that they did not have enough food. The problem was seriously compounded by a bureaucratic problem during the previous eight months: the stipend was paid for only two months, and the remaining funds would not arrive until the end of the financial year (having been used to help address the state's ways-and-means position during the year)—even though the stipend was to be paid out of a donor-supported primary education program. As a result, schools used credit to obtain food, which was likely of low quality and insufficient.

In another village, the nongovernmental organization Gram Vikas constructed residential schools mainly for scheduled tribe children. Applications for accreditation of these schools have been rejected by the government of Orissa on technical grounds, despite good academic results. One month before the visit, two Adivasi girls from one of the Gram Vikas schools entered a Sanskrit recitation competition and won first and second place. Their prizes were replaced by "special awards" once the judges became aware of the girls' origin, and first and second place were reawarded to others.

Any review of the programs for deprived groups has to comment on the wide range of programs—partly state driven, partly centrally sponsored—with many overlapping areas and objectives. In fact, there has been little in-depth and systematic review of the programs. In the case of Orissa, at least, the push for these programs is largely from the top down. Few, if any, programs have arisen out of bottom-up pressure—though there are many examples of innovative bottom-up projects at the local level. The underuse of funding in plan schemes, as highlighted in the Orissa budget for 2003–04 (Government of Orissa 2003), equally suggests that there has been little push for improvements in performance (even though the problem is partly caused by the state's inability to share in the costs for the programs).

Too little knowledge is known about the day-to-day operation of the state administration, but an assessment by Xaxa (2003: 45) is probably not far off the mark in Orissa:

> The constitution of course promises to integrate and provide [Adivasis] space for participation and share in state institutions. However, the state administrative machinery, [which] is manned mainly by personnel from the dominant communities, is indifferent, discriminatory, and even hostile to the entry of the tribal people in these modern institutions. They are not only kept excluded but also discriminated through various kinds administrative recruitment procedures and practices.

Rew (2003) observes how governance in Keonjhar shares many of the characteristics described by Bailey in the 1950s, in which the government is an adversary, a solid and person-like entity, and is insensitive to local context. Little suggests that existing programs help redress the differences in power, and the programs arguably reinforce such problems as long as implementation remains top-down.

Special Area Program: KBK

As in the case of the centrally sponsored programs for scheduled castes and tribes, center-state relations are important in the second major policy intervention, which was designed specifically to address the underdevelopment of the southwestern area of Orissa, the KBK (Kalahandi-Bolangir-Koraput) region. The KBK region has had a great deal of attention from political leaders, including Indira Gandhi, who visited Kalahandi in 1966, and Rajiv Gandhi, who traveled there in 1985. In 1988, the Area Development Approach for Poverty Termination (ADAPT) was initiated. ADAPT was revived after intervention by Prime Minister Narashima Rao and the minister for agriculture in 1991 and was redesigned into the Revised Long-Term Action Plan in 1995. This multisectoral and long-term plan has connectivity and literacy as core objectives. Allocation is Rs 6,000 crore[24] over nine years, and over time the central government allocation for Orissa increased to 100 percent of total funding.

Existing reviews of the program do not show an optimistic picture. The program adds to the number of mushroomed programs that have overlapping objectives overstretch the bureaucracy. Implementation has been extremely slow, and spending in the first years very low—leading to a substantial redesign. A Planning Commission–sponsored study (IAMR 2003) found that the program's headquarters was understaffed. Use of funds, which during previous years had been 75 to 80 percent, varied greatly across the multisectoral program. Many of the agriculture-related schemes appeared unsuccessful and had little effect. A program of mobile health units was hampered by the lack of road access—many would argue unsurprisingly. Programs that were seen to be relatively successful included the emergency feeding, education, drinking water initiatives, as well as some of the poverty alleviation schemes. This outcome suggests that performance has been best mostly in areas of residual social policy, where vested interests are smallest.

A more in-depth review of the program is desirable. Observations indicate that remarkably little has happened even though KBK has long been in the political debate. It is important to emphasize that the lack of performance is not a natural phenomenon but is due to a lack of sustained pressure within the system or among beneficiaries to make things work. Moreover, the program does not address the underlying problems of unequal power relations. Hence, it may do some good, but it cannot be expected to address the stark disparities.

Social Mobilization as a Precondition for Breaking Unequal Structures?

Thinking about the question of the causes of inequality leads to constant shifts in the question of why these disparities are so stark and have prevailed over time. Income inequality across Orissa is linked to disparities in health and education—regional as well as social group disparities—that are mirrored in political relations. To a great extent, these disadvantages overlap and are overdetermined. The disparities by themselves are not random but are the outcomes of historical developments, which in principle are contingent. However, in Orissa—compared with other Indian states—they have not involved a significant transformation of the social structure.

The key institutions that have determined the livelihoods of the poor in Orissa (which are primarily dependent on access to land and forests) have historically been characterized by exploitative relations. These institutions have been only minimally transformed over the past five decades, because peasants have remained largely unconnected to political power. Adivasis are even more remote from political influence because their access to land and forests is still insecure, and local administration is often absent or colludes with local power holders.

It is against this backdrop that, this chapter argues, the potential success of pro-poor policies and programs needs to be assessed. Effects of programs on people who lack basic access to livelihood opportunities are likely to be limited if the institutions responsible for such programs are shaped by the same historical inequities that they are expected to address. The lack of success in addressing disparities, despite the existence of formal institutions and programs, is caused by a lack of accountability that, in turn, is caused by a lack of social mobilization and a lack of interest by policy makers and the elite in a broad social base. This conundrum revolves around five institutional features: a traditional and unchallenged elite, the mixed record of decentralization, low political awareness, weak social mobilization, and unproven reforms and donor support.

A Traditional and Unchallenged Elite

An understanding of the disparities in Orissa, as well as the assessment of the potential to reduce them, needs to take into consideration the continued dominance of the coastal-based elite—perhaps 200 families. This elite operates in the context of a young state with a fluent identity, where the social structure has not seen the churning and the economic base has not seen the rural transformation that has taken place in practically every other Indian state. Orissa does not have the law-and-order problems found in many of the surrounding states (neither problems of caste nor problems of a Naxalite nature, though events in early 2004 suggest an intensification of activities of the latter), but this lack of social activism appears to be a case of unchallenged, unaccountable, and unresponsive policies. Significantly, many of the challenges have come from outside Orissa—including, for example, positive actions by the Supreme Court—but in the decentralized Indian structure, such challenges will have little sustained effect without a strong lead at the state level.

Apart from the political and economic elite, the administrative elite plays an important role in these dynamics. An equally small group dominates the state administration. The group's interaction with subaltern groups needs to be seen in the context of a cultural history of the entry of outsiders associated with very repressive regimes. Key questions remain: Why have the representatives of deprived groups in state- and national-level politics done so little difference to change exploitative structures (particularly with respect to the forests)?[25] Why is representative democracy by itself not sufficient? To what extent and under what conditions have such representatives become part of the exploitative structures?

The Mixed Record of Decentralization

With regard to the multiple sources of disparities in well-being—forest access, land rights, and program implementation—the wide-ranging powers of local government have the potential to effect substantial progress. However, in India as elsewhere, decentralization has had a mixed record on poverty reduction and social justice. These differences can be caused by the various national policies and the contexts in which decentralization is situated, as well as, within India, the different levels of support that state governments (and political parties) have given to the implementation of national legislation. Evidence shows that Orissa has done little to strengthen local capacity for democracy, a problem that is partly fueled by a self-fulfilling prophecy that democracy will not work but probably also by the existence of vested interests that want to maintain power and access to rent-seeking opportunities.

Functions and powers of the locally elected panchayati raj institutions (PRIs) have become extensive. In the case of tribal areas, decisions regarding transfers of land, management of access to forests, and strategies for expansion of primary education prescribe important roles for elected functionaries at the district level and below. For example, a recent decision was made to hand over the responsibility of the Public Distribution System outlets to the panchayat secretary. Orissa introduced a fourth level of decentralization—of *pali sabha* below the panchayat. There is a mandatory semiannual consultation with the entire village on proposed development programs. Moreover, the powers of elected functionaries at the district level are significant, taking over many of the roles and responsibilities of the district collector, who administers the district.

However, development of decentralization in Orissa has been limited as a consequence (as well as a cause) of the lack of success in reducing disparities. The civil service has shown much skepticism of and resistance to decentralized structures, and capacity building has been all but absent. A participatory study highlighted that the panchayat was, for many people, the most important local institution, because it coordinates and sanctions development schemes. However, it was also perceived to be the most corrupt institution, and the distance to its offices was perceived to be great (Praxis Institute for Participatory Studies 2002). The effect of the

PRIs' role in managing forest access remains largely unknown, but a study by the Institute for Socio-Economic Development (2002) showed very low awareness of the PESA act that prescribes the role of PRIs.

Low Political Awareness

Political awareness in Orissa is low, and little has been done to change this problem. A Centre for Development Studies survey (Kumar 2001) showed that the poor take a great interest in the political system, as indicated by high voter turnouts, but their knowledge is limited. Although many people could name the *sarpanch* (village head), only 22 percent of the "very poor" could name the country's prime minister (compared with 78 percent of the upper class) and just 39 percent could name their Legislative Assembly member. Exposure to media is extremely limited: only 6 percent of the very poor read newspapers, and only 17 percent listen to the radio.

This lack of awareness is both a cause and consequence of the political power imbalance. Strong evidence suggests that illiterate women and men have an interest in politics—as election turnouts indicate—and can become capable local leaders, but the power imbalances hinder any serious mobilization of these potentials. The charge of 1991 Mishra Commission report (discussing starvation deaths in Kalahandi) that the state administration is lax, is corrupt, and colludes with locally powerful interests seems pertinent (Jayal 1999): the people of Kalahandi did not mobilize to protest against acute hunger and were unaware of their constitutional rights and entitlements.

Weak Social Mobilization

The number of nongovernmental organizations (NGOs) in Orissa would in itself contradict an assessment of lack of political awareness and ought to provide a more positive assessment of the potential for development. There have indeed been many cases of strong advocacy. Consider, for example, the NGO efforts related to Chilka Lake, the advocacy of land rights by the NGO Gram Vikas, the long-standing advocacy and development efforts by Agragamee, and the state-level efforts of the Centre for Youth and Social Development.

However, it is generally recognized that civil society is weak in Orissa. In the few cases where strong advocacy has occurred, policy debates have become polarized, thereby creating a common perception that NGOs are antidevelopment. Probably most of the organizations lack a social base, and commercial interests play an important role (a situation that was made worse, if not created, by the availability of funding after the supercyclone of October 1999). The adversarial attitudes of officials are partly justified, but the lack of space provided to civil society organizations is also partly responsible for this situation.

A "thickening" of civil society has by and large not happened, and none of the pathways of effective social organization, as identified by Fox in his research on Mexico, have emerged (cited in Bebbington and others 2006). A few reformist officials are present in government circles, but they must fight defensive battles, as highlighted by the blacklisting of Agragamee (which was reversed by a few reformist individuals). There are few cases of collaboration between external and local civil society actors. Many of the significant players come from outside the state, often appearing during calamities. Subsequently, they may set up local organizations, but the number of such cases is limited, and the effect of such organizations is restricted because the unfavorable environment. In addition, analysis of policy responses—for example, of starvation deaths—highlights that, in the most extreme situation, bottom-up mobilization is unlikely to happen. Government responses have a strong charity character and promises by political leaders still—despite decades of nondelivery—do play a role, but deeply ingrained local power relations greatly reduce any potential for effective social mobilization.

Unproven Reforms and Donor Support

The fiscal crisis and adjustment over the past decade have given disparities a new dimension, including the enhanced role of actors outside the state—foreign donors but particularly the central government. It is not possible to assess whether the reforms will reduce the disparities described in this chapter. In any case, within the fiscal reforms there are as many risks as there are possibilities, and much depends on the content and sequencing of governance reforms.

However, it is worth highlighting that the content of recent fiscal reforms is largely determined by elite interests and that such reforms have had to face elite resistance. The power reforms of the early 1990s—the only reforms in which external support was accepted—were implemented partly because of a lack of a significant rural lobby. Although this situation may be efficient, it also indicates the lack of a social base. Current reforms of public sector enterprises—as well as opposition to those reforms—are largely indifferent to the disparities highlighted in this chapter. Delays in proposed reforms—and, for example, the sequencing of particular reforms (the forest corporation will not undergo reform in the near future)—arguably reflect the interests of parts of the system that work against the poor. Resistance to the reforms has been strong, but that resistance arises from a very small proportion of the population, and political disputes over reforms are no reflection of interests of marginalized segments of the population.

Notes

1. *Institutions* are defined, broadly, as rules and structures that determine (enable or limit) human interaction in economic, social, and political spheres. An understanding of institutions needs to take into account their formal structures, the informal rules of the game, and the ways these complexities become constituted through social interactions and mobilization.
2. The chapter will use both the more appropriate terms, *Adivasis* and *Dalits*, and the equivalent administrative terms, *scheduled tribes* and *scheduled castes*, respectively. It should be emphasized that these groups are also very heterogeneous, and that, for example, differences between (minority) scheduled tribes in Orissa and scheduled tribes in the northeast, where they form the majority, are enormous. Moreover, the administrative categories themselves as created during colonial rule have shaped a large part of the political and perhaps social group dynamics in India.
3. Further investigation may change the regional comparisons, as was shown by the rural–urban comparison for adjusted poverty in Deaton's (2003a) analysis.
4. Sen and Himanshu (2004) provide a somewhat optimistic relative picture of Orissa's performance in poverty reduction but confirm its falling behind between 1993/94 and 1999/2000, and south Orissa is one of the NSS regions with increasing poverty between the 43rd and 55th rounds of the survey.
5. It is possible to further disaggregate the NSS data, to the level of the 13 districts as they existed in 1991, though the sample may be low for reliable estimates. This also emphasizes the heterogeneous character within the regions described earlier and shows the extremes to be even further apart: the estimated poverty headcount in Puri is 22 percent, whereas in Koraput it is almost four times as high (80 percent).
6. Calculations of calorie-deficient households show lower levels of poverty in Orissa compared with other states, smaller differences across regions, and a decline in all the NSS regions. Hence, the value of food consumption (prices) may not be adequately recorded, possibly because of dependence on the Public Distribution System.
7. For a discussion of regional inequalities, see Bandyopadhyay (2003), Deaton and Drèze (2002), Noorbakhsh (2003), and Purfield (2006).

8. Government of Orissa (2002: 1/17). Low coverage and inefficiency in irrigation (coupled with decline in traditional irrigation systems) are seen as major causes for this poor performance.
9. In the 1990s, district domestic product varied between Rs 3,727 per capita in Kalahandi to Rs 7,763 in Sundargarh. These data are from the Directorate of Economics and Statistics, Bhubaneswar, quoted in NCDS (2004: table 8.1).
10. Simple comparisons (de Haan and Dubey 2003) suggest that income poverty correlates with illiteracy at the level of Orissa's districts; moreover, female illiteracy correlates with the percentage of women receiving skilled attention during pregnancy for the current 30 districts. Regional data also show, as expected, that infant mortality levels are worse in the poorer parts of Orissa. The correlation between female illiteracy and child immunization is less than the correlation between female literacy and incidence of skilled birth attendance.
11. These statistics were calculated by the author from NSS data 1999/2000. It needs to be noted that these NSS data may not be the most reliable regarding landownership patterns, and special surveys exist.
12. Relative to other castes, and if other factors are held constant, a household is more likely to be poor if it belongs to one of the deprived groups. The marginal increase in the probability is highest for STs, and this increase is larger in Orissa (39 percent) than in India on average (30 percent).
13. This information is based on a presentation by Satish Agnihotri at a poverty-monitoring workshop, NCDS, Bhubaneswar, in February 2003.
14. This information is supported by development indicators from the Regional Centre for Development Cooperation for 1999 and 2000 (IFAD n.d.).
15. In analyzing such institutions and including the question of different performance across Indian states, this chapter builds on the typology developed in Harriss (1999), which distinguishes four types of states: (a) those where upper caste or class dominance has persisted (including Orissa); (b) those where this dominance has been challenged and where the Congress Party has collapsed; (c) those where this dominance has been challenged, but without the collapse of the Congress Party; and (d) those with strong political representation of lower castes and classes (such as Kerala and West Bengal). The comparison builds strongly on Mohanty (1989/90).
16. During the early 1990s, Orissa was among the states with the largest amount of potential foreign investment—most of which did not materialize (S. Jha, United Nations Development Programme, personal communication).
17. Initiatives by the panchayat raj secretary (in 2004) to make disaggregated administrative data available on the government of Orissa's Web site are a case in point.
18. Data on teacher absenteeism do not show worse performance in Orissa than in, for example, Andhra Pradesh, according to data presented at the Global Development Network Conference in New Delhi, January 2004 (quoted in *Economic and Political Weekly*, February 28, 2004).

19. Orissa's per capita spending on social programs is below India's average, but as a percentage of the state domestic product, it is well above the Indian average (9 percent versus 6 percent) (Dev and Mooij 2002; Mehrotra 2004).
20. See Xaxa (2001) for results of tribal groups in particular, and see Hurst (2002) regarding women's local political participation.
21. It is crucial to differentiate policies for Dalits from those for Adivasis—although many of the policy instruments and policy language tend to conflate the two. In the programs for Adivasis, the question of assimilation and integration versus autonomous development has played a key role from the late colonial period onward—and strongly so in the thinking of Jawaharlal Nehru. This debate often neglects the key fact that although Adivasis have been integrated into the wider economy and society, this integration has taken place on very disadvantageous terms.
22. A block is an administrative unit below the district level.
23. It has been suggested that the large proportion of tribals, and hence the relatively large allocations, in Orissa may lead to a greater likelihood of rent seeking (S. Thakur, personal communication).
24. One crore equals 10 million.
25. Orissa's population is heterogeneous, and Adivasis consist of many different and dispersed groups, but other states in India have equally heterogeneous populations, and constitutional provisions for reservation of positions in political and educational structures should have guaranteed a better representation of subaltern interests. Orissa has been marked by a particularly strong lack of substantive democracy, extremely limited realization of rights of deprived groups, and a very limited drive by the elite to incorporate wider segments of the population into a vision of development.

References

Agarwal, B. 1995. "Gender, Environment, and Poverty Interlinks in Rural India: Regional Variations and Temporal Shifts, 1971–1991," UNRISD DP62, United Nations Research Institute for Social Development.

Alam, J. 1999a. "Is Caste Appeal Casteism? Oppressed Castes in Politics." *Economic and Political Weekly* 34 (13): 757–60.

———. 1999b. "What Is Happening Inside Indian Democracy?" *Economic and Political Weekly* 34 (37): 2649–56.

Bailey, F. G. 1957. *Caste and the Economic Frontier: A Village in Highland Orissa*. Manchester, U.K.: Manchester University Press.

———. 1963. *Politics and Social Change: Orissa in 1959*. Berkeley and Los Angeles: University of California Press.

Balagopal, K. 2000. "A Tangled Web: Subdivision of SC Reservation in AP." *Economic and Political Weekly* 35 (13): 1075–81.

Bandyopadhyay, S. 2003. "Convergence Club Empirics: Some Dynamics and Explanations of Unequal Growth across Indian States." WIDER Discussion Paper 2003/77, United Nations University, World Institute for Development Economics Research, Helsinki.

Bebbington, A., L. Dharmawan, E. Fahmi, and S. Guggenheim. 2006. "Local Capacity, Village Governance, and the Political Economy of Rural Development in Indonesia." *World Development*, 34 (11): 1958–76.

Centre for Youth and Social Development. 2002. "Time Spent by People below Poverty Line in Accessing Public Service." Centre for Youth and Social Development, Bhubaneswar, India.

Currie, B. 2000. *The Politics of Hunger in India: A Study of Democracy, Governance, and Kalahandi's Poverty*. Chennai, India: Macmillan.

Datt, G., and M. Ravallion. 2002. "Is India's Economic Growth Leaving the Poor Behind?" *Journal of Economic Perspectives* 16 (3): 89–108.

Deaton, A. 2003a. "Adjusted Indian Poverty Estimates for 1999–2000." *Economic and Political Weekly* 38 (4): 322–26.

———. 2003b. "Prices and Poverty in India: 1987–2000." *Economic and Political Weekly* 38 (4): 362–68.

Deaton, A., and J. Drèze. 2002. "Poverty and Inequality in India: A Re-examination." *Economic and Political Weekly* 37 (36): 3729–48.

de Haan, A., and A. Dubey. 2003. "Extreme Deprivation in Remote Areas in India: Social Exclusion as Explanatory Concept." Paper presented at the Chronic Poverty and Development Policy Conference, University of Manchester, Manchester, U.K., April 7–9.

Dev, S. M., and J. Mooij. 2002. "Social Sector Expenditures and Budgeting: An Analysis of Patterns and the Budget Making Process in India in the 1990s." Working Paper 43, Centre for Economic and Social Studies, Hyderabad, India.

Government of Orissa. 2002. "Draft Tenth Five-Year Plan, 2002–2007." Bhubaneswar, India.

———. 2003. "Orissa Budget 2003–2004 at a Glance." Finance Department, Bhubaneswar, India.

Harriss, J. 1999. "Comparing Political Regimes across Indian States: A Preliminary Essay." *Economic and Political Weekly* 34 (48): 3367–77.

Hurst, E. 2002. "Political Representation and Empowerment: Women in the Institutions of Local Government in Orissa after the 73rd Amendment to the Indian Constitution." Heidelberg Paper in South Asian and Comparative Politics 6, University of Heidelberg, Heidelberg, Germany.

IAMR (Institute of Applied Manpower Research). 2003. "Evaluation Study of RLTAP in the KBK Region in Orissa." Study sponsored by the Planning Commission, Delhi.

IFAD (International Fund for Agricultural Development). n.d. "Second Orissa Tribal Development Programme Formulation Report: Annex 1, Lessons

Learned from Other IFAD Assisted Tribal Development Projects." IFAD, Rome.

Institute for Socio-Economic Development. 2002. "Poor and Marginalised People in Orissa." Institute for Socio-Economic Development, Bhubaneswar, India.

Jayal, N. G. 1999. *Democracy and the State: Welfare, Secularism, and Development in Contemporary India*. Delhi: Oxford University Press.

Kaviraj, S. 2000. "Democracy and Social Inequality." In *Transforming India: Social and Political Dynamics of Democracy*, ed. F. R. Frankel, 89–119. New Delhi: Oxford University Press.

Kijima, Y., and P. Lanjouw. 2003. "Poverty in India during the 1990s: A Regional Perspective." Policy Research Working Paper 3141, World Bank, Washington, DC.

Kumar, S. 2001. "Study of Political Systems and Voting Behaviour of the Poor in Orissa." Report prepared for the U.K. Department for International Development, New Delhi.

Mander, H. 2004. *The Ripped Chest: Public Policy and Poor People in India*. Bangalore, India: Books for Change.

Manor, J. 1998. "Orissa." Part of a series of papers on electricity reform written for the World Bank, Washington, DC.

Mearns, R. 1999. "Access to Land in Rural India: Policy Options." Policy Research Working Paper 2123, World Bank, Washington, DC.

Mehrotra, S. 2004. "Reforming Public Spending on Education and Mobilising Resources: Lessons from International Experience." *Economic and Political Weekly* 39 (9): 987–97.

Mohanty, M. 1990. "Class, Caste, and Dominance in a Backward State: Orissa." In *Dominance and State Power in Modern India: Decline of a Social Order*, ed. F. Frankel and M. S. A. Rao, 321–67. Delhi: Oxford University Press.

NCDS (Nabakrushna Choudhury Center for Development Studies). 2004. "Orissa Human Development Report." Draft report, sponsored by UNDP and Planning Commission, Bhubaneswar, India.

Noorbakhsh, F. 2003. "Spatial Inequality and Polarisation in India." CREDIT Research Paper 03/6, University of Nottingham, Nottingham, U.K.

Panda, M. 2002. "Poverty in Orissa: A Disaggregated Analysis." Paper prepared for the National Conference on Control and Dynamical Systems, Workshop on Poverty Monitoring, Bhubhaneswar, India, February.

Panda, P. K. 1997. "Female Headship, Poverty and Childwelfare: A Study of Rural Orissa, India." Centre for Development Studies, Thiruvananthapuram, India.

Pandey, B. 1998. *Depriving the Underprivileged for Development*. Bhubaneswar, India: Institute for Socio-Economic Development.

Pati, B. 1993. *Resisting Domination: Peasants, Tribals, and National Movement in Orissa 1920–50*. New Delhi: Manohar.

———. 2003. *Identity, Hegemony, Resistance: Towards a Social History of Conversions in Orissa, 1800–2000*. New Delhi: Three Essay Collective.

Pradhan, J. 1993a. "The Distorted Kalahandi and a Strategy for Its Development." *Social Action* 43 (July–September): 295–311.

———. 1993b. "Drought in Kalahandi: The Real Story." *Economic and Political Weekly* 28 (22): 1084–88.

Praxis Institute for Participatory Studies. 2002. "The Accountable State." Report prepared for Government of Orissa, Bhubaneswar, India.

Purfield, C. 2006. "Mind the Gap: Is Economic Growth in India Leaving Some States Behind?" IMF Working Paper WP/06/103, International Monetary Fund, Washington, DC.

Rew, A. 2003. "Why Has It Ended Up Here? Development (and Other) Messages and Social Connectivity in Northern Orissa." *Journal of International Development* 15 (7): 925–38.

Saxena, N. C. 2001. "Empowerment of Tribals through Sustainable Natural Resource Management in Western Orissa." Report for the International Fund for Agricultural Development and U.K. Department for International Development, New Delhi.

———. 2003. "Livelihood Diversification and Non-Timber Forest Products in Orissa: Wider Lessons on the Scope for Policy Change?" ODI Working Paper 223, Overseas Development Institute, London.

Sen, A., and Himanshu. 2004. "Poverty and Inequality in India." *Economic and Political Weekly* 39 (38): 4247–63 and 39 (39): 4361–76.

Sengupta, J. 2001. "State, Market, and Democracy in the 1990s: Liberalization and the Politics of Oriya Identity." In *Democratic Governance in India: Challenges of Poverty, Development, and Identity*, ed. N. Gopal and S. Pai. New Delhi: Sage.

Sundaram, K., and S. K. Tendulkar. 2003. "Poverty in India in the 1990s: An Analysis of Changes in 15 Major States." *Economic and Political Weekly* 38 (14): 1385–93.

Weisskopf, T. E. 2004. "Impact of Reservation on Admissions to Higher Education in India." *Economic and Political Weekly* 39 (39): 4339–49.

World Bank. 2000. "Poverty in Orissa: Diagnosis and Approach." Orissa Policy Notes, World Bank, Washington, DC.

Xaxa, V. 2001. "Protective Discrimination: Why Scheduled Tribes Lag Behind Scheduled Castes." *Economic and Political Weekly* 36 (29): 2765–83.

———. 2003. "Adivasis in India." Paper prepared for U.K. Department for International Development, New Delhi.

PART III

INSTITUTIONAL TRANSITIONS AND PATHWAYS TOWARD EQUITY

CHAPTER 5

Indigenous Political Voice and the Struggle for Recognition in Ecuador and Bolivia

José Antonio Lucero

> "They say this is the lost decade [*una década perdida*] for Latin America; we say that it is a decade in which Ecuadorian Indians have won [*una década ganada*]."
>
> —Luis Macas, President
> Confederation of Indigenous Nationalities of Ecuador[1]

Indigenous struggles in Ecuador and Bolivia provide instructive and challenging cases of the politics of (in)equity in that conditions of economic and political crisis (the "lost decade") coincided with the emergence of a striking indigenous political voice (a decade in which "Indians won," as Luis Macas puts it). Ecuador and Bolivia are often described as among the more economically and politically troubled countries in the Americas. These two Andean states are sometimes called the poorest countries in the hemisphere, because a majority of people in each country live below the poverty line (Ecuador 67 percent and Bolivia 63 percent). With the more comprehensive metric of the Human Development Index (HDI), these states fare a bit better, but they are still decidedly in the bottom half of medium human development countries: Ecuador occupies 100th place and Bolivia 114th in the HDI rankings of 177 countries (UNDP 2004: 140–41). Politically, inchoate party systems in both countries have done a poor job of representing the interests of the excluded sectors of society, and massive social protests have driven democratically elected presidents from office (in 1997 and 2000 in Ecuador; in 2003 and 2005 in Bolivia).[2]

Despite—or indeed because of—these gloomy indicators, one area in which these countries lead the continent is the strength of indigenous social movements. Rightly described as the poorest of the poor, indigenous people in these countries have, over the past three decades, formed local, regional, and national organizations that have challenged their long-standing neocolonial marginalization. Mass protests and marches have forced multicultural development into the mainstream of politics; bilingual education, collective rights, and "development with identity" agendas have become institutionalized in the structures of states and the language of national constitutions. Indigenous people have also won representation in municipalities, in regional and national legislatures, and at the highest levels of government. They have occupied cabinet ministries, the vice presidency, and even the presidency.[3] These achievements are even more remarkable when one considers that it was not until late in the 20th century that obstacles to universal suffrage were lifted and indigenous people were fully enfranchised.

This chapter briefly explores the common conditions that enabled indigenous people to challenge the terms of recognition in Ecuador and Bolivia, as well as the contrasting contexts that have produced different patterns of indigenous political action in these states. In addition, the chapter argues that indigenous actors in Bolivia have achieved more in their development encounters than their counterparts in Ecuador. Much of this claim rests on the recent election and policy accomplishments of Evo Morales in Bolivia, who as this chapter is being written (December 2006) has just completed his first year in office. This claim is in many ways contentious, because until very recently one could have asserted precisely the opposite: that Ecuadorian indigenous actors, especially the Confederación de Nacionalidades Indígenas del Ecuador (Confederation of Indigenous Nationalities of Ecuador, or CONAIE), had achieved remarkable national unity and political influence, whereas Bolivian movements have historically been more regionally fragmented and politically divided. Since 2000, however, the rearticulation of indigenous movements in each country has led to a reversal of fortune that can be illustrated by the electoral achievements of two indigenous leaders. In the 2005 Bolivian presidential elections, Aymara *cocalero* leader Evo Morales won 53.7 percent of the vote, the first time that any candidate has won an outright majority victory. In the 2006 presidential election in Ecuador, the Kichwa CONAIE leader Luis Macas won a meager 2.7 percent of the vote.

The following sections will describe the trajectory of indigenous organizations and struggles in Ecuador and Bolivia, provide some explanation for the variation in movement outcomes, and finally suggest some implications for considering development possibilities in times of multicultural neoliberalism. One interpretation of the mixed picture that emerges in both countries, where gains in indigenous political voice coexist with durable economic inequality, is the possibility of equity tradeoffs—that is, stronger indigenous political gains may result in increased discrimination that keeps poverty gaps high and the returns of education low. A recent World Bank study indicated that this kind of equity tradeoff may be more pronounced in Bolivia than in Ecuador. Yet the victory of Evo Morales, some dramatic policy initiatives, including the nationalization of the hydrocarbon sector (especially natural gas), and a strong economy have had distributional implications that provide reason to reconsider this tradeoff thesis. Even in Ecuador, where indigenous actors have encountered more difficulty as of late, it is possible to formulate a more optimistic interpretation, in that a lag may exist between political and economic gains as indigenous peoples in the Andes and Amazon cultivate greater "capacities to aspire"[4] (Appadurai 2004).

Building Movements: Exclusion, Organization, and Opportunity

Indigenous movements are not limited to Ecuador and Bolivia but constitute a regionwide return of the Indian from Chiapas to Chile. The scholarship on this resurgence of indigenous mobilization has emphasized the political and economic context that allowed indigenous communities to scale up protests in unprecedented ways.[5] The organizational capacity of indigenous communities is an important background explanatory variable as the norms and practices of solidarity and trust help overcome collective-action problems. The persistence of local associational networks is in part due to the unintended consequences of state policies during years of corporatist and populist approaches to what used to be called the "Indian problem." In the middle of the 20th century, governments throughout the region sought to modernize the terms of recognition by "rebaptizing Indians as peasants" (Albó 1994: 57). As states created local spaces for peasants to organize, often in legally recognized rural unions, cooperatives, or communities, it was possible for rural people to employ a Janus-faced posture in which they showed a productive peasant face to a modernizing state but inwardly cultivated local Quechua, Aymara, and other indigenous identities and practices.

The experience of state corporatism, though stronger in Bolivia than in Ecuador, habituated rural highland populations in both countries to think in the terms of class struggles and to organize in unionlike structures. During the 1960s and 1970s, the tactics and rhetoric of the main Andean indigenous federations—ECUARUNARI (Kichwa acronym for roughly the Awakening of the Ecuadorian Indian) in Ecuador and the Confederación Sindical Única de Trabajadores Campesinos de Bolivia (Sole Confederation of Rural Workers of Bolivia, or CSUTCB) in Bolivia—were quite similar. The great debate among highland organizations was over how to harmonize class and ethnic identities—how to "see with both eyes," as the Aymara leader and later Bolivian Vice President Victor Hugo Cárdenas put it. Over time, both external political events (the fall of the Berlin Wall and the crisis of the international Left) and internal ones (the intellectual influence of Indianista nationalist writers such as Fausto Reinaga) "Indianized" class identities and struggles.

In contrast to the class-intensive identities of the indigenous highlands, the lowlands were more hospitable to ethnic alternatives. Indeed, throughout the central Andean republics, "[T]he areas where the ethnic federation has proliferated are precisely those areas which were peripheral to, or outside of, the integrative horizons which have swept the Andean region over the past several millennia" (Smith 1985: 17).

What Smith (1985) has called the "myth of the vast Amazonian emptiness" had many negative consequences for lowland populations, yet the relatively weak presence of the national state provided indigenous people with greater room to craft political identities and organizations that were distinct from the dominant traditions of the state and the Left. The Amazon has been the crucible in which the language of indigenous peoples and nationalities (*pueblos y nacionalidades*) was forged in both Ecuador and Bolivia.

Thus, it should be of little surprise that the first indigenous ethnic federations in the Americas emerged in the Amazonian regions in the 1960s. The first was the Shuar Federation, organized in Ecuador in 1964. Amazonian organizing in Ecuador continued through the 1970s and culminated with the 1980 establishment of the Confederación de Nacionalidades Indígenas de la Amazonia Ecuatoriana (Confederation of Amazonian Nationalities of Ecuador, or CONFENIAE). Although a regional Amazonian organization emerged later in Bolivia (in the 1980s and 1990s), the Confederación de Pueblos Indígenas de Bolivia (Confederation of Indigenous Peoples of Eastern Bolivia, or CIDOB) quickly acquired a surprising political presence given that it represented only 2 percent of the national indigenous population.

The economic shocks of the 1980s and the accompanying structural adjustments provided a catalyst for mobilization as the old corporatist, developmentalist state quickly retreated from the countryside. The subsidies and credits that agrarian reform had made available were drastically diminished, and life in the rural countryside became much harder. This economic transition, though, coincided with a political transition, because the 1980s were also a decade of democratization. In the language of social movement theorists, the political opportunity structures became more permissive at the very moment that economic pressures were getting more oppressive. No longer part of corporatist mediating structures, indigenous people were able to move beyond "ventriloquist" forms of representation (subordinate to political parties, the church, or the state) and to find their own national political voice (Guerrero 1994). Though third parties such as missionaries or nongovernmental organization (NGO) workers often helped indigenous people scale up their struggles by providing access to additional social networks, these nonindigenous allies remained backstage, conscious that these were indigenous movements. Over the course of the 1980s, indigenous people in both Ecuador and Bolivia built powerful regional and national organizations that began to attract increasing international attention in a post-1989, post–Berlin Wall world in which new social movements around identity seemed to be displacing the old movements of class.[6]

Despite the striking similarity of regional styles in both Ecuador and Bolivia, the national configurations of indigenous protest are quite distinct. In the Ecuadorian case—something true of no other Latin American case—the largest highland and lowland indigenous confederations (ECUARUNARI and CONFENIAE, respectively) have, since 1986, been part of the same national confederation. The emergence of the national indigenous confederation, CONAIE, is essentially the convergence of two parallel organizational struggles. In Bolivia, such a convergence has not occurred, and indigenous movements remain "fragmented in structure" Whitehead (2001: 11). The three main national organizations operate in distinct geographic and ecological zones of the country: the labor union–style CSUTCB in the highlands, the coca grower federations in the tropics and valleys, and the ethnic CIDOB in the lowlands.

Throughout the 1990s, CONAIE in Ecuador and CIDOB in Bolivia had the most success politically, in part because of their ability to combine "pluricultural" discourses with tactics that stressed both contestation and negotiation. As Jorge León (2000, 2004, 2005) has noted, protest in the Andes has become a part of the political system, in that mobilization and negotiation are routinized and regular sites of interaction between state and indigenous leaders. As often happens in social movement environments, other organizations appropriated the lessons that leading organizations provided in the competition for visibility, resources, and loyalty. Despite a wide range of actors, interviews with social scientists, policy makers, development practitioners, and indigenous activists reveal clear, shared understandings about the representative organizations in Bolivia and Ecuador, which are summarized in table 5.1. As table 5.1 shows, what Smith (1985) would call "ethnic federations" have become the leading models for collective action. Even the more laborlike federation of coca growers, many of whom were formerly miners relocated by neoliberal reforms in the 1980s, over time crafted a more ethnic discourse that articulated indigenous symbols, such as the sacred coca leaf, with indigenous themes like sovereignty and territory.

Negotiating Neoliberal and Multicultural Reform: States and Movements

The strength of indigenous mobilization has shaped development and political agendas in some striking ways. Through these mobilizations and subsequent negotiations, CONAIE in Ecuador obtained important spaces in the national political system, gaining control of the Directorate of Bilingual Education; the Consejo de Desarrollo de las Nacionalidades y Pueblos de Ecuador (Development Council of the Nationalities and Peoples of Ecuador, or CODENPE); and the Office of Indigenous Health. It also gained a central role in the World Bank–supported Program for the Development of Indigenous and Afro-Ecuadorian Peoples (PRODEPINE). In Bolivia, four councils of bilingual education for Aymara, Guarani, Quechua, and "multiethnic" Amazonian peoples, as well as a Ministry of Peasant and Indigenous Affairs (with an indigenous vice minister), are among the spaces that have been opened since the mid-1990s by intercultural reforms. These state spaces have further institutionalized relationships between indigenous people and international donors, including multilateral and state institutions, such as the World Bank, the Inter-American Bank, the Danish International Development Agency (DANIDA), and the U.K. Department for International Development (DfID), as well as international NGOs, such as Oxfam-America (United States) and Ibis (Denmark).

Table 5.1. Types and Relative Representational Strengths of Indigenous Organizations in Bolivia and Ecuador

Representational strength	Type of organization		
	Ethnic	Labor	Religious
High	CONAIE[a] (Ecuador) CIDOB[b] (Bolivia)	Cocaleros[c] (Bolivia)	
Moderate	CONAMAQ[d] (Bolivia), 2000–present	CSUTCBe (Bolivia), 1970s–1985 CSUTCB[e] (Bolivia), 2000–present FENOCINf (Ecuador)	FEINE[g] (Ecuador), 1998–present
Low	CONAMAQ[d] (Bolivia), 1990s	CSUTCB[e] (Bolivia), 1990s FEI[h] (Ecuador)	FEINE[g] (Ecuador) 1980–98

Source: Author's elaboration based on various interviews cited in Lucero (forthcoming).

a. CONAIE, the Confederación de Nacionalides Indígenas del Ecuador (Confederation of Indigenous Nationalities of Ecuador), is the leading indigenous organization in Ecuador and has become a model of social and political activism for indigenous organizations throughout the region.

b. CIDOB, the Confederación de Pueblos Indígenas de Bolivia (Confederation of Indigenous Peoples of Eastern Bolivia), is the main organization of the Bolivian lowlands, where a minority of Bolivia's indigenous population lives. Despite these demographics, CIDOB is the organization that has the greatest support and recognition from international funders and the Bolivian state.

c. *Cocaleros* stands for the Cocalero Federations of Cochabamba, which are nominally part of the CSUTCB. Under the leadership of Evo Morales (who won the 2005 presidential elections in Bolivia), they have acquired great independent strength in mobilizing protests against U.S.-backed coca eradication programs.

d. CONAMAQ, the Consejo Nacional de Ayllus y Markas de Qullasuyu (National Council of Ayllus and Markas of Qullasuyu), was established in the late 1990s in the highlands of Bolivia. It reconstitutes and confederates the pre-Columbian forms of highland communities that were often ignored in times of compulsory rural union organizing. CONAMAQ has had some difficulties in establishing credibility despite support from prominent international funders.

e. CSUTCB, the Confederación Sindical Única de Trabajadores Campesinos de Bolivia (Sole Confederation of Rural Workers of Bolivia), was the leading organization of the Bolivian highlands until internal conflicts and an outdated class discourse generated a crisis in the 1990s. At the end of the millennium, the CSUTCB regained strength in antineoliberal protests.

f. FENOCIN, the Federación Nacional de Organizaciones Indígenas y Negras (Federation of Peasant, Indigenous, and Black Organizations), is a leftist, multiethnic, class-based, rural organization in Ecuador. It was prominent in struggles over agrarian reform in the 1970s and 1980s, but recently it has been eclipsed by the ethnic-based platforms of CONAIE.

g. FEINE, the Consejo de Pueblos Indígenas Evangélicos del Ecuador (formerly Federación de Evangélicos Indígenas del Ecuador, or Evangelical Indigenous Federation of Ecuador), is a national-level organization that promotes indigenous issues and Christian spiritual development. It has been seen in the past as pro-government and opposed to protest, but since 1998, it has taken a more active place in social movement politics.

h. FEI, the Federación Ecuatoriana de Indios (Ecuadorian Federation of Indians), was founded in the 1940s by the Ecuadorian Communist Party. Although it was an important early organization, it has little support in society or state.

Electorally, indigenous people have also taken advantage of state reforms and changing political conditions to gain important representation in local and national elected office. After a decade of refusing to take part in elections, in 1996 CONAIE allied with nonindigenous social movements and formed the Pachakutik Pluricultural Movement. Pachakutik has won between 6 and 10 percent of the national vote in elections since 1996, though it won just over 2 percent in the 2006 presidential elections in Ecuador. Several high-profile Pachakutik mayors, such as Auki Titwaña of Cotacachi, have been praised for their inclusionary, grassroots models of municipal development.

Even after the failed coup of 2000, in which CONAIE leaders and elements of the reform-minded military forced Jamil Mahuad out of office and held power for only a few hours, Pachakutik continued to be an important part of Ecuadorian politics. In perhaps a natural follow-up to the 2000 indigenous-military coup, Pachakutik and CONAIE decided to support the presidential candidacy of one of the main figures of the coup, Lucio Gutiérrez. Gutiérrez won the 2002 elections and included two historic CONAIE-Pachakutik leaders, Nina Pacari and Luis Macas, in his cabinet. Indigenous people were at the very center of political power, but not for long. In 2003, differences over Gutiérrez's policy toward the International Monetary Fund and the United States resulted in public disagreements between Pachakutik and the president. After only a few months, Gutiérrez dismissed the indigenous ministers, and CONAIE was once again an opposition movement, not a governing partner. Gutiérrez, however, was better able than other presidents to co-opt indigenous leaders and divide the movement. He named former CONAIE president Antonio Vargas as his minister of agriculture and chose a leader from the FEINE, or Consejo de Pueblos Indígenas Evangélicos del Ecuador (formerly the Federación de Evangélicos Indígenas del Ecuador, or Evangelical Indigenous Federation of Ecuador) as executive secretary of CODENPE. CONAIE found itself divided and for the first time in a decade had difficulty mobilizing its communities for protests. Remarkably, in the wave of popular mobilizations that toppled Gutiérrez after he tried to close down and pack the Supreme Court, CONAIE was noticeable for its absence. An Informe Confidencial (2003) poll conducted in 2003 found that 58 percent of Ecuadorians had "little or no confidence" in the indigenous movement. In the 1990s, CONAIE was often named as one of the institutions that enjoyed the greatest public confidence. Several analysts suggest that this shift in public perception can be traced to the 2000 coup and the ill-fated cogovernment with Gutiérrez—political missteps from which the movement has yet to recover fully.[7]

In Bolivia, the participation of indigenous people in government has had a different history, though 2000 was also something of an inflection point. Until then, and especially during the 1990s, political incorporation was directed largely from above, because ruling elites in Bolivia set the terms of political participation to a greater extent than their Ecuadorian counterparts, who were forced to react to mobilizations from below. For example, the rise of Aymara leader Victor Hugo Cárdenas to the vice presidency was made possible by the selection of a candidate and former planning minister, Gonzalo Sánchez de Lozada, from the dominant party, Movimiento Nacionalista Revolucionario (Nationalist Revolutionary Movement, or MNR). This administration (1993–97), however, led to further multicultural openings, most notably in the Law of Popular Participation (Ley de Participación Popular, or LPP) and Agrarian Reform Law (Ley del Instituto Nacional de Reforma Agraria, or INRA). President Sánchez de Lozada (known almost universally as "Goni") made many enemies when the LPP transferred state funds from regional development corporations to local municipalities.

In addition, the legislation recognized the legal right of indigenous people (as indigenous people) to participate in local governance. Local electoral contests became meaningful in unprecedented ways as municipalities, for the first time in republican history, actually had significant resources to administer. INRA allowed the titling of indigenous territories (*tierras comunitarias de origen*, or TCOs), hence permitting state recognition of indigenous political voices and spaces, though many question the effects of this kind of recognition. As Ricardo Calla, sociologist and former minister of campesino and indigenous affairs has written, both LPP and INRA have resulted less in "state decentralization but rather in the state decentralizing indigenous and rural reality" (Calla 2003: 256).[8] This decentralization can be interpreted either as the empowerment of grassroots indigenous communities that have indeed become more important in local spaces or as the "divide and conquer" strategies of a dominant power that seeks to dilute indigenous power on the local level rather than confront it in national mobilizing structures.

The incentives for working with parties in each country, then, were different in the 1990s. In more centralized Ecuador, national social movement activity was seen as more important than national party politics. Moreover, changes in electoral laws in the 1990s gave indigenous people the option to participate in elections as independents, keeping their distance from traditional parties. By the 1990s in Bolivia, a decentralized political system combined with stricter restrictions on electoral participation (only formally recognized parties could run candidates) pushed indigenous candidates toward traditional (and often clientelistic) parties.

Yet municipal elections are now vital and indigenous and peasant candidates have participated like never before. In the 1995 Bolivian municipal elections, the first election after popular participation, 29 percent of local seats (464 of 1,724) were won by indigenous and *campesino* candidates (Albó 2002). Indigenous candidates participated with a wide variety of political parties, and after a 2004 law allowed independent electoral groupings to participate, indigenous people had even more options, thus creating a very mixed picture of indigenous political representation at the local level. Indigenous voice was amplified, if still fragmented.

At the same time, the municipalization of party politics was a major problem for the normal practices of traditional clientelistic political parties that were accustomed to dividing the electoral spoils nationally and regionally. The ability to sustain multiparty coalitions was hurt by the rise of local politics (Albó 2002). In addition, the deaths of the leaders of various Bolivian political parties—including Hugo Bánzer (Acción Democrática Nacional, or National Democratic Action); Carlos Palenque (Conciencia de Patria Movimiento Patriótico, or Conscience of Fatherland Patriotic Movement); and Max Fernandez (Unión Cívica Solidaridad, or Civic Solidarity Union)—created an additional blow to the traditional political party system (Van Cott 2003, 2005).

Since 2000, however, a series of "wars"—first over the privatization of water in Cochabamba, then over taxes, and finally over the exportation of natural gas—has changed the dynamic in Bolivia. Although this cycle of contention will be discussed later, for now suffice it to note that the massive uprisings prompted by different Bolivian governments all served to delegitimize existing neoliberal policies and the political elites who implemented them. Over time, well-organized indigenous parties have been able to take advantage of new opportunities on the local level as well as the crises of traditional parties of both left and right. Most notably, the nearly defunct Movimiento al Socialismo (Movement toward Socialism, or MAS) was taken over by a sector of the *cocalero* movement and established itself as the leading political party in the country. In the 2004 municipal election, the MAS won over 18 percent of municipal council seats, which in a very crowded field put it in first place. In the 2005 presidential election, the MAS won an even more impressive victory, capturing a majority of the popular vote, an accomplishment never before seen in Bolivian political history. Meanwhile, the traditional parties of the past two elected presidents, the MNR (Goni's party) and the Acción Democrática Nacional (Banzer's party) teetered on the verge of disappearance (Gisselquist 2005; Van Cott

2005). Thus, popular participation has had ambivalent political effects: it has made Bolivian politics more decentered and fragmented, yet allowed the emergence of organized indigenous political actors such as the MAS.

Explaining Ecuadorian Unity and Bolivian Fragmentation

For the purpose of this chapter, it is important to describe the diversity of indigenous actors. Why has indigenous contention achieved relative unity in Ecuador and been more divided in Bolivia? This difference is best understood in relation to political and cultural opportunities, which are "given" by existing political systems and rules of the game and "made" through the interaction of indigenous and nonindigenous actors. More precisely, these contrasting opportunities are visible in the regionalized nature of political power, the discursive construction of indigenous subjects, and the contrasting strategies of radical contestation and more conciliatory negotiation.

Region and Movement

To understand this difference in indigenous political geographies, one should consider the geography of dominant power. Indigenous politics in Ecuador offer a mirror image to dominant elite arrangements. Although political and economic elites cluster around the poles of coastal Guayaquil and highland Quito, the Amazon, for much of the nation's history, was a faraway site of war (with Peru) or a promised land of resource explorations (for oil). The state's relative neglect of the Ecuadorian lowlands allowed indigenous actors greater degrees of freedom in consolidating regional organizations that could confront the threats of outside forces such as highland colonizers and multinational oil companies. In Bolivia, lowland groups had less room to maneuver, largely because of the central place of the lowland Santa Cruz in the distribution of power in the country.

The regional structures of opportunity—with regard to the existence of regional elite opposition—were more favorable in Ecuador than in Bolivia (see table 5.2). In Ecuador, strong indigenous organizations emerged first in an Amazonian region that was relatively marginal to national elites, which were concentrated in other regions.[9] In the highlands, indigenous organizations emerged later, especially after agrarian reform weakened landed elites that had controlled prior systems of ethnic administration. In Bolivia, in contrast, lowland CIDOB became a strong force only in the 1990s, long

Table 5.2. Ecuador and Bolivia: Region and Timing in Indigenous Mobilization

	Ecuador	Bolivia
Indigenous population[a] (approximate % of nationals)	25	62
Largest indigenous groups	Highlands: Kichwa (85–90% of total Indian population) Lowlands: Shuar, Kichwa, and 10 smaller groups	Lowlands: Quechua and Aymara (98% of total Indian population) Lowlands: Guarani, Quechua, Aymara, and 35 other groups
Non-Indian elite regional cleavages	Coast (Guayaquil) Highlands (Quito)	Eastern lowlands (Santa Cruz) Highlands (La Paz)
Indian regional cleavages	Lowlands and highlands (coastal groups weak)	Lowlands, valleys, and highlands
Timing of indigenous political organizations	1. Lowland (1960s) 2. Highlands (1970s) 3. National (1980s)	1. Highlands (1970s) 2. Lowlands (1980s) 3. Valleys (1980s)
Patterns of indigenous representation	Relative unity (Pan-regional CONAIE)[b]	Fragmentation along regional and ideological lines (Lowlands: CIDOB; valleys: Cocaleros; highlands: CSUTCB and CONAMAQ)

Source: Lucero forthcoming.

a. Indigenous population figures are disputed and should be treated with caution. The Latin American Demographic Center estimates that 56.8 percent of Bolivians and 29 percent of Ecuadorians are indigenous. The Instituto Indigenista Internacional has higher estimates: 63 percent for Bolivia and 40 percent for Ecuador. Although 2001 census data reinforce the view that indigenous people are a majority of Bolivians (62 percent), they yield a controversially low 7 percent for Ecuador. See Gonzalez (1994) and Layton and Patrinos (2006).

b. As table 5.1 suggests, there are other national organizations, though they are less powerful than CONAIE.

after the highland groups that had become prominent in the 1970s. Why? Part of the reason lies in location: CIDOB emerged in the very center of the economically strong and politically conservative region of Santa Cruz. Lowland indigenous groups, explains Kevin Healy (2001: 75), were literally "surrounded by powerful white and mestizo cattle ranchers, large commercial farmers, agrobusinesses, and timber enterprises whose holdings had been bolstered by government and international aid." The presence of powerful regional elites created an obstacle to indigenous political participation in lowland Bolivia that did not exist in lowland Ecuador.

The relatively late entrance of Bolivian lowland groups has important implications for the possibilities of a unifying national movement. Unlike Ecuador, where lowland and highland indigenous elites were in contact for decades (the Shuar Federation had an office in Quito in the 1970s), a lowland indigenous elite did not emerge in Bolivia until the late 1980s, with significant help from a local NGO known as Apoyo para Campesinos Indígenas del Oriente de Bolivia (Support for the Peasant-Indigenous People of Eastern Bolivia). By 1985, the successive blows of economic crisis and neoliberal economic reform had cut the legs from under the structure of the highland Bolivian Left, most notably in the mining sector but also in the CSUTCB. This crisis in the highlands enabled the rise of powerful movements in the valley (around the *cocaleros*) and in the lowlands (confederated in CIDOB) but made a national confederation less likely.

Terms of Recognition: Constructing Nationalities, Peoples, and Indígenas

It is widely agreed that the language of indigenous ethnicity has eclipsed the old language of peasant class identity, yet what is less remarked on is the variety of pan-ethnic indigenous subjects that have emerged in Latin America. Movements have crafted broad pan-Indian categories to unite often very different local indigenous communities, and some movements are more successful than others. Perhaps the most obvious difference, in Ecuador the term *nacionalidad indígena* applies easily and comfortably across highland and lowland settings; in Bolivia, *indígena* is usually reserved for lowland native groups, whereas the numerically superior Quechuas and Aymaras are more often described (and describe themselves) as *pueblos originarios* (roughly, "first nations"). Space limitations preclude a thorough exploration of these discursive differences,[10] but briefly they are also part of the history of regionalized contention and indigenous strategy. In creating a national organization, Amazonian and Andean indigenous elites in Ecuador and Bolivia consciously deployed the idea of indigenous nationalities to acknowledge the cultural distinctiveness, political equality, and aspirations of different groups (especially the smaller groups in the Amazon). In informal and formal indigenous networks, the idea of nationality was embraced by key Andean and Amazonian elites that were able to overcome regional tensions in forming CONAIE. Despite initial resistance to the idea of multiple Ecuadorian nationalities, this language was later accepted by nonindigenous elites.[11] As most scholars agree, and as non-CONAIE leaders lament, the hegemony of CONAIE in setting the terms of indigenous representation is striking. *Hegemony* is used here not only because one wants to highlight, following Antonio Gramsci, the cultural and political power of CONAIE, but also because various informants used this term to describe the strength of CONAIE. Often, though, the term took different hues. For rival organizations, CONAIE had an "exclusionary hegemony" (personal interview with P. De la Cruz, Federación Nacional de Organizaciones Campesinas, Indígenas y Negras, Quito, June 21, 1999). For some multilateral development agencies, CONAIE had a "necessary hegemony" (personal interview with J. Pérez, Fondo Indígena, La Paz, November 10, 1999).

In Bolivia, the relatively late political emergence of lowland *indígenas* to social movement politics meant different possibilities for discursive and organizational consensus. CIDOB is the main Bolivian lowland organization, but in terms of members it is much smaller than the highland "rural worker" CSUTCB. CIDOB has long been fearful of being swallowed by its Andean counterpart. Moreover, because of the Amazonian bias of international aid, CIDOB had little economic incentive to partner with the CSUTCB. With the added environmental interest in the Amazon, lowland groups are often positioned relatively advantageously in international networks. "The greening of Indian rights," explains Brysk (1994: 36), "also reinforced the disproportionate international attention to Amazonian indigenous groups vis-à-vis their more numerous but less remotely situated peers [in the highlands]."

Another important factor also affected indigenous recognition: Amazonians were not only more "green" but also less "red." Hans Hoffmeyer, director of Ibis, explains that Ibis had to make a choice about its target population; it chose indigenous people, one of the few NGOs to define its target groups in this way. Explaining why Ibis works with CIDOB but does not work with the highland CSUTCB, Hoffmeyer put the choice in the following terms: "Between the ethnic and class discourses, we chose the ethnic. It was with these eyes that we saw the situation and thus excluded work with the unions" (personal interview with H. Hoffmeyer, La Paz, November 16, 1999). It should also be pointed out that in adopting a more radical, anti-imperialist posture, the CSUTCB is also less likely to look for funding from actors such as Ibis and Oxfam. In the valleys and tropics, the *cocaleros* were often at odds with the law, making them risky partners for many (though certainly not all) NGOs. Thus, it is important to think about not only the structures of opportunities but also the agency and strategy of particular indigenous actors.

Strategies: Contestation and Negotiation in the New Millennium

Indigenous people in Latin America have centuries-long traditions of both "resistance and accommodation" with regard to dominant power.[12] Both strategies characterize Ecuadorian and Bolivian movements, often with mixed results. Since its 1990 mobilization, CONAIE has on several occasions paralyzed national roads and convoked peaceful but potent uprisings. These protests provided CONAIE with important political capital that it could use in negotiating a series of agreements with elites over indigenous and nonindigenous issues. As Zamosc (2004: 139) has pointed out, over time the demands of CONAIE have become less and less "indigenous" in taking on large questions of economics (oversubsidies, privatization, and structural adjustment). Within CONAIE, there is disagreement over the right mix of contestation and negotiation: lowland groups are often seen as more *gobiernista* (pro-government) and are willing to go to the negotiating table, while highland actors are more likely to take to the streets. As we will see, the same tension exists in Bolivia, yet in Ecuador the existence of a national organization provides an institutionalized way to overcome these divisions, at least most of the time. That unity became much more fragmented when President Gutiérrez and CONAIE ended their alliance.

Gutiérrez was highly capable of dividing the indigenous movement by reaching out to former CONIAE president Antonio Vargas, who became his minister of social welfare (and was denounced as a traitor by CONAIE), as well as to other indigenous actors, including FEINE and sectors of the Amazon still loyal to fellow Amazonian Antonio Vargas. Within the office of CONAIE and throughout Ecuador, one hears concerns about a severe organizational crisis that was all too obvious in a noticeably small uprising that CONAIE convoked at the beginning of 2004 to protest Gutiérrez's policies.

Bolivia's indigenous movement was also entering a critical juncture at the turn of the millennium. In the period of neoliberal multiculturalism, CIDOB was often favored by state and international actors, because other actors, such as the CSUTCB or *cocaleros*, were seen as clinging to old-fashioned class-based politics, obstructionist tactics, and anti-imperialist rhetoric. Speaking of the CSUTCB, the director of Ibis suggested in 1999 that "their discourse has expired, the union says no to everything, the state is always the enemy" (personal interview with H. Hoffmeyer, La Paz, November 16, 1999). Generally, one can say that international organizations and the state see CIDOB, and not the CSUTCB, as the most viable national indigenous actor in the elaboration of development and conservation programs (personal interviews with H. Hoffmeyer, La Paz, November 16, 1999; J. Pérez, La Paz, November 10, 1999; M. Pérez, Santa Cruz, Bolivia, October 28, 1999; M. Scurrah, Miami, Florida, United States, March 17, 2000). A high-ranking official of the Vice Ministry of First Nations and

Indigenous Peoples, himself a former CSUTCB leader, explained how CIDOB consistently outshone the CSUTCB:

> In every project of the Vice Ministry, we invite organizations to a two-day seminar and say here is the proposal. When we held the last one, the CIDOB assumes ownership of the project. [CIDOB officials say,] "We have been fighting for this for years, marching. This project is ours, not the governments." Not the CSUTCB, it keeps throwing rocks, but it doesn't reject the programs either. (Personal interview, M. Morales, La Paz, September 18, 1999)

When Victor Hugo Cárdenas was vice president of Bolivia, he echoed this sentiment by declaring that the different responses that CIDOB and the CSUTCB had toward the INRA indicated who the pragmatic and responsible indigenous actors were:

> In first place come the [lowland] indigenous people because they have good leaders and advisors. They receive around six million hectares in titles of original community lands (TCOs). They are net winners, and I congratulate them. The second winners are the agricultural businessmen because they achieved a 60 percent reduction in taxes ... and I myself am surprised by this victory.... They also achieved positive advantages for the titling of their land.... The only sector that won nothing was the CSUTCB because of the mediocrity and incapacity of their leadership. (*La Presencia*, October 10, 1996, as cited in Condo 1998)

CIDOB may remain an important development actor, but in political terms, recent events have moved Bolivia from a period of neoliberal multiculturalism to one of neoliberal backlash. Since 2000, a series of "wars"—first over the privatization of water in Cochabamba, then over taxes, and finally over the exportation of natural gas—has changed the dynamic in Bolivia, as well as views about the incapacity of the CSUTCB. The cycle of protests began with the ill-considered privatization plan that in some cases resulted in a 400 percent increase in the cost of water in local communities. This uprising set off a wave of subsequent protests in the valley by the *cocaleros*, under the leadership of Evo Morales, as well as blockades in the high plains, led by the radical *indianista* leader of the CSUTCB, Felipe Quispe. In the elections of 2002, indigenous voices were also heard loudly as the parties of Morales (MAS) and Quispe (Movimiento Indígena Pachakutik) combined to win 27 percent of the vote, a much higher percentage of the vote than indigenous parties have ever won in Bolivia (Van Cott 2003).

Though Sánchez de Lozada returned to the presidency (narrowly defeating Evo Morales), his support quickly vanished as he pursued widely unpopular tax hikes and a plan to export gas through the nation's historic enemy, Chile. Popular discontent reached the point where hundreds of thousands of protesters took to the streets and demanded Sánchez de Lozada's resignation. Aymara leader Felipe Quispe escalated his rhetorical assaults by calling for an independent Aymara state. Violence from the Bolivian state only made matters worse, and the president was forced to step down from office and leave the country in October 2003. His vice president, Carlos Mesa, took over the presidency and moved cautiously and pragmatically.

Unlike his predecessor, President Mesa resisted calls to use state violence to halt the frequent blockades and protests. Instead he appealed to the force of public and political elite opinion by threatening to resign. It was a telling indicator that the most threatening move this executive could make was to tender his resignation. Fearful of the ensuing vacuum and increasingly weary of social protest, significant numbers of middle- and upper-class citizens mobilized for a while to prevent Mesa's resignation. In June 2005, Mesa offered his resignation to Congress for the last and final time. Eduardo Rodríguez, the former president of the Supreme Court, became head of a caretaker government that took Bolivia to the historic elections of December 2005, which resulted in the stunning first-round victory of *cocalero* leader Evo Morales. Morales had come in a close second in 2002, but very few people foresaw Morales's winning by an outright majority victory in the first round. Since democracy returned to Bolivia in the early 1980s, no candidate until Evo had ever won a majority of the popular vote, and thus (until now) a second-round election, which took place in Congress and was characterized by deal making and maneuvering, usually decided Bolivian elections. The 2005 election, though, put an end to a pattern of elections in which the people voted but never finally decided on the leader. In 2005, they decided to vote for Evo, for nationalization of natural gas resources, and against the U.S. war on drugs. Evo moved boldly, though pragmatically. In a forceful symbolic move, he "nationalized" gas with the high-profile assistance of the Bolivian armed forces on May 1, 2006, securing many fields where Brazilian, Spanish, and other transnational firms were working. Yet the actual maneuvering was pragmatic: nationalization did not mean a complete takeover, but something more like a renegotiation of the amount of the revenue that would go to the foreign firms and the amount that would remain with the state.

The inflection point for indigenous politics in the Andes occurred in 2000. In Ecuador, an alliance between CONAIE and sectors of the military in January 2000 resulted in a short-lived junta and then two years later led to a slightly longer-lived coalition between CONAIE and Gutiérrez. These failed partnerships have jeopardized a decade's worth of political capital as non-CONAIE indigenous leaders occupy spaces in the government and in international programs like PRODEPINE. These national events may not necessarily be a negative development for the livelihood of indigenous communities; more research is needed to explore the local repercussions. Yet it is clear that CONAIE, both as an actor in civil society and as a protagonist in "ethnodevelopment," has suffered a setback. In Bolivia, the more radical elements of the movement—the former guerrilla Quispe and, to a much more significant degree, the *cocalero* leader Morales—became central actors in indigenous politics. CIDOB may, like CONAIE, still be relevant in the politics of development, but it is less central to the politics of protest.

Seeing Equity and Development Possibilities: Tradeoffs of Voice and Equity?

Despite these contrasts, it is clear that strong indigenous political organizations are having important effects in the political economies of both Ecuador and Bolivia. But what does this mean for indigenous livelihoods? In countries with significant indigenous populations, being indigenous increases the possibility of being poor (see table 5.3). Moreover, discrimination against indigenous people seems to be increasing—or at least not

Table 5.3. Percentage Increase in Probability of Being Poor, If Indigenous, Controlling for Other Common Predicators of Poverty

Country	Early 1990s (%)	Latest available year (%)
Bolivia	16	13
Ecuador	—	16
Guatemala	11	14
Mexico	25	30
Peru	—	11

Source: Hall and Patrinos 2006: 223.
Note: "Data are the marginal effects of an indigenous indicator in a logit regression, which estimates the percentage by which an individual's likelihood of being poor increases as a result of being indigenous, controlling for other factors, including age, household composition, region, employment status, and education level. These estimates were not generated for Ecuador or Peru in 1994" (Hall and Patrinos 2006: 223).

declining. A preliminary and pessimistic possibility that emerges in recent World Bank studies suggests that, in both countries, greater indigenous mobilization may invite social discrimination, which keeps wages down, keeps poverty gaps high, and limits the returns to schooling.

Noting growing discrimination in Bolivia, Landa and Fernández (2006: 53) state this possible interpretation directly:

> Indigenous groups across Bolivia increased prominence throughout the 1990s, resulting in broad success in legislative elections and the effective overthrow of the President early in the following decade. That increased prominence may be associated with employers more frequently recognizing and penalizing indigenous workers.

Although this hypothesis is plausible, it demands more empirical research before it can be confirmed or rejected. However, there are various reasons for skepticism about the logic behind the claim that greater voice has either generated a backlash or hurt the economic possibilities for indigenous peoples in the Andean and Amazonian republics.

First, there is historical evidence that suggests that indigenous protest does not necessarily create anti-indigenous feelings. In Ecuador, for example, it was striking that at the height of the country's worst economic crisis, in 1999, public opinion data revealed relatively high levels of support for the main indigenous confederation, CONAIE, even as it paralyzed the streets of the nation. In fact, polls revealed that it was the third most trusted institution in the country, behind the church and the military.[13]

Second, in cases where increases in anti-indigenous feeling have been documented, it is important to disaggregate the backlash and see precisely where and why those feelings have been on the rise. In Bolivia, existing data provide a striking geographic and class map of discrimination against Aymaras and Quechuas. As figure 5.1 illustrates, discrimination rises as one moves from the largely indigenous high plains to the departments of the lowlands or *media luna* (the half-moon shaped part of the country that includes Pando, Beni, Santa Cruz, and Tarija) and as one moves from lower- to higher-income groups.

In addition, there may be important reasons and evidence to justify turning this perversity thesis on its head.

Finding Equity through Voice?

It is important to point out that the emergence of strong indigenous movements may also have net positive effects on equity over the medium and

Figure 5.1. Discrimination against Aymaras and Quechuas in Bolivia

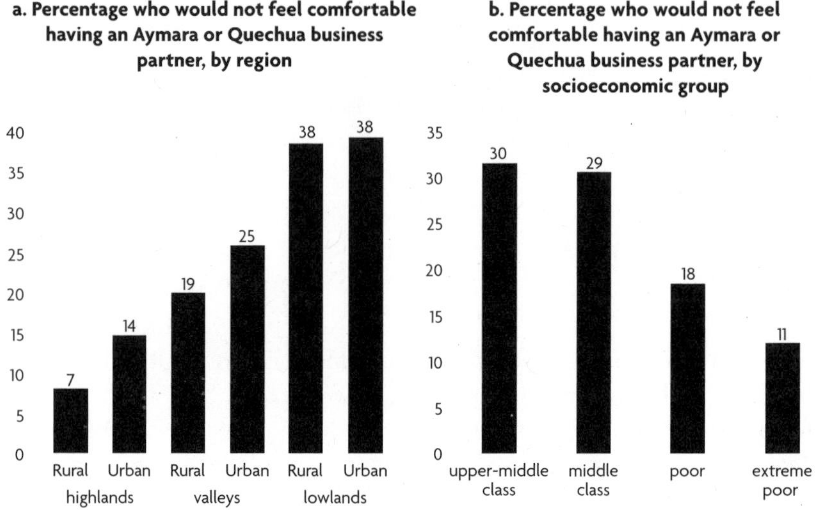

Source: UNDP 2004.

long term. The opposing thesis discussed above—that stronger voice invites stronger discrimination—is troubling, not only for its family resemblance with a kind of "blame the victim" logic, but also because it neglects the increased opportunities that indigenous struggles have forged. Politically, the presence of indigenous representatives at all levels of government is itself a substantively important achievement in securing public attention to indigenous concerns that were often invisible. Perhaps more fundamentally, the emergence of indigenous people as political actors carries the promise of challenging what Appadurai (2004) calls the "terms of recognition," in which the dominant cultural descriptions of certain groups are themselves part of the structures of subordination and poverty. Challenging these constraints involves cultivating what Appadurai (2004) calls the poor's "capacity to aspire," which he describes as a kind of metacapacity that enables the poor to work on increasing other capabilities by envisioning alternative political and economic horizons.

Reading accounts of the mobilizations of indigenous people in the Andes, one can sense (though not measure) such dreaming and note shifts in the capacity to aspire. Indigenous people, who were often prisoners of neocolonial social hierarchies, were often forced to occupy (literally) subordinate spaces at the back of buses and marginal spaces of cities and towns.

The uprisings of the 1990s, which often took main plazas, cathedrals, and other public spaces, allowed a reconsideration of the "proper places" of Indians, which now include parliaments and presidential palaces (León 1994). Moreover, ordinary indigenous people have a sense of possibility that was unknown before the 1990s. "I didn't know there were so many of us" was a common expression in the historic 1990 uprising in Ecuador (J. León, personal interview, Quito, March 3, 1999). Subsequent mobilizations have increased the political visibility of indigenous people and their political and economic concerns.

The electoral victory of Evo Morales provides perhaps the most resounding rebuke of the perversity thesis. In just over a year, the "indigenous-popular" government of Morales has made various policy shifts that have radically altered the political economic possibilities of indigenous people. Although Morales's government has also generated increasing opposition, largely in the lowlands (the *media luna* departments mentioned earlier), Morales continues to enjoy high public approval ratings—67 percent in November 2006 (*La Razón* 2006). This popularity owes something to the most ambitious and controversial measure of the first term: the nationalization of the hydrocarbon sector. As mentioned previously, this nationalization was unlike the nationalizations of the past century, in that the property of transnational firms was left untouched. Rather, nationalization meant contract renegotiations with Brazilian, Spanish, and other transnational companies that dramatically increased the percentage of income that would go to the Bolivian government (see table 5.4).

Table 5.4. Legal Changes in Bolivian State Share of Hydrocarbon Rents

Law	Bolivian state share of hydrocarbon rents (%)	Average annual income (US$ million)
Law 1689 (in effect through Sánchez de Lozada government)	"Megafields": 18 (plus IUH)[a] Other fields: 18 (plus IUH)	250
Law 3958 (Mesa government)	"Megafields": 50 (plus IUH)[a] Other fields: 50 (plus IUH)	500
Law 28701 (Evo Morales, transitional nationalization period)	"Megafields": 82 (plus IUH)[a] Other fields: 50 (plus IUH)	700
Law 2870 (nationalization with new contracts)	"Megafields": 84[b] Other: 50[b]	1,300 (projected)

Source: La Razón (2006: 15).

a. IUH (*impuesto a la utilidades de empresa*) is the capital tax on corporations.

b. These rates are variable and will fluctuate between 50 and 84, depending on various factors that were written in the new contracts. The amount that companies will invest, however, will not vary and is set by the contracts.

Higher international prices have also meant a windfall year for the economy overall, as Bolivia, though still one of the poorest countries, has under Morales found itself with a budget surplus, something that none of the neoliberal governments of the 1980s or 1990s ever accomplished. The new revenues from natural gas, oil, and other natural resources translate into greater resources generally—but also specifically for local-level development initiatives. The direct tax on hydrocarbons will mean significant increases in the municipal budgets of all the departments, further decentralizing the distribution of national resources. Specifically, the nationalization and accompanying taxes will result in a 44-percent increase in municipal funds for La Paz, 44 percent for Santa Cruz, 46 percent for Cochabamba, 62 percent for Potosi, 82 percent for Chuquisaca, 112 percent for Oruro, 120 percent for Beni, 150 percent for Tarija, and 832 percent for Pando (*La Razón* 2006).

In addition to the nationalization initiatives, the Morales government, with the help of indigenous marches, has also passed a new law on agrarian reform that will allow for the expropriation and redistribution of lands that are not being used productively. This law, unlike the nationalization law, will likely create greater social conflicts, because landowners of large estates in the lowlands will not let their lands go without serious opposition. Dealing with this opposition will be one of the great challenges of the Morales government in 2007 and beyond. Yet for indigenous people, it is another sign that the change in government has advanced the promise of decolonization.

In Ecuador, the indigenous movement has been unable to translate its victories in the mobilization of the 1990s into electoral gains as dramatically as Bolivia. The indigenous party, Pachakutik, still has representation in Congress and several municipalities, but it decided against making a formal alliance with the main leftist candidate, Rafael Correa, in the 2006 presidential election. Having been burned by the alliance with Lucio Gutiérrez, CONAIE and Pachakutik decided to support the candidacy of CONAIE president Luis Macas, who captured slightly more than 2 percent of the vote. Correa, however, was able to beat the conservative populist Alvaro Noboa and has promised to govern with the poor in mind. A leftist economist, Correa has already signaled that he follows the example of Evo Morales and Hugo Chavez in putting national interests before those of foreign oil companies.

Also, he inherits a state apparatus that has been shaped by the previous struggles of indigenous movements. The establishment of transnational "ethnodevelopment" initiatives, such as CODENPE and PRODEPINE, in which indigenous actors are involved at various levels of policy making, may also help expand opportunities for indigenous people. Yet before embracing an optimistic future too quickly, one must address significant critiques about the implications of ethnodevelopment efforts. First, critics such as Victor Bretón and others have raised skepticism that PRODEPINE is simply an analgesic meant to silence more radical questioning of dominant neoliberal orthodoxy. According to the social-capital methodology of PRODEPINE, the crucial indigenous actors involved are not the national-level actors discussed here, but rather the intermediate second-level organizations that link local communities and national confederations. Choosing these organizations may make sense in looking for the densest layer of associational life capable of carrying out development programs, yet using social capital as a guide to policy intervention may also mean that, paradoxically, the areas that get the most help are not the ones with the greatest needs, but the ones with the greatest abilities. Operating at the second level and away from the more politically vocal third-level (national) organization also keeps important policy questions away from political debate (Bretón 2002).

Second, several indigenous leaders argue that PRODEPINE is a good start but that it picks the wrong terms of recognition with regard to development strategies and tactics. Strategically, many indigenous leaders argue that the program should recognize indigenous people not as organizations (which reflect the contingencies of politics and place) but as nationalities and pueblos (which reflect aspirations of autonomy and self-governance). Thinking more of the Spanish models of plurinationality than of Eastern European ones, several indigenous leaders I have interviewed see the strengthening and recognition of indigenous nationalities as the most important long-term political project to alter the structures of inequality and advance the process of decolonization.

Perhaps the most damning critique of PRODEPINE can be found in the difficulties that kept its second phase (PRODEPINE II) from being realized. Although this theme deserves more detailed treatment, key problems can be summarized here. According to indigenous leaders and former PRODEPINE staff members, the complications that blocked the continuation of the next phase of this ethnodevelopment program had to do with the instability of the government, the increased competition among indigenous organizations for resources, a lack of clarity and transparency in the planning and execution of projects, and political opportunism.

These critiques are worth taking seriously as the World Bank continues to formulate new strategies for poverty reduction and enters the next phase of ethnodevelopment thinking. As we move to conclude with some recommendations, though, it is worth keeping in mind Appadurai's (2004) reminder that meaningful change with regard to equity is often slow. As he notes, one of the great paradoxes and resources of the poor is that, in conditions of urgency and emergency, they are capable of great patience: "In helping to negotiate emergency with patience, the capacity to aspire guarantees an ethical and psychological anchor, a horizon of credible hopes, with which to withstand the deadly oscillation between waiting and rushing" (Appadurai 2004: 81–82). Thus, perhaps the best provisional answer to the perversity thesis that greater indigenous political voice may invite great economic exclusion may lie in the nurturing of the (meta)capacity to aspire, which, over time, can strengthen indigenous people's ability to rectify more than 500 years of dramatically disadvantageous terms of recognition.

Conclusions and Recommendations

Over the past three decades, movements in Ecuador and Bolivia have grown increasingly powerful and have made great gains in political voice. Different structures of opportunity in each country, however, have made Ecuadorian indigenous movements more unified than Bolivian ones. Although more fragmented, Bolivian movements have been more contentious as conflicts over water, taxes, and coca have given new life to more radical contestation. Despite the increase in voice, indigenous people face severe socioeconomic conditions. As Hall and Patrinos (2006) note, gaps in health, economic opportunity, and education continue to separate indigenous and nonindigenous people. Narrowing these persistent gaps requires both sustained research and action. In conclusion, here are three possible avenues:

1. *Pursue more research on possible equity tradeoffs.* Although some argue that the increasing protest of indigenous movements may increase discrimination and thus have a perverse effect on equity, the opposite may be true if increased indigenous voice can challenge the terms of recognition that have fueled discrimination against indigenous people for centuries. Understanding these relationships, though, requires better economic and ethnographic data so that broad trends can be identified and cultural and social mechanisms understood.

2. *Include "pragmatic" and "radical" voices.* One of the lessons of the political resurrection of figures such as Felipe Quispe and, even more significantly, Evo Morales might be called the limits of "neoliberal multiculturalism." In times of extreme economic and political crisis, the (perhaps unintended) use of ethnodevelopment policies to favor "pragmatic" indigenous actors over "radical" ones can backfire, as it did in the explosive water, gas, and tax wars in Bolivia.[14] Put more positively, development and governance agendas work best when most inclusive. Conversely, extreme indigenous demands, like the Aymara separatism of Felipe Quispe, have the greatest audience when political and social orders are most exclusionary. Thus, strategies that reach out across the radical-pragmatic divide have the most promise for long-term gains in productive political voice.
3. *Rethink terms of recognition, collectively.* More efforts should be made to cultivate indigenous peoples' capacities to aspire in ways that respond to local conditions and not external agendas. One of the ironies of PRODEPINE, with its social-capital focus, is that it ends by privileging external criteria (social-capital indexes) over a plurality of local alternatives (for example, nationalities and pueblos, indigenous Evangelical churches, and municipalities). Although the reasons behind these choices are good, there should be greater opportunities for the participation of a wide range of indigenous people, from various ideological and organizational traditions, to collectively deliberate over the terms of recognition. Greater efforts should also be made to identify some terms of recognition (such as gender) that may be underemphasized in current debates. These kinds of deliberations may themselves enhance the (meta)capacities and capabilities of indigenous people to participate in the forging of more equitable alternative futures.

Notes

1. These words from Macas serve as the epigraph for the Bebbington and others (1992) volume titled *Actores de una década ganada* (roughly, "Actors of a Winning Decade"). This chapter follows Bebbington and his colleagues in revealing some good news from the so-called lost decade of the 1980s: the rise of indigenous political voice.
2. On party systems, see Conaghan (1995), Gamarra and Malloy (1995), and Van Cott (2003, 2005). On the overthrow of Jamil Mahuad in Ecuador in

2000, see Lucero (2001). For a pessimistic account of the phenomenon of "interrupted presidencies" in Latin America, see Valenzuela (2004).

3. In Bolivia, Victor Hugo Cárdenas was vice president in the mid-1990s under Sánchez de Lozada, and Evo Morales won the presidency in 2005 after coming in a close second to Sánchez de Lozada in the 2002 elections.
4. The "capacity to aspire" is Appadurai's (2004) argument for the importance of voice, as will be discussed later.
5. This explanation has been most clearly articulated by Yashar (1998, 2005). See also Albó (1991) and Zamosc (1994).
6. That an old (500-plus years) Indian identity could be part of the rise of new social movements is one of the many paradoxical characteristics of movements and the literature about them.
7. For more on the changing fortunes of CONAIE, see León (2005) and Lucero (forthcoming).
8. In addition, lowland indigenous organizations were seen as benefiting more from INRA than highland groups that rejected the law.
9. This is not to say that Amazonian indigenous peoples in Ecuador faced no adversaries—quite the contrary. Oil and timber companies were powerful and disruptive forces, but as a classic enclave setting, these opponents were targets against which to mobilize, as opposed to the more pervasive webs of local elites like those in the Bolivian lowlands. To use Gramscian metaphors, there were more trenches in lowland Bolivia than in Ecuador to block collective action.
10. A more thorough discussion can be found in Lucero (2002, forthcoming).
11. Consider the place of nationality in an executive decree of 1998:

    > It is the duty of the National Government to promote the harmonization of the secondary laws and institutional structure of the State with the existing Political Constitution guaranteeing the exercise of the collective rights of the nationalities and pueblos.... Exercising the powers provided by the current Constitution, [the President of the Republic] decrees ... the Creation of the Council for the Development of the Nationalities and Pueblos of Ecuador. (Executive Decree 386, December 11, 1998)

12. A useful long-term look is provided in the essays collected by Stern (1987).
13. A 1999 poll asked, "In which institution do you have the most trust?" Responses were church—28.44 percent, military—25.97 percent, CONAIE—12.66 percent, government—2.6 percent, labor unions—2.3 percent (cited in Lucero 2001: 65).
14. For more on the postmulticultural moment of indigenous politics and development in Bolivia, see Postero (2006); for a comparative Andean exploration, see Lucero (forthcoming) and Andolina, Laurie, and Radcliffe (forthcoming). Key writings on neoliberal multiculturalism include Gustafson (2002), Hale (2002), and Van Cott (forthcoming).

References

Albó, X. 1991. "El retorno del indio." *Revista Andina* 9 (2): 299–357.

———. 1994. "And from Kataristas to MNRistas? The Surprising and Bold Alliance between Aymaras and Neoliberals in Bolivia." In *Indigenous Peoples and Democracy in Latin America*, ed. D. L. Van Cott, 55–81. Washington, DC: Inter-American Dialogue.

———. 2002. *Pueblos indios en la política*. La Paz: Plural/CIPCA.

Andolina, R., N. Laurie, and S. Radcliffe. Forthcoming. *Multiethnic Transnationalism: Indigenous Developments in the Andes*. Durham, NC: Duke University Press.

Appadurai, A. 2004. "The Capacity to Aspire: Culture and the Terms of Recognition." In *Culture and Public Action*, ed. V. Rao and M. Walton, 59–84. Stanford, CA: Stanford University Press.

Bebbington, A., H. Carrasco, L. Peralvo, G. Ramón, V. H. Torres, and J. Trujillo. 1992. *Los actores de una década ganada: Tribus, comunas y campesinos en la modernidad*. Quito: Comunidec/Abya-Yala.

Bretón, V. 2002. "Cooperación al desarrollo, capital social y neo-indigenismo en los Andes ecuatorianos." *Revista Europea de Estudios Latinoamericanos y del Caribe* 73 (October): 43–63.

Brysk, A. 1994. "Acting Globally: Indian Rights and International Politics in Latin America." In *Indigenous People and Democracy in Latin America*, ed. D. L. Van Cott, 29–54. New York: St. Martin's Press.

Calla, R. 2003. *Indígenas, política y reformas en Bolivia: Hacia una etnologia del Estado en América Latina*. Guatemala City: Instituto Centroamericano de Prospectiva e Investigación.

Conaghan, C. 1995. "Politicians against Parties: Discord and Disconnection in Ecuador's Party System." In *Building Democratic Institutions: Party Systems in Latin America*, ed. S. Mainwaring and T. Scully, 434–58. Stanford, CA: Stanford University Press.

Condo, F. 1998. *La Marcha del siglo: Marcha de las naciones originarias, el tiempo del instrumento político*. La Paz: Alkamiri.

Gamarra, E., and J. Malloy. 1995. "The Patrimonial Dynamics of Party Politics in Bolivia." In *Building Democratic Institutions: Party Systems in Latin America*, ed. S. Mainwaring and T. Scully, 399–433. Stanford, CA: Stanford University Press.

Gisselquist, R. 2005."Bolivia's 2004 Elections." *Focal Point* 4 (1): 1–2.

Gonzalez, M. L. 1994. "How Many Indigenous People." In *Indigenous People and Poverty in Latin America: An Empirical Analysis*, ed. G. Psacharopoulos and H. A. Patrinos, 21–40. Washington DC: World Bank.

Guerrero, A. 1994. "Una imagen ventrílocua: El discurso liberal de la 'desgraciada raza indígena' a fines del siglo XIX." In *Imágenes e imagineros: Representaciones de los indígenas ecuatorianos, siglos XIX y XX*, ed. B. Muratorio, 197–252. Quito: FLACSO-Ecuador.

Gustafson, B. 2002. "Paradoxes of Liberal Indigenism: Indigenous Movements, State Processes, and Intercultural Reform in Bolivia." In *The Politics of Ethnicity: Indigenous Peoples and Latin American States*, ed. D. Maybury-Lewis, 267–306. Cambridge, MA: Harvard University Press.

Hale, C. 2002. "Does Multiculturalism Menace: Governance, Cultural Rights, and the Politics of Identity in Guatemala." *Journal of Latin American Studies* 34 (3): 485–524.

Hall, G., and H. A. Patrinos. 2006. "Key Messages and an Agenda for Action." In *Indigenous People, Poverty, and Human Development in Latin America: 1994–2004*, ed. G. Hall and H. A. Patrinos, 221–40. Hampshire, U.K.: Palgrave Macmillan.

Healy, K. 2001. *Llamas, Weaving, and Organic Chocolate*. Notre Dame, IN: University of Notre Dame Press.

Informe Confidencial. 2003. *La confianza en las instituciones*. Unpublished report. Quito: Informe Confidencial.

Landa, F., and W. Fernández. 2006. "Bolivia." In *Indigenous People, Poverty, and Human Development in Latin America: 1994–2004*, ed. G. Hall and H. A. Patrinos, 40–66. Hampshire, U.K.: Palgrave Macmillan.

La Razón. 2006. *Anuario: 30 Noticias para la historia*. La Paz: *La Razón*.

Layton, H. M. and H. A. Patrinos. 2006. "Estimating the Number of Indigenous People in Latin America." In *Indigenous People, Poverty, and Human Development in Latin America: 1994–2004*, ed. G. Hall and H. A. Patrinos, 25–39. Hampshire, U.K.: Palgrave Macmillan.

León, J. 1994. *De campesinos a ciudadanos diferentes*. Quito: CEDIME/Abya-Yala.

———. 2000. "La crisis de un sistema político regionalizado en Ecuador." In *La crisis ecuatoriana: Sus bloqueos económicos, políticos y sociales*, ed. M. F. Cañete, 87–109. Quito: CEDIME/IF.

———. 2004. "La democracia real versus la democracia idealizada: Ecuador de 1978 a 2003." *Revista Política* 1 (January): 1–35.

———. 2005. "Los pueblos indígenas y su participación gubernamental, 2002–2003." In *Participación política, democracia y movimientos indígenas en los Andes*, ed. J. León and others, 11–38. La Paz: PIEB/IFEA/Embajada de Francia.

Lucero, J. A. 2001. "Crisis and Contention in Ecuador." *Journal of Democracy* 12 (2): 59–73.

———. 2002. "Arts of Unification: Political Representation and Indigenous Movements in Ecuador and Bolivia." Ph.D. diss., Princeton University, Princeton, NJ.

———. Forthcoming. *Voices of Struggle, Struggles of Voice: Indigenous Representation in the Andes*. Pittsburgh, PA: University of Pittsburgh Press.

Postero, N. G. 2006. *Now We Are Citizens: Indigenous Politics in Postmulticultural Bolivia*. Stanford, CA: Stanford University Press.

Smith, R. C. 1985. "A Search for Unity within Diversity: Peasant Unions, Ethnic Federations, and Indianist Movements in the Andean Republics." *Native Peoples and Economic Development*, ed. T. MacDonald, 5–38. Cambridge, MA: Cultural Survival.

Stern, S., ed. 1987. *Resistance, Rebellion, and Consciousness in the Andean Peasant World*. Madison: University of Wisconsin Press.

UNDP (United Nations Development Programme). 2004. *Human Development Report 2004: Cultural Liberty in Today's Diverse World*. New York: UNDP.

Valenzuela, A. 2004. "Latin American Presidencies Interrupted." *Journal of Democracy* 15 (4): 5–19.

Van Cott, D. L. 2003. "From Exclusion to Inclusion: Bolivia's 2002 Elections." *Journal of Latin American Studies* 35 (4): 751–76.

———. 2005. *From Movements to Parties: The Evolution of Ethnic Politics*. Cambridge, MA: Cambridge University Press.

———. Forthcoming. "Multiculturalism against Neoliberalism in Latin America." In *Multiculturalism and the Welfare State*, ed. K. Banting and W. Kymlicka. Oxford, U.K.: Oxford University Press.

Whitehead, L. 2001. "Bolivia and the Viability of Democracy." *Journal of Democracy* 12 (2): 6–16.

Yashar, D. 1998. "Contesting Citizenship in Latin America: Indigenous Movements and Democracy in Latin America." *Comparative Politics* 31 (1): 23–42.

———. 2005. *Contesting Citizenship: Indigenous Movements and the Postliberal Challenge in Latin America*. Cambridge, MA: Cambridge University Press.

Zamosc, L. 1994. "Agrarian Protest and the Indian Movement in the Ecuadorian Highlands." *Latin American Research Review* 29 (3): 37–68.

———. 2004. "Indigenous Movements and Class Struggles in Ecuador (1992–2002)." In *The Struggle for Indians Rights in Latin America*, ed. N. G. Postero and L. Zamosc. Brighton, U.K.: Sussex Press.

CHAPTER 6

Cash Transfers for Older People Reduce Poverty and Inequality

Armando Barrientos

Only a handful of developing countries have established large-scale noncontributory pension programs for older people (Schwarz 2003), but in the past decade such programs have been introduced in Bangladesh, Bolivia, Lesotho, and Nepal.[1] This policy option is important for developing countries concerned with confronting the inequalities faced by the elderly for several reasons. These reasons include the rapid unfolding of the demographic transition, the incidence of old-age poverty, and the accumulated evidence on the relative effectiveness of the programs (Barrientos 2003a; Bertranou, Solorio, and van Ginneken 2002; Willmore 2007). Moreover, in industrial countries, pension programs provided the foundation on which social security systems were built. This chapter examines the role that noncontributory pension programs could play in developing sustainable and effective institutions for poverty and inequality reduction in developing countries. It draws on the rich experiences of first of South Africa and then of Brazil, which have two of the older and larger programs of this type in the South, and on the experience of Bangladesh, which is a low-income country with a newly established program.

The chapter addresses two sets of related issues. First, it examines the evolution of noncontributory pension programs as institutions for poverty and inequality reduction. A key objective is to identify the main factors explaining the establishment, growth, and sustainability of these programs in the context of societies with high levels of inequality. Second, it evaluates the available evidence on the extent to which noncontributory pension programs reduce poverty, facilitate household investment, and reduce inequality. The chapter takes as a given that many of the elderly are caught in inequality traps. Rather than exploring how those traps emerge and are reproduced, the chapter is concerned with exploring (similar to chapters 5 and 7) the political economy underlying the emergence of particular instruments and institutions that address the sources and effects of the traps and then considering how effective such instruments are in weakening inequality traps and their effects.

The chapter is divided into three sections and a conclusion. The first section outlines summary information on the nature of noncontributory pension programs in the three countries. The second section explores the emergence and institutionalization of the programs and describes some implications for the establishment of institutions for equity and development in developing countries. The final section discusses available evidence on the incidence of noncontributory pension programs on poverty, household investment, and equity. The main findings are summarized in the conclusion.

Noncontributory Programs in South Africa, Brazil, and Bangladesh

This section provides a brief description of noncontributory pension programs in three countries.

South Africa

In South Africa, a monthly social pension is paid to men age 65 and older and to women age 60 and older. Benefit entitlements of around US$70 are means tested on the incomes of the individual beneficiary and his or her spouse, but not on the incomes of other household members. In 1993, slightly more than 1.5 million old-age pensions were paid, with 1.2 million paid to blacks (van der Berg 2001), but the number of beneficiaries rose to 1.9 million in 2003. The program is reasonably well administered and reaches the poorer rural areas. The program is funded through general taxation; it absorbed 60 percent of social security expenditure and 1.4 percent of the gross domestic product (GDP) in 2002. It is widely acknowledged that the old-age pension has had a significant influence on poverty among South Africans (Ardington and Lund 1995) and that it has produced a substantial redistribution of income in the country (Committee of Inquiry into a Comprehensive System of Social Security for South Africa 2002).

Brazil

The two noncontributory pension programs in Brazil were established in their current form by social security reforms that began in 1991. The rural old-age pension, Prêvidencia Rural (PR), benefits men from age 60 and women from age 55 who worked in informal employment. Whereas before 1991 only heads of household were entitled to a pension, the reforms extended entitlement to all qualifying workers, thereby expanding coverage to female rural workers who were not heads of household. The monthly value of the pension benefits was raised from one-half minimum wage to one minimum wage (around US$70). Entitlement is conditional on workers demonstrating an engagement in agricultural or subsistence production and on their not having contributed to social insurance or acted as employers. The contributory requirement is replaced by proof of economic activity.[2] A key aspect of the program is that pension entitlements do not require earnings or inactivity tests.

In urban areas, provision of old-age assistance pensions is much less developed. A social assistance pension known as the Renda Mensal Vitalícia (RMV) was introduced in 1974. That pension pays a flat-rate benefit of one-half minimum wage to older people and people with disabilities who cannot provide for themselves. To be entitled to the RMV, individuals need to be 70 years of age or older and have at least 12 months of contributions to social insurance. In January 1996, a new social assistance pension, the Beneficio de Prestação Continuada (BPC), was introduced under the 1988 constitution. The BPC pays one minimum wage to people age 65 and older and people with disabilities who live in urban or rural areas with per capita household income no greater than one-fourth minimum wage. Entitlement, including the means test, is reviewed every two years. The conditions for entitlement under the BPC are tougher than those under the PR.

In December 2000, 4.6 million beneficiaries received an old-age pension under the PR, 0.3 million old-age beneficiaries under the RMV, and 0.4 million old-age beneficiaries under the BPC.[3] The fiscal cost of the PR, including disability pensions, has been estimated at 1 percent of gross domestic product (GDP) (Schwarzer and Querino 2002b), whereas the cost of the RMV and BPC together should be around 0.2 percent of GDP, given the smaller number of beneficiaries. Excluding disability pensions, a reasonable estimate of the cost of providing old-age noncontributory pensions in Brazil is 1 percent of GDP.

Bangladesh

The Old-Age Allowance Scheme (OAAS) was introduced for the first time in Bangladesh in 1997 to 1998. A separate program, the Assistance Program for Widowed and Destitute Women (APWDW), was established later. The OAAS pays a monthly allowance of around US$2 (Tk 100) to the 10 oldest and poorest members (5 men and 5 women) of each ward of each union, which is the lowest-level district in Bangladesh. The APWDW adds another five beneficiaries per ward. The programs are financed from general government revenues, through budgetary allocations in the five-year plan. The annual budget allocation for the OAAS is Tk 500 million, or around 0.02 percent of GDP. If the APWDW is included, the total cost rises to 0.03 percent of GDP. There are 40,311 wards in 4,479 unions in the country, so the targeted number of beneficiaries for the OAAS when the program is fully operational is 403,110. The APWDW adds another 201,555 beneficiaries.

The Ministry of Social Welfare manages the programs. The programs are, therefore, targeted at the extremely poor and destitute (Begum 2003; Rajan, Perera, and Begum 2003). In addition, beneficiaries must be landless with an annual income below US$50. Selection of beneficiaries is necessary because not enough allowances are available to cover all poor, older people. Wards committees do the selection on the basis of the age, economic status, and health status of prospective beneficiaries. The ward committees include public officials, elected representatives, local elites, and at least one social welfare officer. Early evaluations have concluded that the programs are well received by local communities and that they are reasonably well targeted, but they are insufficient in number to cover the poor groups that need the allowance. Moreover, the amount of the benefit is insufficient to pull beneficiaries above the poverty line (Begum 2003).

Noncontributory Pensions as Institutions for Equity and Development

Given their scale and budgetary significance, these noncontributory pension programs can clearly be viewed as institutions for promoting equity and poverty reduction. But why and how did they emerge and become institutionalized? This section examines the main factors explaining their establishment, development, and sustainability in South Africa and Brazil, the two countries in which this process of institutionalization and institutional change is most advanced.

Development of Noncontributory Pensions in South Africa and Brazil

In South Africa, the social pension can be traced to 1928, when means-tested old-age grants were introduced for whites and colored people.[4] Blacks were explicitly excluded. The pension was extended to blacks in 1944, but with lower entitlements and stricter conditions. Despite its discriminatory basis, the social pension had significant implications for the development of social policy in South Africa. As noted in a report by the Committee of Inquiry into a Comprehensive System of Social Security for South Africa (commonly known as the Taylor report), the extension of the social pension to blacks embodied a universal, if discriminatory, principle, in contrast to apartheid's labor-welfare nexus, which focused on protecting "the labour market position of white workers" (Committee of Inquiry into a Comprehensive System of Social Security for South Africa 2002: 8). After legislation established full parity in entitlements in 1996, the social pension has been looked on as a basis for development of a comprehensive social security system in South Africa.

The extension of the social pension to include blacks led to a rapid increase in the number of pension recipients, but because of different entitlements, the share of benefit expenditure going to black beneficiaries lagged. The share of blacks among pension beneficiaries rose to 60 percent in 1958, 70 percent in 1978, and 81 percent in 1993. In contrast, the share of total benefit value received by those beneficiaries was just 19 percent, 43 percent, and 67 percent in those same respective years. The shift to parity was achieved through a combination of a reduction of benefit levels and a tightening of the means test for whites, plus a rise in the level of benefit for blacks. These changes were made possible by a favorable set of institutional and political factors (van der Berg 1997). In the context of apartheid, discrimination in the labor market made the social pension of marginal value to whites, and it lowered the degree of opposition to the changes compared with the response to changes in other areas of public expenditure. As van der Berg (1998: 6) notes, equalization "was thus most readily accomplished where political resistance to reducing white benefit levels was the least … [and] the small number of whites who qualified under the means test were poor and politically marginal." The implications for public finances of incorporating blacks presented greater difficulty, but the large differential in benefit levels for whites and blacks, together with increases in budget allocation, smoothed out the changes. Enlightened officials and those opposed to the apartheid regime supported universalization of the social pension along nonracial lines. They were persuaded that the social pension had a strong effect on poverty among blacks—especially those in rural areas. The politicians were fully aware of the instrumental value of the social pension, as it helped "confer political legitimacy on the homeland system and the tricameral parliament" (van der Berg 2001: 188). Cash transfers also provided a much-needed injection of liquidity into the homelands, thus helping to stem migration to South Africa's urban centers.

In Brazil, the right to social security was incorporated into the constitution in 1934, but it specifically excluded rural and informal workers. This situation led to the development of social insurance institutions for specific groups of workers—a common scenario in countries in the region. The scenario was consonant with the import substitution industrialization model of development, which was dominant in Latin America and which relied on a strong state redirecting resources from agriculture to industry. Such models were sustained by political alliances involving the middle classes and workers in formal employment (Barrientos 2004). The development of rural social movements in the 1950s and 1960s led to the formation in the 1960s of the Ligas Campesinas (Peasant Leagues), which agitated for agrarian reform. The progressive government of João Goulart responded in 1963 by establishing the Estatuto do Trabalhador Rural (Statute of the Rural Worker), which set up the Fundo de Assistência e Previdência do Trabalhador Rural (Assistance Fund for Rural Workers, or FUNRURAL). This program to provide limited social insurance for rural workers was financed by a 1 percent tax on the sale of rural produce. FUNRURAL was intended more as a political or programmatic intervention than a full-fledged social insurance for rural workers, and its financial base was inadequate.

The military government that took power in 1964 initially downgraded FUNRURAL, restricting it to providing health insurance. Interestingly, the military later restructured and expanded FUNRURAL. A new program called Programa de Assistência ao Trabalhador Rural (Rural Workers' Assistance Program, or PRORURAL) was set up in 1971 to be managed by FUNRURAL. Under the restructured program, old-age cash transfers were made to rural and informal workers, age 65 and older, who were heads of household. The benefit was equivalent to one-half of the minimum wage. Schwarzer (2000) outlines four key factors explaining this change of policy, the first two of which repeat factors identified by van der Berg (2001) for the South African case:

- Enlightened officials who were committed to the policies of the International Labour Organization pushed for the universalization of social insurance. This effort at the same time helped secure a unified administrative social security system under their control.

- Cash transfers were seen as an effective means to stem migration into the cities and as a stimulus to the local rural economy and to the development of basic services infrastructure in the countryside.
- The military saw instrumental value in the program in terms of reducing social unrest and opposition to the restructuring of the agricultural sector.[5]
- The policy was also seen as a means of co-opting the rural trade unions into the state. (Rural trade unions played a key role in identifying beneficiaries in the absence of contributory or administrative registers among informal workers. They also provided and arranged health care.)

In urban areas, establishment of a noncontributory pension program was more difficult because of concerns, especially within the government and trade unions, that such a program would undermine the contributory social insurance program. However, in 1974/75, the military government introduced a social assistance pension for destitute elderly people and people with disabilities, the RMV, which paid one-half minimum wage to those age 70 and older with no other means of support. This program applied to both rural and urban areas, but it required at least 12 months of contributions to formal social insurance. Given the strong opposition to noncontributory pensions, the program was implemented with considerable caution (Schwarzer 2000).

The end of two decades of military dictatorship led to a fundamental rethinking of social security and to a renewal of the social contract enshrined in the 1988 constitution. The constitution restated the right to social protection for all but now included informal and rural workers and households (Delgado and Cardoso 2000a). It also embodied a commitment to an integrated system covering social insurance and social assistance. Legislation introduced in 1991 to 1993 produced significant changes in the rural and urban noncontributory pension programs. The PR replaced FUNRURAL and PRORURAL in 1993. The PR extended entitlements to all age-qualified individuals and doubled benefits to one minimum wage. The RMV was replaced for new beneficiaries in January 1996 by the BPC. The BPC gradually reduced the age of entitlement from 67 to 65 years of age in 2005 and included a means test threshold set at a per capita household income of one-fourth of the minimum wage. Unlike the RMV, the BPC does not require a contribution record, but the program's entitlement is to be reviewed every two years.

In both South Africa and Brazil, the emergence of noncontributory pension institutions has to be explained both in political economic and in technocratic terms. In each country, these institutions emerged because of a gradual shift in relationships of power in society—a shift that itself reflects broader political and economic changes, in ways similar to those described by Boix in chapter 8. At the same time, the programs emerged because of the prior existence of mechanisms that, while not conceived as instruments to foster transitions to equity, constituted a base on which to design institutions with this goal. Finally—also in ways similar to those noted by Boix—these institutional transitions were facilitated by the presence of reformist technocrats in the government easing them along and defending them within broader processes of policy debate and design.

The social pension in South Africa and the PR in Brazil also demonstrate that solidarity institutions can emerge in deeply unequal societies, suggesting that even under extreme circumstances institutionalized inequalities can be broken. In South Africa, the social pension expanded into a nonracially discriminatory program in the midst of the highly discriminatory and unequal institutions of apartheid. In Brazil, the PR developed in the context of institutions that explicitly excluded informal and rural workers and that were based on the contributory principle. The PR developed against these two overriding principles of welfare provision and is perceived as a key program in extending social protection to informal workers (Delgado and Cardoso 2000a; Schwarzer and Querino 2002b).

Unconventional Nature of Noncontributory Pensions

In industrial countries, a stylized model of the development of solidarity institutions engaged in welfare production is graphically described as ever-expanding concentric circles centered on formal and unionized workers and on a narrow range of benefits in which old-age and retirement pensions are dominant. Over time, more vulnerable workers and their households were co-opted, and the range of contingencies covered expanded.[6] The path of development of welfare institutions can be described as moving "from the strong to the weak." In contrast, the nature and dynamics of noncontributory pension programs appear to follow an altogether different path.

Mulligan and Sala-i-Martin (1999b, 1999c) have sought to develop a positive theory of programs that support the old across a range of industrial and developing countries. They do so by identifying common characteristics in the relevant programs. They find that the strongest common feature is that such programs induce retirement, and they conclude that the "main lesson from cross-country and historical comparisons of programs for the elderly is that ... programs appear to be strongly related to labor markets—'contributions' are a function of labor income, while benefits are a function of labor income and labor force status" (Mulligan and Sala-i-Martin 1999a: 11). This conclusion implies that the vast majority of programs for the elderly cannot be described as antipoverty and equity-enhancing programs. The noncontributory programs under examination here are very different. In all three countries, noncontributory pension programs were adopted specifically to deal with old-age poverty, are not directly linked to labor market,[7] do not require earnings-related contributions, and most important do not explicitly require withdrawal from the labor force except for implicit constraints arising from the means test in South Africa. They are explicitly antipoverty cash-transfer programs based on age (Case and Deaton 1998).

For Brazil, the adoption of noncontributory pension programs arises from the failure of social insurance or occupational pension plans to extend beyond workers in formal employment. This point is obvious but far reaching. In Latin America, in particular, the expectations implicit in social policy in the post–World War II period were that social insurance schemes would gradually co-opt more vulnerable groups until universal coverage was achieved. Not only have these expectations not materialized, but also coverage of contributory pension programs shrank in the 1980s and 1990s (Barrientos 2004).

Developing countries appear incapable of replicating the "strong to the weak" path observed in industrial countries. The experiences of Brazil and South Africa suggest one important explanation: entrenched inequality precludes the gradual co-option of more vulnerable groups into social insurance institutions.[8] In Brazil, rural–urban and formal–informal divisions set definite limits to the expansion of social insurance. In South Africa, racial discrimination further entrenched inequality.[9]

Why the Focus on Old-Age Poverty?

It is an interesting to ask why concerns with poverty and pension programs for the elderly take priority over welfare programs for other vulnerable groups.[10] The priority afforded to support for the older poor is sometimes questioned on efficiency grounds.[11] It can also be questioned in the context of maximizing poverty reduction expenditure.[12] Yet evidence from attitudinal surveys across societies and age groups suggests that concerns over old-age poverty are strong and widely shared.[13] Also there is a direct association between old age and poverty (Barrientos, Gorman, and Heslop 2003), and this finding is as true for developing countries today as it was true for developed countries as they industrialized. In relative terms, stronger concerns with old-age poverty and greater political support for programs assisting poor older people can be accounted for in a number of ways, and the points that follow fail to exhaust those provided by the related literature. Atkinson (1995) suggests that support for poor older people by the population at large is more likely to be forthcoming because old age is more easily verifiable than, say, involuntary unemployment and because adverse work incentives are less likely in the case of older people. Mulligan and Sala-i-Martin (1999b) note that noncontributory pensions are compatible with incentives in that recipients are less likely to alter their labor-supply or saving behavior.[14] Lund (1999) suggests that support for older people is more likely to be forthcoming because most people expect to be old one day but perhaps do not expect to be unemployed, to be a single parent, or to have a disability.[15]

In chapter 3, Moncrieffe discusses how communities and groups can sustain and reinforce poverty and inequality. She urges us to question the way in which group formation, through classifications and labels, is socially constructed. These issues are important in the context of old age and older people. The discussion in this chapter suggests that sympathy for older people has something to do with the fact that membership is an inevitable outcome of the life course, though the historical emergence of noncontributory pension programs also shows that attitudes to the old and their needs have changed over time. Put another way, the emergence of these programs suggests a change in the meanings associated with category "old"—a change that has allowed a challenge to the (in part) culturally ascribed inequalities faced by the old. Likewise, perceptions of thresholds (that is, when is one considered old?) are also culturally defined, as are assumptions about dependency in old age commonly attached to this threshold. There is arguably also a relationship between changes in these meanings and shifts in eligibility thresholds defined by noncontributory pensions.

What Kind of Institutional and Political Environment Made Possible the Development of Noncontributory Pensions in the Countries Studied?

Remarkably, important similarities exist in the political economy and performance reasons provided to explain the extension of noncontributory pension programs in South Africa and Brazil. These similarities merit enumerating because some of them (particularly those linked to the political economy of institutional change) point to important factors that can foster institutional transitions toward equity and that also resonate with factors identified in other chapters in this volume.

Among the political economy reasons are the following:

1. In both South Africa and Brazil, enlightened government officials committed to universalizing welfare institutions supported the extension of noncontributory pension programs (Delgado and Cardoso 2000a; van der Berg 1997). In the case of Brazil, government officials also aimed to consolidate and control the disparate administrative bodies engaged in social security. Both Ross (in chapter 7) and Boix (in chapter 8) also suggest the importance of such reformist officials in the private and public sectors.
2. Perhaps more important, in both countries the noncontributory pension programs involved an explicit redistribution from urban to rural areas, which was justified by the need to prevent or reduce migration from rural to urban areas. In this context, cash transfers to poor older people appeared to be a politically acceptable instrument to inject purchasing power into rural areas. This outcome is interesting because one could think of other, perhaps more effective, means of encouraging rural development. One possible explanation is that pensions, as opposed to other types of transfers, are less likely to create work disincentives.
3. In both countries, unpopular regimes saw noncontributory pensions as instrumental in reducing social unrest, which, in South Africa, arose from the homelands system and, in Brazil, arose from agricultural liberalization and landlessness. This background is important in explaining why regimes otherwise strongly opposed to redistribution in fact supported it in these two countries. Indeed, just as Lucero notes in chapter 5 in connection with Bolivia and Ecuador, political mobilization appears to be a necessary precondition for many of the changes that address either the causes or effects of institutionalized

inequalities. In South Africa and Brazil, political mobilization was an important factor in the extension of noncontributory pension programs. Although the mobilization was not directly about addressing old-age poverty, preexisting programs and institutions provided a channel through which some form of support for those most affected by discrimination, poverty, and vulnerability could be reached. Noncontributory pensions provide an example of how social protection institutions can be adapted to meet changing conditions and needs and can be extended to groups that were originally excluded. The introduction of the child support grant in South Africa was made possible by wide public support for the social pension.[16]

4. A renewal of the social contract was also key in the extension of noncontributory pension programs in both countries. In South Africa, this renewal occurred with the gradual dismantling and final fall of apartheid, and in Brazil, it occurred with the enactment of the 1988 constitution after two decades of dictatorship. These events encouraged debate and consensus around the need to establish and uphold rights to social protection for all. Such occurrences resonate strongly with Boix's discussion in chapter 8 of the role of strengthening of the welfare state and social expenditure in facilitating Spain's transition to democracy. The development of social protection institutions can be a significant factor in facilitating political, social, and economic transformation while emerging partly because of broader social and political economic pressures.
5. The programs embed a range of desirable dimensions of redistribution. Noncontributory pensions combine redistribution to the poor with life-course redistribution. As noted previously, social preferences on life-course redistribution are strong, suggesting that those institutional transitions that are most culturally resonant are more likely to succeed (an observation that relates to points made by Moncrieffe in chapter 3). They also combine urban–rural redistribution, reflecting equity considerations combined with instrumental or functional considerations, such as the perceived need to reduce migration to urban centers.

In addition, reasons related to the design and effects of these programs have favored their growth:

- Noncontributory pensions are especially effective in addressing old-age poverty among women. They can, therefore, play a role in reducing discrimination and exclusion.

- Noncontributory pensions are perceived to be effective; they are reasonably well targeted (more strictly, they are tagged on the old rather than targeted); abuse of the system is not a significant issue; and the administration of the benefit is reasonably effective and low cost.[17] This aspect will be covered in more detail in the next section below.
- Noncontributory pensions have proved flexible in responding to problems arising from social and economic change. HIV/AIDS in South Africa, as well as labor migration, have led to a rise in the share of households without middle-age members and in which grandparents take up a role of primary caregiver. The social pension is generally perceived to be an effective and key instrument for supporting these households. In Brazil, PR is generally agreed to have played an important role in facilitating economic transformation in the rural sector and in protecting households from the adverse effects of such change (Delgado and Cardoso 2000b).

The following section discusses these dimensions in much more detail, showing ways in which these programs have reduced both poverty and inequality.

Poverty, Household Investment, and Equity

The findings from a number of studies indicate that the incidence of noncontributory pension programs is strongly associated with positive outcomes on a wide range of variables. Noncontributory pension programs can reduce poverty among older people and their households, can enable investment in human and physical capital within beneficiary households, can strengthen intergenerational solidarity and transfers, can insure poorer rural communities against the adverse effects of agricultural reform, and can encourage local economy activity. This section considers some of the evidence.

Pension Income and Poverty

A small number of studies have focused on the effects of noncontributory pension programs in Brazil and South Africa on poverty. Ardington and Lund (1995) and Lund (1999) have identified the poverty reduction and promotion effects of the social pension in South Africa and have traced the expanding literature. Case and Deaton (1998: 132) looked at this issue in the context of a 1993 nationwide household dataset and confirmed that the social pension has large effects on poverty. In Brazil, researchers at the Instituto de Pesquisa Econômica Aplicada (Institute of Applied Economic Research) have investigated the influence of the rural old-age pension and have concluded that it has significant effects on poverty (Delgado and Cardoso 2000a, 2000c; Schwarzer 2000; Schwarzer and Querino 2002b). No studies have been published on the effects on poverty of the urban noncontributory pension program in Brazil or the noncontributory programs in Bangladesh.

With data from dedicated household surveys in Brazil and South Africa,[18] reliable and comparable estimates of old-age poverty can be constructed (Barrientos 2003b). These estimates are applied to two measures of household income: one measure incorporating all household income and a second measure excluding pension income. The difference in the poverty estimated on these two measures of household income yields an estimate of the programs' effect on poverty.[19] The comparison answers a hypothetical question: what would be the incidence of poverty among households with older people if the pension benefit were withdrawn? The poverty estimates presented here are based on adult equivalent household income, which is obtained by applying an equivalence scale to aggregate household income. The adjustment takes account of the comparative "cost" of children (0.5 of an adult's cost) and economies of scale in the household (extra adults count for 0.75 of the first one). The poverty lines used were the levels of the pension benefit at the time of the survey.

The comparison of poverty measures with the full income of the household and after subtracting pension income is presented in figure 6.1 for the South Africa (panel a) and Brazil (panel b), respectively. The figures are in the TIP ("Three 'I's of Poverty") format (Jenkins and Lambert 1997) and provide a representation of the incidence, intensity, and inequality dimensions of aggregate poverty. The horizontal axis shows the cumulative share of households, ranked from the poorest on the left to the richest on the right. The vertical axis measures the cumulative sum of the average poverty gap. A point on the TIP curve shows the cumulative sum of the poverty gaps of the poorest households up to the corresponding point on the horizontal axis averaged across the entire sample of households. For nonpoor households, the poverty gap is zero; hence, the point at which the TIP curve becomes horizontal indicates the share of the population who are poor on the horizontal axis (the incidence of poverty), and the average poverty gap for the sample of households on the vertical axis (the intensity of poverty). The degree of concavity of the curve indicates the inequality

Figure 6.1. TIP Curves for South Africa and Brazil

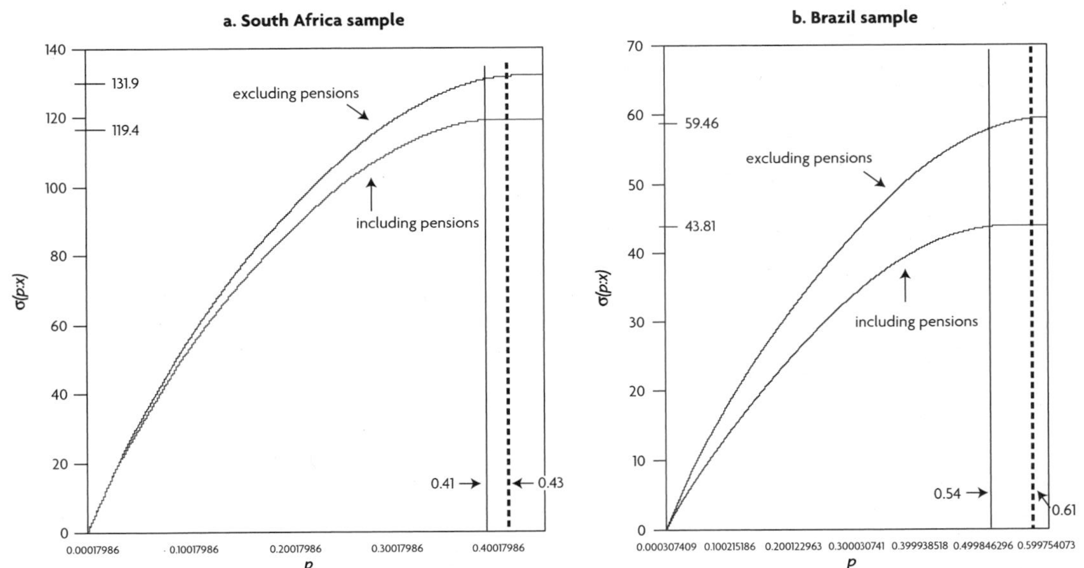

Source: Author's calculations.

Note: The panels of the figure are in TIP format (Jenkins and Lambert 1997) and provide a representation of the incidence, intensity, and inequality dimensions of aggregate poverty. The distribution of incomes *y* in a population of *n* units can be ranked in ascending order as $y_1, y_2, \dots, y_n$. The horizontal axis shows the cumulative percentiles of households *p* arranged from the poorest to the left to richest to the right. The poverty gap is the difference between a unit, a unit *i*'s income *yi*, and the poverty line *z*. More precisely, the vertical axis shows the cumulative sum of average poverty gaps *G*(*p*;*z*). The vector of poverty gaps is defined by $g_{yi = \max}[z - y_i, 0]$, and the cumulative poverty gap curve adds the poverty gaps from the poorest units divided by the sample of units—that is, $TIP(g;k/n) = \Sigma^k_{i=1} g_{yi}/n$, for integer values $k \leq n$. For nonpoor units, the poverty gap is zero; thus, the point at which the TIP curve becomes horizontal indicates the share of the population who are poor on the horizontal axis. The length of the curve, therefore, indicates the incidence of poverty. The point at which the TIP curve becomes horizontal also indicates on the vertical axis the cumulative average poverty gap. The height of the curve, therefore, provides an indicator of the intensity of poverty. The degree of concavity of the curve indicates the inequality dimension of aggregate poverty. If the incomes of the poor were equally distributed—and, therefore, poverty gaps were equal—the curve would be a straight line.

dimension of aggregate poverty. If the incomes of the poor were equally distributed—and, therefore, poverty gaps were equal for all households—the curve would be a straight line.

Figure 6.1 shows that the withdrawal of the pension income—in the absence of second-order effects—would increase the incidence, intensity, and inequality of poverty. For South Africa, panel a shows that withdrawing the pension income would have a marginal effect on the incidence of poverty, increasing the poverty headcount from 41 to 43 percent among individuals in the sample (households with older people), but a much larger effect on the average poverty gap, from R$119.40 to R$131.90, an increase of 10.4 percent. For Brazil, panel b shows that withdrawing the pension income would lead to a rise in the incidence of poverty in the sample of households with older people from 54 to 61 percent. It would also have a large effect on the average poverty gap, which would increase from R$43.80 to R$59.40, an increase of 35.6 percent.

In interpreting the figures showing the effect of noncontributory pensions on poverty, one must keep in mind that the analysis is premised on pension income being shared within the household[20] and is based on adult equivalent household income. The smaller effect of the noncontributory pension on poverty incidence in South Africa reflects the larger household size in that sample, with pension income divided more extensively than in Brazil.[21] The stronger effect from withdrawing pension income on the average poverty gap than on poverty incidence is encouraging, because it suggests that pension income works better at lifting the incomes of the poorest than at taking those just below the poverty line above it.[22]

In Bangladesh, household data from the 2000 Bangladesh Demographic and Health Survey enable a limited analysis of the incidence of the noncontributory pension programs on poverty. It is possible to identify in the data beneficiaries of the OAAS and APWDW. The brief analysis that follows targets exclusively households in the sample with at least one member age 57 or older—the age of eligibility for the OAAS. Looking at these households is helpful in seeking to identify the beneficiaries of the old-age cash transfer program within the subset of households with an eligible member.

Recall that the program specifies a fixed number of beneficiaries per ward, with beneficiaries selected by local committees. The 2000 Bangladesh Demographic and Health Survey does not capture data on household income or expenditure, but a range of household asset variables enables the construction of a wealth index, which can be used to classify households according to their socioeconomic status.[23] Table 6.1 shows the location of noncontributory pension beneficiaries within quintiles of households

Table 6.1. Location of Households in Bangladesh with Noncontributory Pension Beneficiaries among Households with a Member Age 57 or Older, 2000

Quintiles of wealth index	Distribution of households with a pension beneficiary in each quintile (%)	Share of households in each quintile having a pension beneficiary (%)
Quintile 1 (lowest)	39.6	6.4
Quintile 2	37.6	6.0
Quintile 3	15.8	2.5
Quintile 4	5.9	0.8
Quintile 5 (highest)	1.0	0.2

Source: Author's calculations from Bangladesh Demographic and Health Survey 2000 data.
Note: Eligible beneficiary households are those with at least one member age 57 or older. Figures are for a weighted sample of these households.

classified according to the wealth index. If the households in the lowest two quintiles are considered poor, the figures show that the program is reasonably well targeted: 77.2 percent of households with a beneficiary are in the lowest two quintiles. The probability of having a pension beneficiary in the household is significantly higher for households in those two quintiles (at 6.4 percent for the lowest and 6.0 percent for the second-lowest quintiles) than for better-off households.

Although the noncontributory pension programs in Bangladesh score reasonably well on vertical poverty reduction efficiency, leakages to the nonpoor are one-third or less. Also their coverage of the poor (horizontal poverty reduction efficiency) is low, with only 6.4 percent of eligible households in the poorest quintile being able to access the cash transfer.

Noncontributory Pensions and Household Investment

There is growing evidence on the extent to which noncontributory pensions facilitate household investment in human and physical capital. Such investment is a consequence of higher household income and of the regularity and reliability of pension benefits, which enable households to plan for the future.[24] This finding is important in the context of persistent inequality and poverty. To the extent that noncontributory pensions can facilitate asset accumulation in beneficiary households, such pensions could have longer-term effects on poverty and inequality.

Delgado and Cardoso (2000c) argue strongly that the PR in Brazil has been effective in generating a transformation of subsistence agriculture into sustainable household production. (They define *sustainable household production* as production capable of generating a surplus.) They find that a significant proportion of beneficiaries of the rural pension in

Brazil reported using part of their pension to purchase seeds and tools to support agricultural production. Barrientos and Lloyd-Sherlock (2003) did not find a similar effect in South Africa, but findings from qualitative surveys reveal a great deal of informal economic activity among pensioners. The regularity of pension payments and the links to financial providers improve access to credit by beneficiary households. This result is reported for South Africa (Ardington and Lund 1995) and for Brazil. Schwarzer and Querino (2002b: 15) note that "the electronic banking card that each beneficiary receives is often used as proof of creditworthiness." Studies in Brazil (Schwarzer 2000) and South Africa (Ardington and Lund 1995) report that beneficiary households invest in improvements in their housing after first receipt of the pension.

Enrollment rates of school-age children have been found to be higher among pension beneficiary households for South Africa (Duflo 2003) and for Brazil (Carvalho 2000). In South Africa, the main reason given by pensioners for sharing their pension benefit with relatives living elsewhere was to finance the costs of education (Barrientos and Lloyd-Sherlock 2003). The health status of children and older people is higher in beneficiary households in South Africa (Case 2001).

Some studies have focused on households dynamics associated with pension receipt. Studies for South Africa find evidence that household dynamics around the time of first pension receipt are consistent with labor migration of younger household members (Bertrand, Mullainathan, and Miller 2003; Edmonds, Mammen, and Miller 2001).

No comparable evidence is available for Bangladesh, where the pension benefit is much lower and the coverage of the program is very limited. As with most developing countries, extensive coresidence suggests that, at least potentially, noncontributory pension programs in Bangladesh could facilitate household investment. According to data from the Bangladesh Demographic and Health Survey 2000, more than four-fifths of households with a member age 57 or older and two-thirds of households with a pension beneficiary also contain children below the age of 15.

Conclusion

This chapter set out to examine two sets of related issues: first, the development of noncontributory pension programs over time as institutions for poverty and inequality reduction and, second, the evidence of the effectiveness of such programs at reducing poverty and inequality.

The discussion noted that noncontributory pension programs in South Africa and Brazil developed against adverse institutional environments: racially discriminatory social policy in South Africa and segmented social insurance in Brazil. Over time, they followed a different path from that shown by contributory pension programs: insofar as they show a focus on poverty, their entitlements are not directly determined by labor market factors, and they do not encourage retirement from the labor force. Their evolution has not followed the "strong to the weak" dynamics of social security systems in industrial countries. The development of noncontributory pension programs reflects widely held concerns with old-age poverty, and they are a core foundation of solidarity institutions. Instrumental factors combined with natural reservoirs of political support and social contract renewals can explain the expansion of noncontributory pension programs in South Africa and Brazil in the 1990s. The political economy factors underlying the emergence of these programs resonate with factors identified in the chapters 5 and 8 as important for equity-enhancing institutional transitions.

There is mounting evidence that noncontributory pension programs are effective in reducing poverty and facilitating household investment. The latter is particularly significant in the context of concerns with inequality. A range of studies using a variety of methods and datasets concludes that pension receipt is associated with household investment in human, physical, and social capital, especially in terms of investment in the human capital of coresident children. This finding suggests that noncontributory pension programs can have longer-term effects on poverty and inequality.

Notes

1. *Noncontributory pension programs* are programs providing regular transfers in cash to older people in which entitlements are not based on a lengthy record of contribution to a pension plan. They include cash transfers for older people in poverty, assistance pensions, and old-age grants. Noncontributory pension programs often include disability and survivor pensions, which are not discussed in this chapter.
2. The partial integration of rural pensions within the social insurance system in Brazil has generated uncertainty regarding the conditions for entitlement for rural pensions in the future. The legislation replaces, for rural workers, the contribution record requirement with a requirement of economic activity (including household and informal production), but only for the period 1992 to 2007.

3. These figures exclude beneficiaries of disability pensions under the three programs.
4. In South Africa, blacks are described as *Africans* and persons of mixed race as *colored people*.
5. Schwarzer and Querino (2002a: 74) note that the referral process for accessing FUNRURAL pensions involved local officials; hence, "holding a position such as local director of FUNRURAL in small towns was an important way of promoting a political career in those days."
6. See Atkinson (1995) for a discussion of social insurance.
7. However, economic activity is a factor in the identification of PR beneficiaries.
8. Bourguignon (1998: 28) discusses how inequality undermines middle-class support for insurance pooling.
9. Alesina, Glaeser, and Sacerdote (2001) suggest that an important reason the United States does not have European-style welfare states is the heterogeneity of its population groups.
10. Mulligan and Sala-i-Martin (1999a, 1999b, 1999c) pursue this issue in detail in the context of contributory programs.
11. James (2001: 170), for example, notes that "one can argue that priority for social assistance should be given to young families with children, who have their entire lives ahead of them."
12. In the context of South Africa, van der Berg (2002) suggests that changes in poverty and vulnerability require a remodeling of social assistance with a greater focus on unemployment. For Brazil, Paes de Barros and Carvalho (2004) argue for the need to rebalance social expenditure away from pensions and toward families with children (Paes de Barros and Carvalho 2004).
13. See, for example, the evidence from Latinobarómetro suggesting that a higher proportion of respondents support greater public expenditure on pensions (83.7 percent) than on unemployment insurance (73.4 percent) or defense (32.4 percent) (de Ferranti and others 2000: 4). Support for pensions is also shown to be consistent across age groups.
14. Younger household members could do so, however. See the next section for evidence on the incidence of pension receipt on the labor supply of older people. See also Jensen (2004) for a discussion of "crowding out."
15. Some explanations proffered for the strong pension programs in industrial countries do not apply to developing countries—for example the view that pension programs in industrial countries are supported by a gerontocracy (Mulligan and Sala-i-Martin 1999a), which is sustained by powerful interest groups that represent older people with considerable leisure time and that are unified around a single issue.
16. Grassroots organizations of older people in South Africa have been very effective in campaigning on HIV/AIDS issues.

17. In fact, some administrative issues are associated with the programs' delivery and cost in South Africa (Van Zyl 2003), as well as with corruption and poor targeting in Brazil (Saboia 2003), but these problems are not of a scale capable of undermining political support for the programs.
18. Details on the surveys can be found in Barrientos and Lloyd-Sherlock (2003a).
19. The estimates are imperfect because they do not account for second-order effects from the withdrawal of the pension benefit. To the extent that the withdrawal of the benefit encourages other household members to pursue additional income-generating activities, the poverty reduction effects of the noncontributory pension program are overestimated. But to the extent that the pension income supports income-generating activities, the estimates from this approach underestimate the effects of the program on poverty. This aspect is discussed further later in the chapter.
20. This factor was confirmed by survey responses to questions on pension and income sharing.
21. Median household size was three in Brazil and five in South Africa.
22. The TIP curve shows the effect of pension income on the poverty gap averaged across the full sample, but a measure of the effect of pension income on the poverty gaps of the poor only is also appropriate. Withdrawing pension income would increase the poverty gap of the poor by 81 percent in South Africa and by 40 percent in Brazil (Barrientos 2003b).
23. There is a "correspondence between a classification of households based on the asset index and a classification based on consumption expenditures" (Filmer and Pritchett 2001: 115).
24. Economic theory predicts that regular income streams raising a household's permanent income are more likely to lead to saving and investment than one-off or uncertain transfers.

References

Alesina, A., E. Glaeser, and B. Sacerdote. 2001. "Why Doesn't the U.S. Have a European-Style Welfare State?" Discussion Paper 1933, Harvard Institute of Economic Research, Cambridge, MA.

Ardington, E., and F. Lund. 1995. "Pensions and Development: Social Security as Complementary to Programmes of Reconstruction and Development." *Development Southern Africa* 12 (4): 557–77.

Atkinson, A. B. 1995. "Social Insurance." In *Incomes and the Welfare State: Essays on Britain and Europe*, ed. A. B. Atkinson, 205–19. Cambridge, U.K.: Cambridge University Press.

Barrientos, A. 2003a. "Pensions and Development in the South." *Geneva Papers on Risk and Insurance* 28 (4): 696–711.

———. 2003b. "What Is the Impact of Non-contributory Pensions on Poverty? Estimates from Brazil and South Africa." Chronic Poverty Research Centre/ Department of Economics and Public Policy Working Paper 33, Institute for Development Policy and Management, University of Manchester, Manchester, U.K.

———. 2004. "Latin America: Towards a Liberal-Informal Welfare Regime." In *Insecurity and Welfare Regimes in Asia, Africa, and Latin America*, ed. I. Gough, G. Wood, A. Barrientos, P. Bevan, P. David, and G. Room, 121–68. Cambridge, U.K.: Cambridge University Press.

Barrientos, A., M. Gorman, and A. Heslop. 2003. "Old Age Poverty in Developing Countries: Contributions and Dependence in Later Life." *World Development* 3 (3): 555–70.

Barrientos, A., and P. Lloyd-Sherlock. 2003. "Non-contributory Pensions and Poverty Prevention: A Comparative Study of Brazil and South Africa." Institute for Development Policy and Management and HelpAge International, Manchester, U.K.

Begum, S. 2003. "Pension and Social Security in Bangladesh." Bangladesh Institute of Development Studies, Dhaka.

Bertrand, M., S. Mullainathan, and D. Miller. 2003. "Public Policy and Extended Families: Evidence from Pensions in South Africa." *World Bank Economic Review* 17 (1): 27–50.

Bertranou, F., C. Solorio, and W. van Ginneken. 2002. *Pensiones no-contributivas y asistenciales: Argentina, Brazil, Chile, Costa Rica y Uruguay*. Santiago: International Labour Organization.

Bourguignon, F. 1998. Social Protection in Industrial Countries: Which Lessons for LAC Countries?" World Bank, Washington, DC.

Carvalho, I. 2000. "Household Income as a Determinant of Child Labor and School Enrollment in Brazil: Evidence from a Social Security Reform." Massachusetts Institute of Technology, Boston.

Case, A. 2001. "Does Money Protect Health Status? Evidence from South African Pensions." NBER Working Paper 8495, National Bureau of Economic Research, Cambridge, MA.

Case, A., and A. Deaton. 1998. "Large Scale Transfers to the Elderly in South Africa." *Economic Journal* 108 (450): 1330–61.

Committee of Inquiry into a Comprehensive System of Social Security for South Africa. 2002. *Transforming the Present—Protecting the Future*. Draft consolidated report. Pretoria: Committee of Inquiry into a Comprehensive System of Social Security for South Africa.

de Ferranti, D., G. E. Perry, I. S. Gill, and L. Servén. 2000. "Securing Our Future in a Global Economy." Washington, DC: World Bank.

Delgado, G. C., and J. C. Cardoso, eds. 2000a. *A Universalização de Direitos Sociais no Brazil: a Prêvidencia Rural nos anos 90*. Brasilia: Instituto de Pesquisa Econômica Aplicada.

———. 2000b. "Condicões de reproducão econômica e combate à pobreza." In *A Universalização de Direitos Sociais no Brasil: a Prêvidencia Rural nos anos 90*, ed. G. C. Delgado and J. C. Cardoso, 63–80. Brasilia: Instituto de Pesquisa Econômica Aplicada.

———. 2000c. "Principais Resultados da Pesquisa Domiciliar sobre a Previdência Rural na Região Sul do Brasil." Texto para Discussão 734, Instituto de Pesquisa Econômica Aplicada, Rio de Janeiro, Brazil.

Duflo, E. 2003. "Grandmothers and Granddaughters: Old-Age Pensions and Intrahousehold Allocation in South Africa." *World Bank Economic Review* 17 (1): 1–25.

Edmonds, E., K. Mammen, and D. Miller. 2001. "Rearranging the Family? Household Composition Responses to Large Pension Receipts. Dartmouth College, Hanover, NH.

Filmer, D., and L. Pritchett. 2001. "Estimating Wealth Effects without Expenditure Data—or Tears: An Application to Educational Enrollments in States of India." *Demography* 38 (1): 115–32.

James, E. 2001. "Coverage under Old Age Social Security Programs and Protection for the Uninsured: What Are the Issues?" In *Shielding the Poor: Social Protection in the Developing World*, ed. N. C. Lustig, 149–74. Washington, DC: Brookings Institution Press and Inter-American Development Bank.

Jenkins, S. P., and P. J. Lambert. 1997. "Three 'I's of Poverty Curves, with an Analysis of U.K. Poverty Trends." *Oxford Economic Papers* 49 (3): 317–27.

Jensen, R. 2004. "Do Private Transfers 'Displace' the Benefits of Public Transfers? Evidence from South Africa." *Journal of Public Economics* 88 (1–2): 89–112.

Lund, F. 1999. "Understanding South African Social Security through Recent Household Surveys: New Opportunities and Continuing Gaps." *Development Southern Africa* 16 (1): 55–67.

Mulligan, C. B., and X. Sala-i-Martin. 1999a. "Gerontocracy, Retirement, and Social Security." NBER Working Paper 7117, National Bureau of Economic Research, Cambridge, MA.

———. 1999b. "Social Security in Theory and Practice (I): Facts and Political Theories." NBER Working Paper 7118, National Bureau of Economic Research, Cambridge, MA.

———. 1999c. "Social Security in Theory and Practice (II): Efficiency Theories, Narrative Theories, and Implications for Reform." NBER Working Paper 7119, National Bureau of Economic Research, Cambridge, MA.

Paes de Barros, R., and M. Carvalho. 2004. "Targeting as an Instrument for a More Effective Social Policy." Foro de Equidad Social, Washington, DC.

Rajan, S. I., M. Perera, and S. Begum. 2003. "Economics of Pensions and Social Security in South Asia: Special Focus on India, Sri Lanka, and Bangladesh," Centre for Development Studies, Thiruvanapuram, India.

Saboia, J. 2003. "Relatório final de pesquisa de campo sobre benefícios não-contributivos para os idosos no Brasil." Instituto de Economia da Universidade Federal do Rio de Janeiro, Rio de Janeiro, Brazil.

Schwarz, A. M. 2003. "Old Age Security and Social Pensions." World Bank, Washington, DC.

Schwarzer, H. 2000. "Impactos socioeconômicos do sistema de aposentadorias rurais no Brazil: Evidências empíricas de un estudio de caso no estado de Pará." Texto para Discussão 729, Instituto de Pesquisa Econômica Aplicada, Rio de Janeiro, Brazil.

Schwarzer, H., and A. C. Querino. 2002a. "Beneficios sociales y los pobres en Brasil: Programas de pensiones no convencionales." In *Pensiones no contributivas y asistenciales*, ed. F. Bertranou, C. Solorio, and W. van Ginneken, 63–124. Santiago: Oficina Internacional del Trabajo.

———. 2002b. "Non-contributory Pensions in Brazil: The Impact on Poverty Reduction." Extension of Social Security Paper 11, Geneva: Social Security Policy and Development Branch, International Labour Organization.

van der Berg, S. 1997. "South African Social Security under Apartheid and Beyond." *Development Southern Africa* 14 (4): 481–503.

———. 1998. "Ageing, Public Finance, and Social Security in South Africa." *Southern African Journal of Gerontology* 7 (1): 3–9.

———. 2001. "Social Policy to Address Poverty." In *Fighting Poverty: Labour Markets and Inequality in South Africa*, ed. H. Bhorat, M. Leibbrandt, M. Maziya, S. van der Berg, and I. Woolard, 171–204. London: Zed Press.

———. 2002. "Devising Social Security Interventions for Maximum Poverty Impact." *Social Dynamics* 28 (2): 39–68.

Van Zyl, E. 2003. "Old Age Pensions in South Africa." *International Social Security Review* 56 (3–4): 101–28.

Willmore, L. 2007. "Universal Pensions for Developing Countries." *World Development* 35 (1): 24–51.

CHAPTER 7

Mineral Wealth, Conflict, and Equitable Development

Michael L. Ross

In theory, new mineral wealth should offer governments a chance to boost economic growth and reduce inequality.[1] In practice, it often leads to a type of inequality trap: mineral production produces heightened inequalities, which lead to violent conflict; violent conflict tends to scare off investment outside the minerals sector, which might have otherwise reduced inequalities. As a result, countries become lodged in an inequality trap, unable to diversify the economy in ways that could reduce inequalities and lower the risk of violent conflict. Countries such as Algeria, Angola, Colombia, the Democratic Republic of Congo, the Republic of Congo, and Nigeria have all suffered from mineral-based inequality traps.

There is nothing inevitable about these traps: mineral-rich countries such as Botswana, Chile, and Malaysia have all avoided them and used their resource wealth to reduce inequality. However, avoiding an inequality trap is not easy and can be done only when the government can navigate a complex series of economic, social, and political challenges.

One of the most difficult challenges is deciding how to deal equitably with the regional or local communities where the extraction occurs.[2] Both the central government and the local communities typically claim ownership of the resources, dispute the other side's claims, and have some ability to slow or block projects they dislike. Mineral firms are often caught between the two sides. When these disputes can be resolved, mineral development can proceed without triggering conflict, but if mineral development proceeds without the resolution of these issues—as in Bolivia, Indonesia,

Papua New Guinea, and Sudan—the result may be political unrest and long-term inequality traps.

This chapter explores the problems and opportunities that governments, firms, and local communities face when they must divide the costs and benefits of a mineral development project. It makes four central arguments:

- Mineral-dependent countries have the highest risk of violent conflict when they have low income levels; when they produce oil or other deep-shaft minerals; and when the mineral-rich region is mountainous, lies on the country's periphery, and harbors people who are ethnically or linguistically distinct from the rest of the country's population.
- Stable democratic institutions can help prevent central–local disputes from becoming violent, but new democracies are often unstable and face high risks of conflict.
- Granting additional rents to the extractive region is often insufficient to avoid conflict.
- To avoid violent conflict in the extractive region, the governments, firms, and local communities should promote transparency, establish multistakeholder dialogues before projects begin, and take special care to protect human rights and security.

In this discussion, a country's mineral dependence is measured as the value of its oil, gas, and hard-rock mineral exports as a percentage of gross domestic product (GDP). In 2000, 53 countries had mineral exports worth more than 5 percent of GDP; they are the *mineral-dependent countries*.[3] About half these states—27 of the 53—had mineral exports worth more than 20 percent of GDP; these *high mineral-dependence countries* are listed in table 7.1.

As table 7.2 shows, most of the mineral-dependent states are found (in descending order) in Sub-Saharan Africa, the Middle East and North Africa, the former Soviet Union, and Latin America. Among the high mineral-dependence states, about 40 percent are in the Middle East and North Africa.

The chapter proceeds as follows. The first section explains why mineral-producing states tend to have atypically high rates of violent conflict. The second section describes six structural factors that can raise or lower the conflict risk in mineral-exporting states. The next section argues that, even in high-risk regions, governments and firms can reduce the conflict risk by promoting transparency, using multistakeholder dialogues, and paying

Table 7.1. High Mineral–Dependence Countries, 2000

Rank	Country	Mineral dependence[a]	Conflict years, 1990–2000[b]
1	Bahrain	63.44	0
2	Qatar	53.37	0
3	Iraq	50.00	7
4	Turkmenistan	49.91	0
5	Gabon	48.83	0
6	Nigeria	48.75	0
7	Saudi Arabia	44.74	0
8	Papua New Guinea	41.52	6
9	Trinidad and Tobago	41.16	1
10	Congo, Rep. of	41.07	5
11	Brunei Darussalam	37.65	0
12	Kazakhstan	36.11	0
13	Libya	35.91	0
14	Algeria	35.75	10
15	Botswana	35.10	0
16	Kuwait	32.41	0
17	Azerbaijan	28.83	4
18	Angola	27.88	11
19	Zambia	27.12	0
20	Liberia	26.76	7
21	Norway	25.97	0
22	Oman	25.65	0
23	Iran, Islamic Rep. of	25.55	8
24	Mongolia	25.45	0
25	Russian Federation	25.38	8
26	Venezuela, R. B. de	23.54	1
27	Yemen, Rep. of	22.32	1

Source: Author's construction. Data on violent conflict come from the Armed Conflict Dataset 2007 that is maintained by the Uppsala Conflict Data Program at the Department of Peace and Conflict Research, Uppsala University, Sweden, and the Centre for the Study of Civil War at the International Peace Research Institute in Oslo, Norway.

a. A country's mineral dependence is calculated as its mineral exports divided by its gross domestic product, multiplied by 100.

b. This column indicates how many years from 1990 to 2000 were marked by violent conflict.

Table 7.2. States by Region and Mineral Dependence, 2000

Region	Not mineral dependent (< 5)	Mineral dependent (> 5)	Highly mineral dependent (> 20)
OECD[a]	19	4	1
Latin America	18	8	2
Sub-Saharan Africa	30	14	7
Middle East and North Africa	8	11	10
Asia	10	4	2
Former Soviet Union	2	9	4
Other	20	3	1
Total	107	53	27

Source: Author's construction.
a. OECD = Organisation for Economic Co-operation and Development.

special attention to human rights and security issues. A brief conclusion summarizes these arguments.

Minerals and Geographic Conflict

Since the seminal work of Collier and Hoeffler (1998), many scholars have found evidence that certain measures of mineral production or exports are linked to civil war. Econometric studies by Collier and Hoeffler (2004), de Soysa (2002), Fearon (2004), Fearon and Laitin (2003), Humphreys (2003), and Ross (2006) all find that oil-exporting states face a higher risk of civil war than states that do not export oil.[4]

Why should mineral exports be correlated with civil war? Many scholars have sketched out theories that link oil and other minerals to conflict. For this study, two are germane.[5]

First, sometimes the minerals-conflict link is spurious. Unlike other types of industries, mining is location specific: firms must go where the minerals are, even if the area is remote or unstable. Manufacturing and service firms tend to stick to countries—and regions of countries—where the infrastructure is good and law and order have been well established; mineral firms do not have this luxury. Hence, we will sometimes find mineral firms working in war-torn regions, even though mineral extraction did not cause the conflict. For example, some countries with long-running civil wars, such as Algeria, Angola, and Liberia, have grown heavily dependent on mineral exports, simply because other types of businesses have been forced to close or relocate to safer countries while mineral firms have stayed behind.

Sometimes, however, mineral extraction is causally linked to violent conflict—partly because mineral wealth seems to heighten the perception of territorial inequalities, which, in turn, can cause secessionist movements. Table 7.3 lists 10 cases of violent separatist movements in regions with significant mineral wealth.[6] In each case, leaders of these movements appeared to believe that mineral rents would raise the benefits—or lower the costs—of attaining independence. As Collier and Hoeffler (2005) suggest, the allure of claiming ownership to valuable natural resources can encourage populations in peripheral regions to establish sovereign states.

One example of a mineral-related secessionist conflict is the rebellion in Indonesia's northwestern province of Aceh. The rebel group—widely known as GAM (Gerakan Aceh Merdeka, or Aceh Freedom Movement)—began in 1976, shortly after the construction of Aceh's enormous natural gas facility. GAM's 1976 "Declaration of Independence" denounced the Indonesian government for stealing Aceh's resource revenues, but it did not criticize the natural gas facility itself, or Mobil (now ExxonMobil), which operates the facility.[7] One of GAM's first acts was to attack the plant. During the subsequent conflict, GAM propaganda often claimed that if Aceh were independent and its citizens could appropriate all of Aceh's gas revenues—instead of sharing them with the rest of the country—the Acehnese would become rich (Ross 2005). After waxing and waning between 1976 and 1998, the Aceh rebellion broke out into a full-scale civil war from 1998 to 2004. Following the tragic tsunami in December 2004, GAM reached a settlement with the Indonesian government in 2005.

A second example is the war in Sudan, which began in 1983, when Sudanese President Gaafar Mohamad Numeiry took a series of measures that upset the delicate balance between the predominantly Muslim north and the heavily Christian and animist south. Among these measures was his decision to place newly discovered oil in the country's south under the

Table 7.3. Mineral Resources and Secessionist Movements

Country	Region	Duration	Mineral resources
Angola	Cabinda	1975–2004	Oil
Congo, Dem. Rep. of	Katanga/Shaba	1960–65	Copper
Indonesia	West Papua	1969–present	Copper and gold
Indonesia	Aceh	1975–2005	Natural gas
Morocco	West Sahara	1975–88	Phosphates and oil
Myanmar	Hill tribes	1983–95	Tin and gems
Nigeria	Biafra	1967–70	Oil
Papua New Guinea	Bougainville	1988–97	Copper and gold
Sudan	South	1983–2004	Oil
Yemen, Rep. of	East and South	1994	Oil

Source: Author's construction.

jurisdiction of the north and to build an oil refinery in the north instead of the south. The Sudan People's Liberation Army subsequently complained that the north was stealing the south's resources, including oil; demanded that work cease on a pipeline to take oil from the south to the refinery in the north; and, in February 1984, attacked an oil exploration base, killing three foreign workers and bringing the project to a halt (see Anderson 1999; O'Ballance 2000). After two decades of combat, the two sides signed a peace accord in May 2004.

Structural Risk Factors

Even when mineral wealth makes secessionist conflict more likely, most of the time mineral extraction does not result in civil violence. Hence, there must be additional factors that help explain why mineral wealth sometimes triggers civil wars. Some of these factors are structural—that is, they are major historical, economic, and geographic features of the region that cannot easily be changed by state policies. Other factors are more tractable and can be readily influenced by the actions of governments, mineral firms, and nongovernmental organizations (NGOs). This section discusses six structural factors that—according to recent studies—are associated with a high civil war risk in mineral-dependent states; these factors help identify the countries and regions that face the highest civil war risk. The next section discusses some of the tractable factors that can alleviate—or exacerbate—the danger of conflict in these high-risk regions.

Poverty

Perhaps the most important structural factor is income per capita in the affected country. Several major studies have shown that civil wars are more likely to occur in poor countries than in rich ones (Collier and Hoeffler 2004; Fearon and Laitin 2003). The mineral-dependent countries in table 7.1 are coded by the number of years (from 1990 to 2000) that they suffered from violent domestic conflict. While wealthy mineral-dependent countries such as Kuwait, Norway, and Qatar have avoided civil war, poor mineral-dependent countries such as Papua New Guinea, Angola, and Algeria have been plagued by it. Indeed, no violent conflict occurred at all in mineral-dependent countries with incomes above the level of Trinidad and Tobago—about US$11,175.

Steady economic growth can also reduce the conflict risk. In Indonesia, for example, the Aceh region—which around 1975 became a major source of liquefied natural gas exports—enjoyed high growth rates throughout the 1970s, 1980s, and early 1990s. Even though the rebel movement periodically attacked government facilities, it was more of a nuisance than a threat to the central government's authority. This situation changed dramatically with the onset of the Asian economic crisis in 1997 and 1998. Aceh's non-petroleum GDP declined by 5.9 percent in 1998 and 2.9 percent in 1999. The crisis also produced a jump in unemployment and underemployment: in 1998 alone, the number of people in Aceh's official labor force dropped 37.3 percent. The economic shock was followed by a dramatic rise in GAM's popular support and military activities (Ross 2005).

Terrain

The second factor is terrain. Several studies have found a strong correlation between the likelihood of rebellion and the presence of mountainous terrain. This correlation can be interpreted in several ways. Perhaps governments find it harder to control mountainous terrain, enabling rebel movements—which are, at least initially, greatly outnumbered by government troops—to hide and persevere (Collier and Hoeffler 2004; Fearon and Laitin 2003). Alternatively, mountainous areas might serve as refuges for minority or dissenting groups. The greater risk of conflict in these regions could reflect historical antagonisms between peoples who live in plains and valleys and minorities groups that have found protection in the adjacent highlands.

Peripheries

The third factor is the location of the extractive region. Separatist movements are more common in regions that lie along a country's borders or are not contiguous with the rest of the country (Fearon and Laitin 2003; Le Billon 2001). All 10 mineral-related conflicts listed in table 7.3 occurred in peripheral regions; 3 of them—in Angola, Indonesia (West Papua), and Papua New Guinea—happened in areas that were not contiguous with the rest of the country. Peripheral regions are more likely to harbor people who identify themselves as ethnically or linguistically distinct from the rest of the population. It is also easier for rebel movements in peripheral regions to get funds and weapons—and to protect themselves from government troops—by crossing the border into neighboring states.

Prior Regional Identity

The fourth factor is prior identity. Separatist movements may be encouraged by mineral wealth, but they do not seem to be created by mineral wealth. In each of the 10 cases in table 7.3, there was a strong sense of regional identity and at least some interest in independence before the mineral wealth was discovered or exploited.

In most cases, this regional identity was rooted in historical or geographic differences from the rest of the country. Cabinda, for example, was governed separately by the Portuguese until 1956; it is also not contiguous with the rest of Angola. Bougainville is geographically closer to the Solomon Islands than the island of New Guinea and was not governed as part of colonial New Guinea until 1886. Aceh was an independent sultanate until the end of the 19th century; the rest of Indonesia (then called the Dutch East Indies) had been subdued by the Dutch many decades—even centuries—earlier. The hill tribes of Myanmar had considerable autonomy under British colonial rule and are ethnically and linguistically distinct from the Burman and Karen peoples of the country's lowlands.

In some cases, the rebellious regions were not originally part of the country whose sovereignty they later rejected: West Papua was under Dutch rule until it was invaded by Indonesia in 1961; Western Sahara was under Spanish rule until 1975, when it was taken over by Morocco (and, for a time, Mauritania); and the People's Democratic Republic of Yemen was a separate country until 1990, when it peacefully united with the Arab Republic of Yemen.

These historical, geographic, and ethnic factors gave people in each of these regions a prior sense of identity that was distinct from—and sometimes opposed to—the national identity of the country to which they were annexed. The presence of mineral wealth added the prospect of great wealth—or perhaps, removed the prospect of great poverty—to the attractions of sovereignty.

Political Institutions

Evidence indicates that stable democratic institutions help countries avoid violent conflicts (Hegre and others 2001; Muller and Weede 1990).[8] When discontented groups can bring about change through peaceful means, such as elections, they may be less likely to resort to violence.

Scotland's movement for political autonomy, which was partly motivated by the value of North Sea oil, provides a good example. Until 1974, there was little support in Scotland for independence or autonomy: in the 1970 general election, the pro-autonomy Scottish National Party received just 11 percent of the Scottish vote and won a single seat in the U.K. Parliament. Yet the sharp rise in oil prices in 1973 and 1974 multiplied the value of North Sea oil and suddenly made Scottish autonomy economically attractive. In the 1974 election, the Scottish National Party adopted the slogan "It's Scotland's Oil"; the party won 30 percent of the Scottish vote and captured 11 seats (Collier and Hoeffler 2005).

Between 1974 and 1998, there was a steady rise in Scottish nationalist activity. Advocates had both violent and nonviolent options. The militant Scottish National Liberation Army was formed in the early 1980s to advance the cause through violence, while others worked through electoral and legislative channels, aligning themselves with the Labour Party. Twenty-four years after the 1974 vote, the peaceful campaign triumphed in 1998 when the U.K. Parliament adopted the Scotland Act, which led to the devolution of considerable powers from London and the opening of Scotland's first parliament since 1707. The availability of peaceful channels for political change made violent options, like those offered by the Scottish National Liberation Army, less attractive.

The East Malaysian states of Sabah and Sarawak also illustrate the merits of democratic governance. In the 1960s and 1970s, Sabah and Sarawak were high-risk areas for a separatist rebellion: they were part of a country that, at the time, was relatively poor; their terrain is mountainous; they are separated from West Malaysia by water; most of their populations are ethnically and linguistically distinct from the peoples of West Malaysia; they had markedly different colonial histories from West Malaysia; and they joined the Malaysian Federation only in 1963, six years after the rest of the country had gained independence. Moreover, Sabah's and Sarawak's natural resource wealth gave both of them an economic incentive to secede: they have both been major timber exporters, and about half of Malaysia's petroleum exports come from off the shores of the two states, even though the state governments get only a 5 percent petroleum royalty. If they were independent, they would—like neighboring Brunei Darussalam—reap a large windfall from oil and natural gas revenues.

Yet there has never been a serious independence movement—violent or nonviolent—in either state since it joined the Malaysian Federation. One reason is that Malaysia is both a stable democracy and a federal state. Both Sabah and Sarawak have local governments with substantial authority: citizens can express any grievances they have—at both the state and federal levels—through the electoral process, and officeholders have incentives to mitigate these grievances, lest they lose their elected positions.

There are important differences, however, between stable democracies and new ones: new democracies are often unstable and may raise unrealistic expectations, which, in turn, can lead to violence. In 1999, Nigeria transited to democratic rule; it also adopted a new constitution that raised the allocation of oil revenues to the oil-rich Niger Delta. Since 1990, the Niger Delta had been marked by confrontations—sometimes violent—between local communities, oil companies, and the federal government over access to oil rents, as well as over environmental and human rights issues. At first, democratization and the promise of greater oil revenues had a palliative effect on the region: the number of protests fell sharply in 2001 and 2002 (Lewis 2004). In 2003, however, renewed fighting broke out when people in one of the Delta communities, the Ijaw, claimed they were not receiving their fair share of oil revenues. The 2003 election did little to resolve the issue; indeed, widespread irregularities occurred at polling stations in the Delta.

Table 7.4 displays public opinion data from three successive Afrobarometer surveys conducted in 2000, 2001, and 2003; it contrasts the responses of Nigerians in the Niger Delta, where oil revenues had risen, with Nigerians from outside the Delta. Despite the infusion of oil revenues, Delta citizens felt their situation had deteriorated—both economically and politically—between 2001 and 2003. Support for Nigeria's democratic government plunged to very low levels, setting the stage for the separatist violence that broke out in the Delta in 2004.

Type of Minerals

The sixth factor is the type of mineral resource. Minerals (and other commodities) can be divided into two groups: *lootable minerals* such as alluvial gemstones, which can be easily extracted by small teams of low-skill workers; and *unlootable minerals* such as oil, which can be extracted only with large capital investments and highly skilled labor.[9]

In the popular media, civil wars are commonly linked to lootable commodities, like diamonds and other gemstones. Between 1990 and 2000, four civil wars were linked to the production of diamonds, and three others were tied to the production of other gemstones; they are listed in table 7.5. Yet the outbreak of conflict is also linked to the production of unlootable minerals—in particular, oil (Ross 2006).

Different types of minerals may be linked to different types of conflict. Unlootable resources, such as oil, natural gas, copper, and gold, seem to be

Table 7.4. Public Opinion in Nigeria

Question	2000	2001	2003
"Are [your group's] economic conditions worse, the same, or better than other groups in this country?" (% saying worse or much worse)			
Niger Delta	13	33	60
Other Nigerians	12	39	31
"Overall, how satisfied are you with the way democracy works in Nigeria?" (% saying fairly or very satisfied)			
Niger Delta	84	47	13
Other Nigerians	84	57	37
"Is 'the ability of ordinary people to influence what government does' better now than under military rule?" (% saying better or much better)			
Niger Delta	63	56	17
Other Nigerians	67	61	43

Source: Lewis 2004.

Table 7.5. Civil Wars Linked to Lootable Minerals, 1990–2000

Country	Duration	Mineral resources
Afghanistan	1992–2001	Lapis lazuli
Angola	1975–2002	Diamonds
Cambodia	1978–97	Rubies
Congo, Dem. Rep. of	1996–99	Diamonds and columbite-tantalite
Liberia	1989–96	Diamonds
Myanmar	1983–95	Gemstones
Sierra Leone	1991–2000	Diamonds

Source: Author's construction.

strongly linked to the onset of secessionist wars. Consider once again the list of mineral-related secessionist conflicts in table 7.3: in all 10 conflicts, the separatist movements fought for control of regions with unlootable resources.[10] Also note the gemstone-related conflicts listed in table 7.5: six of the seven cases are not separatist wars. The conflict in Myanmar, which has both lootable and unlootable minerals, is the sole exception.

At least two reasons explain why unlootable minerals, but not lootable minerals, appear to be linked to separatist conflicts. First, separatist movements may thrive on exaggerated claims about the value of the rents. When locals can acquire and trade the resources themselves—as with gemstones—they may have fairly realistic ideas about the economic value of independence. However, when the economic value of the resource is harder for local peoples to estimate—as with oil and gas—nascent rebel movements may find it easier to exaggerate the value of the region's resources and, hence, the value of independence (Collier and Hoeffler 2005).

This argument is well illustrated by the conflict in Aceh, Indonesia. Since the conflict began in 1976, the rebel movement has made grossly exaggerated claims about the value of the natural gas being extracted from Aceh. In recent years, pro-independence speakers and pamphlets have denounced the "theft" of Aceh's mineral wealth and claimed that, if independent, Aceh would be as wealthy as Brunei Darussalam, the oil-rich Islamic sultanate on nearby Borneo. This claim is misleading: if Aceh were fiscally independent in 1998 and collected all the revenues from natural gas exports, per capita GDP would have risen by about one-third, to US$1,257. This amount would still be more than an order of magnitude below Brunei Darussalam's 1998 per capita income of US$17,600 (Ross 2005).

The second reason is that the extraction of unlootable resources provides relatively few jobs for local unskilled workers. Because oil, gas, and deep-shaft mineral firms tend to use highly skilled labor, they employ few local, unskilled workers and generate relatively little wealth—and hence little popular support—among local communities. They often work in enclaves or, in the case of offshore oil, on rigs at sea. Sometimes, they employ foreign workers exclusively, or nearly so.

The presence of sequestered mineral firms in poor areas can generate extraordinary resentment among local communities for their failure to abide by local reciprocity norms. In many traditional agrarian cultures, rich and poor citizens have reciprocal obligations: wealthy members of the community are obliged to provide the poor with jobs, loans, and other forms of assistance; the poor must offer the rich their fealty (Scott 1976, 1985). Local communities are often obliged to surrender land and water rights to the mineral firm, yet they may get little in return. Mineral firms typically pay little attention to local norms; instead, they focus on their contractual obligations to the central government and their responsibility to create value for their shareholders. The result may be local resentment against the firm for its violation of community norms.

The extraction of lootable resources, by contrast, entails large amounts of unskilled labor and little capital: a shovel and a wood-framed metal screen for alluvial diamonds and a chainsaw for timber. Local, unskilled workers have innumerable opportunities to find jobs and earn money. Because there are few barriers to entry into the mining business and (at most) modest economies of scale, typically many small operations exist, each with relatively small profits. When a resource is unlootable, the rents will go to the firm and the government; when it is lootable, much of these rents will accrue to local peoples.

Ways to Avert Conflicts

Even in high-risk settings, governments, firms, and NGOs can do much to avert conflict. Although there is no single, foolproof formula for avoiding violent disputes, the likelihood of a conflict can be reduced by promoting transparency, developing a multistakeholder dialogue before mineral development begins, and paying special attention to security and human rights issues. Although sharing rents with the affected region may help, it is generally insufficient to prevent conflict and promote equitable development.

Rent Sharing

Some might assume that disputes could be avoided if central and local authorities could agree in advance on how to divide the rents from mining or, in the absence of any explicit agreement, if the central government ensured that the affected region received a larger share of the rents than other regions. Yet violent conflict has still afflicted states that have tried these approaches.

Since Aceh began producing natural gas in 1976, the Indonesian central government has given the region a disproportionate share of development funds in hopes of averting pro-independence sentiment. When support for independence began to swell in mid-1999, the government adopted a law granting Aceh 30 percent of net public income from natural gas. In 2001, a new law raised Aceh's share to 70 percent. None of these arrangements had a measurable effect on the violence.

In Nigeria, the central government has recognized since colonial times that oil-producing regions should receive an extra share of the revenues they generate. The size of this share has been the subject of constant dispute and negotiation: between 1946 and 2003, the formula for allocating oil revenues to the states was reviewed or changed 18 times—about once every three years. The 1999 constitution established a new arrangement that gave oil-producing states a special "derivation grant" worth 13 percent of the revenues from their region. Unfortunately, this arrangement has not reduced violent conflicts among tribal groups for these funds—disrupting both the 2003 elections and the region's oil production.

Transparency

Rebel groups often make exaggerated claims about the economic gains from independence. Transparency can reduce these misperceptions and undercut support for rebellion. The more that communities understand about the real costs and benefits of any mineral project—such as how large revenues are typically offset by large risks and large up-front costs—the less susceptible they will be to false appeals about the advantages of independence.

Transparency also helps restrain government corruption. Mineral-rich governments tend to be highly corrupt (Gylfason 2001; Leite and Weidemann 1999). In 2002, for example, an International Monetary Fund investigation found that the Angolan government could not account for almost US$1 billion in oil revenue over the previous year. Investigations by Global Witness, an NGO based in London, suggest the "missing" revenues may be even larger and seem to disappear on an annual basis.[11] Higher levels of corruption can only fuel popular discontent with the government: when citizens in peripheral regions believe their money is being stolen, they are more likely to prefer independence. Although government corruption cannot be vanquished overnight, it can be reduced through greater transparency.

Several international initiatives are now promoting transparency in the extractive industry. Global Witness, in partnership with other NGOs, has developed a "publish what you pay" campaign, whose goal is to make mineral firms disclose all payments they make to host governments. The U.K. government has developed an Extractive Industries Transparency Initiative, which is working with a wide range of governments, companies, and NGOs to promote transparency in mineral-producing states.

There are limits, however, to the ability of donors to impose transparency measures; the case of Chad offers a good illustration. Chad is one of the world's poorest countries and faces a high risk of conflict because of its low income and unequal division of resources: while political and military power is held by tribes from the north, oil and agricultural land is occupied by tribal peoples in the south.

Although oil was found in Chad in the early 1950s, the country only recently attracted sufficient investment to exploit it. Following extensive negotiations with the World Bank, the Chadian government adopted the Petroleum Revenue Management Law of 1999. The law specified that all the country's oil revenues must be initially deposited in an offshore escrow account; that the account must be subjected to an independent audit annually; that the funds must be spent according to a strict formula that allocates 80 percent to education, health care, social services, rural development, infrastructure, and environmental and water resource management; that 5 percent of the royalties must go to local communities in the oil-producing region; and that the revenue-allocation process must be supervised by a board that includes both government officials and representatives of labor and human rights NGOs.

It is unclear, however, if the Chadian transparency measures are sustainable. The World Bank suspended its loans to the Chad in January 2006, after the government adopted revisions to the Revenue Management Law that abrogated its prior commitments. Loans were resumed in April 2006 after the World Bank signed a memorandum of understanding with the government, but the effectiveness and durability of the original transparency arrangements look fragile at best.

Multistakeholder Dialogues

Pouring money into a disaffected region and offering high levels of transparency may not be enough to avoid conflict; it is certainly not enough to create equitable development. A credible, ongoing dialogue among stakeholders can also help.

One reason that dialogues might be useful is that they may encourage local communities to forge ex ante guidelines for dividing up the rents that will flow to their region. Having such agreements in place can reduce the chance that one group or another will eventually feel disadvantaged. Much of the recent conflict over oil revenues in the Niger Delta, for example, is not between local peoples and the government, but between tribal groups—the Ijaw and the Itsekiri—over how to apportion these funds. Once a cycle of violence and retribution begins, it can be extraordinarily difficult to stop. Hence, ex ante agreements and working dialogues can be very valuable.

A second reason is that local communities care about many other aspects of mineral development besides rents, including environmental pollution, the loss or degradation of their lands, the absence of jobs, and the social and economic consequences of migration to their region. Typically, these concerns are far easier—and cheaper—to address before mineral development begins than after it is under way.

Ignoring local concerns can create unnecessary problems for both firms and governments. In 1997, several local communities in Ecuador sought a meeting with a subsidiary of Mitsubishi, which had opened a mine in their region; they wished to discuss their concerns about deforestation, soil erosion, and pollution. After they were apparently rebuffed for three days by the mine's management, they removed goods and equipment from the mine site and burned the remains (Switzer 2001).

By contrast, firms that respect community concerns can reduce their security costs substantially. In Papua New Guinea, Placer Dome needed to protect nearly 70 kilometers of electrical cables that provided its Porgera mine with power. Instead of hiring a security company, it was able to protect its cable less expensively simply by paying attention to the needs of the communities that lived along the cable's path (Switzer 2001).

A dialogue should not end with a comprehensive agreement; however, it is equally important to have an ongoing forum for resolving problems as they arrive. Mineral-based development always creates problems that local communities cannot anticipate, particularly if the area is poor and isolated. In the Indonesian state of West Papua, for example, Freeport-McMoran crafted a 1974 agreement with the indigenous Amungme peoples—a preliterate culture—that offered them schools, clinics, and markets in exchange for mining rights. Yet within several years, local peoples were engaged in violent confrontations with Freeport-McMoran: despite placing their thumbprints on the contract, they were wholly unprepared for the consequences of mineral development, which transformed the landscape and raised the local population more than 100-fold. A credible, ongoing multistakeholder dialogue—instead of a "once and for all" pact, in which one side was grievously uninformed—might have given communities a constructive way to address these issues as they arose.

Well-crafted agreements can also become outdated over the course of a mining project because of generational changes among local peoples. Between 1968 and 1988, Papua New Guinea's Panguna copper mine—operated by Bougainville Copper Limited (BCL), which was jointly owned by the mining company Rio Tinto and the Papuan government—brought major disruptions to the lives of the people of Bougainville. The mine was located in a region that was unusually poor and remote, even by Papuan standards. Many locals had had little prior contact with the cash economy. The mine's social, economic, and environmental impact was pronounced: villages lost their land; thousands of young Papuan men from other islands came to Bougainville, bringing crime and alcohol abuse with them; local rivers became unfit to drink from; fish disappeared from most of the Kawerong-Jaba river system, covering some 480 square kilometers; and hunting and gathering became more difficult, given the pollution and environmental degradation (Polomka 1990; Thompson 1991).

BCL provided compensation payments to locals for land it leased or damaged. It also made substantial efforts to contribute to the Bougainville economy: it instituted training and scholarship programs, which by 1980 produced a workforce that was 80 percent Papuan and 30 percent Bougainvillean, and it helped establish a wide range of local business ventures, some of which proved successful (Wesley-Smith and Ogan 1992). The development of the mine also led to the construction of roads, to expanded access to education and health, and to a sharp rise in the cash economy. By the late 1980s, BCL claimed that the Panguna operation directly or indirectly provided incomes to 30,000 of Bougainville's 150,000 people (Carruthers 1990).

Yet community support—or at least acquiescence—for the project ultimately deteriorated as provisions in the original contract became outdated. When the original lease was signed in 1967, BCL agreed to a compensation package for local landowners. It was later revised many times in favor of the landowners, the local community, and the regional government. By the late 1980s, this arrangement had come under attack by a new generation of Bougainvilleans, who claimed it was unfair for two reasons. First, only primary landholders received BCL compensation, whereas those who held subsidiary rights—a common practice under traditional tenure systems—received little or nothing (Wesley-Smith and Ogan 1992). Second, there were now intergenerational problems: the money for land compensation went to 850 primary landholders and family heads, but their children, who had come of age during the mining lease, had less direct access to these funds. Because many of the island's traditional cultures had strong egalitarian norms, even small degrees of inequality provoked strong reactions.

After several years of nonviolent disputes over these issues, a small group of frustrated young men formed the Bougainville Revolutionary Army in late 1988 and launched a series of attacks on BCL property. By May 1989, they had forced the Panguna mine to close. The ensuing conflict lasted until 1997 and may have claimed more than 10,000 lives.

In theory, a dialogue need include only local community leaders and the government, which has formal responsibility for handling these issues. In practice, mineral firms must often play a central role in these dialogues. Firms will be blamed for—and will certainly suffer the costs of—conflicts that break out between locals and the national government; hence, they have a strong incentive to find solutions. A 2001 survey found that political instability is a major problem for the mining industry: 78 percent of the firms surveyed said that over the previous five years, political instability—particularly armed conflict—had caused them to refrain or withdraw from otherwise sound investments (Switzer 2001).

Transnational mineral firms can bring important skills to the dialogue process. They have extensive experience with extractive projects and their many externalities; governments often do not. Mineral firms have long time horizons and execute complex, multidecade projects; many governments cannot plan beyond the next election. Governments may also have little credibility in the eyes of affected communities; sometimes, it is easier for outsiders, such as mineral companies, to negotiate with locals. In apartheid South Africa, where the government was viewed as illegitimate among the majority-black population, BP and Rio Tinto formed direct, bilateral partnerships with local communities.

Some mining firms have used dialogues to find innovative ways to head off conflicts. In the Las Cristinas area in the south of the República Bolivariana de Venezuela, Placer Dome has allocated part of its concession to local, artisanal miners and helped train them in mining techniques and business management. In the Philippines, WMC Resources helped indigenous communities gain official recognition from the government, so they could obtain royalty payments and legal protection for their ancestral lands (Switzer 2001).

NGOs can also play a key role in these dialogues. They often have experience in protecting the rights and interests of local communities, which the communities themselves may lack. They may have a level of credibility among local peoples that neither the government nor the mineral firm enjoys; this credibility can be essential to the dialogue's success. NGOs can help administer local development programs that are funded with mining revenues; monitor and sanction the activities of firms, the government, and other actors; convene adversarial parties; and provide early warnings about impending conflicts.

Human Rights and Security

Large-scale mining can lead to conflict when it attracts police and military forces that engage in predatory behavior. In Indonesia, the government has required many large mineral firms to make regular payments to military forces stationed nearby. These military forces often extract payments from others who live or work near the mine site. Occasionally, these military units will serve a useful purpose, but much of the time their presence is simply a pretext for extortion. In several cases, military units may have staged or facilitated attacks on mining firms to extract additional funds.

Even when they refrain from extortion, poorly trained and poorly compensated soldiers and police officers may heighten animosity toward the government and the mining operation. The Indonesian government placed its Military Operations Command (*Kolakops*) for the province of Aceh directly in Lhokseumawe, home of the natural gas facility, instead of in the provincial capital. The large military presence created innumerable tensions in the region. Soldiers assigned to protect the Lhokseumawe facility have periodically been involved in the abduction, torture, and execution of Acehnese in neighboring areas, whom they suspect are sympathetic to or associated with GAM. The presence of the military at the facility—and the military's disregard for human rights—helped spur popular support for the rebels and animosity toward Mobil.

A recent project by BP in West Papua, Indonesia, uses innovative techniques for protecting human rights and avoiding abuses by security forces. West Papua is a high-risk region for mineral development, because of its extreme poverty, mountainous terrain, peripheral location, and sharply distinct culture and history. Indeed, the large copper mine operated by Freeport-McMoran near the town of Timika has been the site of almost constant unrest, in part because of the Indonesian military presence.

To avoid replicating these problems at its new Tangguh natural gas site, BP has engaged in extensive consultations with local communities since the early days of the project. After BP determined that the optimal site for its facilities was near a village of 127 families, it enlisted the World Bank's help in forging a relocation agreement with the community—along with plans for local hiring, restrictions on immigration, sustainable economic development, cultural preservation, and biodiversity conservation.

BP has also insisted that Indonesian security forces remain away from the project area; instead, BP is training local Papuans to create a community-based security force. To give its policies greater credibility, BP has sought independent evaluations of its operations: it has carried out an environmental impact assessment and a human rights assessment and has established an independent advisory panel to subject the noncommercial parts of the project to external scrutiny. Both local and international NGOs have played important roles in developing, monitoring, and critiquing the project. When disputes between villagers, BP, and the government have arisen, they have been resolved nonviolently, often through dialogue and compromise.

Conclusion

The mineral-exporting states of the developing world are troubled by economic volatility, corruption, authoritarian rule, and violent conflict. This chapter has discussed one facet of this resource curse: the conflicts that commonly arise when resource wealth is unevenly distributed around the country. Mineral-based conflicts can create self-perpetuating inequality traps: when high levels of inequality—a common feature of mineral-based development—lead to violent conflict, such violence will deter investment in nonmineral sectors (such as manufacturing and agriculture) that could promote more equitable forms of growth. These inequality traps, however, can be short-circuited by wise policies—in both governments and mineral firms—that promote transparency, multistakeholder dialogues, and special attention to human rights issues.

The problem of conflict in the mineral-exporting states has global repercussions; it has only recently begun to receive the attention it merits. NGOs have taken the lead in publicizing this issue and have placed the "publish what you pay" issue on the global agenda. The United Kingdom's Extractive Industries Transparency Initiative and the Group of Eight have also begun to address the issue, while the World Bank—having just completed a two-year review of its policies in the extractive sector—has pledged to support these initiatives. Still, much remains poorly understood about the resource curse, and many of the problems that face these states remain unaddressed.

Notes

1. The term *minerals* is used here to include oil, gas, hard-rock minerals, and gemstones.
2. Of course, mineral-exporting states confront many other challenges. See Auty (2001); Gelb and associates (1988); Ross (1999, 2001); and Stevens (2003).
3. The data are drawn primarily from the World Bank's (2002) publication *World Development Indicators 2002*. Missing values were replaced by values from earlier years or from other sources.
4. For a review of these and similar studies, see Ross (2004b).
5. Other important arguments linking mineral wealth to civil war include oil wealth leads to state weakness, which, in turn, causes civil war (Fearon 2004; Fearon and Laitin 2003); mineral wealth may encourage foreign intervention, which triggers or exacerbates internal conflict (Ross 2004a); trade shocks,

which disproportionately affect commodity exporters, may lead to civil war (Humphreys 2003); and mineral dependence may reduce a country's level of internal trade, which, in turn, could diminish the conflict-alleviating properties of commercial interaction (Humphreys 2003). Also see Keen (1998), Klare (2001), Le Billon (2001), and Switzer (2001).

6. For sources and coding rules, see Ross (2004a).
7. Indeed, the founder of GAM, Hasan di Tiro, was a businessman who failed in his effort to win a bid for a work contract at the natural gas facility (Robinson 1998).
8. Not everyone agrees; some studies find that once income is accounted for, political institutions have no measurable effect on the likelihood of civil war. See, for example, Collier and Hoeffler (2004) and Fearon and Laitin (2003).
9. The distinction between lootable and unlootable commodities was developed by Collier and Hoeffler (2004) and Le Billon (2001).
10. In Myanmar, the separatist regions had both lootable (gemstones) and unlootable (tin) minerals.
11. On Global Witness's investigation into Angolan state finances, see http://www.globalwitness.org.

References

Anderson, G. N. 1999. *Sudan in Crisis*. Gainesville, FL: University Press of Florida.

Auty, R. M., ed. 2001. *Resource Abundance and Economic Development*. New York: Oxford University Press.

Carruthers, D. S. 1990. "Some Implications for Papua New Guinea of the Closure of Bougainville Copper Mine." In *The Bougainville Crisis*, ed. R. J. May and M. Spriggs, 38–54. Bathurst, Australia: Crawford House Press.

Collier, P., and A. Hoeffler. 1998. "On Economic Causes of Civil War." *Oxford Economic Papers* 50 (4): 563–73.

———. 2004. "Greed and Grievance in Civil War." *Oxford Economic Papers* 56 (4): 663–95.

———. 2005. "The Political Economy of Secession." In *Negotiating Self-Determination*, ed. H. Hannum and E. Babbitt, 37–60. Lanham, MD: Lexington Books.

de Soysa, I. 2002. "Paradise Is a Bazaar? Greed, Creed, and Governance in Civil War, 1989–99." *Journal of Peace Research* 39 (4): 395–416.

Fearon, J. D. 2004. "Why Do Some Civil Wars Last So Much Longer Than Others?" *Journal of Peace Research* 41 (3): 275–301.

Fearon, J. D., and D. D. Laitin. 2003. "Ethnicity, Insurgency, and Civil War." *American Political Science Review* 97 (1): 75–90.

Gelb, A., and associates. 1988. *Oil Windfalls: Blessing or Curse?* New York: Oxford University Press.

Gylfason, T. 2001. "Natural Resources, Education, and Economic Development." *European Economic Review* 45 (4): 847–59.

Hegre, H., T. Ellingsen, S. Gates, and N. P. Gleditsch. 2001. "Toward a Democratic Civil Peace? Democracy, Political Change, and Civil War, 1816–1992." *American Political Science Review* 95 (1): 33–48.

Humphreys, M. 2003. "Natural Resource, Conflict, and Conflict Resolution: Uncovering the Mechanisms." *Journal of Conflict Resolution* 49 (4): 508–37.

Keen, D. 1998. "The Economic Functions of Violence in Civil Wars." Adelphi Paper 320, International Institute of Strategic Studies, London.

Klare, M. T. 2001. *Resource Wars*. New York: Metropolitan Books.

Le Billon, P. 2001. "The Political Ecology of War: Natural Resources and Armed Conflicts." *Political Geography* 20 (5): 561–84.

Leite, C., and J. Weidmann. 1999. "Does Mother Nature Corrupt? Natural Resources, Corruption, and Economic Growth." IMF Working Paper WP/99/85, International Monetary Fund, Washington, DC. http://www.imf.org/external/pubs/ft/wp/1999/wp9985.pdf.

Lewis, P. 2004. "Identity and Conflict in Nigeria's Niger Delta: New Evidence from Attitude Surveys." Paper presented at the annual meeting of the American Political Science Association, Chicago, September 2.

Muller, E. N., and E. Weede. 1990. "Cross-National Variation in Political Violence." *Journal of Conflict Resolution* 34 (4): 624–51.

O'Ballance, E. 2000. *Sudan, Civil War, and Terrorism 1956–1999*. New York: St. Martin's Press.

Polomka, P. 1990. "Bougainville: Perspectives on a Crisis." Strategic and Defence Studies Centre, Research School of Pacific Studies, Australian National University, Canberra.

Robinson, G. 1998. "Rawan Is as Rawan Does: The Origins of Disorder in New Order Aceh." *Indonesia* 66 (October): 127–56.

Ross, M. L. 1999. "The Political Economy of the Resource Curse." *World Politics* 51 (2): 297–322.

———. 2001. "Does Oil Hinder Democracy?" *World Politics* 53 (3): 325–61.

———. 2004a. "How Does Natural Resource Wealth Influence Civil War? Evidence from 13 Cases." *International Organization* 58 (1): 35–67.

———. 2004b. "What Do We Know about Natural Resources and Civil War?" *Journal of Peace Research* 41 (3): 337–56.

———. 2005. "Resources and Rebellion in Indonesia." In *Understanding Civil War: Evidence and Analysis*, ed. P. Collier and N. Sambanis, 35–58. Washington, DC: World Bank.

———. 2006. "A Closer Look at Oil, Diamonds, and Civil War." *American Review of Political Science* 9 (1): 265–300.

Scott, J. C. 1976. *The Moral Economy of the Peasant*. New Haven, CT: Yale University Press.

———. 1985. *Weapons of the Weak*. New Haven, CT: Yale University Press.

Stevens, P. 2003. "Resource Impact: Curse or Blessing?—A Literature Survey." *Journal of Energy Literature* 9 (1): 1–42.

Switzer, J. 2001. "Armed Conflict and Natural Resources: The Case of the Minerals Sector." Minerals, Mining, and Sustainable Development Report 12, International Institute for Environment and Development, London. http://www.iied.org/mmsd/mmsd_pdfs/jason_switzer.pdf.

Thompson, H. 1991. "The Economic Causes and Consequences of the Bougainville Crisis." *Resources Policy* 17 (1): 69–85.

Wesley-Smith, Terence, and Eugene Ogan. 1992. "Copper, Class, and Crisis: Changing Relations of Production in Bougainville." *The Contemporary Pacific* 4: 407–30.

World Bank. 2002. *World Development Indicators 2002*. Washington, DC: World Bank.

CHAPTER 8

Spain: Development, Democracy, and Equity

Carles Boix

In the past half century, Spain has undergone a dramatic and, by most counts, successful political and economic transformation from relative underdevelopment and authoritarianism to wealth and democracy. In the immediate aftermath of World War II, which resulted in the reestablishment of democracy in Western Europe, Spain remained a culturally and diplomatically isolated country, governed by authoritarian institutions. Moreover, whereas democratic Europe experienced a period of rapid economic growth and growing trade integration, Spain was burdened by the destruction yielded by its civil war in the 1930s, as well as the pursuit of autarkic policies and a long history of relative poverty. Following the decision to liberalize its economy in the late 1950s, Spain quickly transformed into a modern manufacturing- and service-based economy. It experienced unprecedented levels of prosperity, massive urbanization, and a growing middle class. This rapid and massive economic growth dissolved most of the social tensions that had blocked the introduction of democracy in the past. With the death of its dictator, Francisco Franco, in 1975, Spain embarked on a peaceful transition to democracy. In turn, the process of democratization transformed the political economy of Spain even further—a still heavily regulated state gave way to an increasingly liberalized, open economy. In part to respond to the demands unleashed by competitive elections but also as a result of that deregulation, the Spanish state grew to perform an important compensatory role similar to any European welfare state. The economic and political transformation was successful and almost complete. However, as the conclusion of this chapter points out, two central issues remain unresolved to date: the territorial organization of the state and the performance of the labor market.

This successful transition to economic and political modernity is particularly relevant, theoretically and from the viewpoint of policy makers, because Spain stands as one of the few countries that has managed to move peacefully from underdevelopment and authoritarianism to democracy and prosperity in the past few decades. Most of today's wealthy democracies (concentrated in Europe and North America) were already industrialized and had liberal political regimes by the middle of the 20th century. Except for a few Asian countries and, more recently, some small Eastern European nations, the rest of the world—which was either underdeveloped, undemocratic, or both a few decades ago—still has a long way to catch up with the industrial West.

Although case studies offer a chance to dwell on the details of the historical development of either a particular country or a set of events and to track the motives and interactions of the agents who made the decisions that shaped the outcomes under study, they are inherently limited in their ability to adjudicate between different theoretical accounts. To minimize this problem, this chapter follows two strategies. First, taking Spanish history as if it were a time series, this chapter engages in several temporal comparisons. It examines why democracy failed in the 1930s but succeeded 40 years later. It debates what caused the economic policy shift of 1959. It also evaluates the expansion of the Spanish public sector in the 1970s and 1980s by looking at the factors that remained unchanged and the factors that varied with the construction of a modern welfare state. Second, this chapter makes extensive reference to a broader theoretical literature and to cross-national empirical studies. The emphasis on theory garners particular strength in the concluding section of the chapter.

To examine the story of Spain's economic and political transitions, the chapter is organized as follows. The first two sections explore the nature and causes of the economic underdevelopment of Spain since the 19th century, as well as the violent collapse of its brief democratic experiment in the early 1930s. The third section depicts the Franco regime—particularly the heavily regulated economy in place until the late 1950s, the decision to liberalize in 1959, and the period of rapid growth that followed. This section explores the causes of that economic policy shift and argues that although the exact timing was probably random, the policy consolidation was not. The fourth section describes the democratic transition that followed the death of Franco in 1975. In particular, it emphasizes the conditions (economic growth and the formation of a broad middle class in the 1960s) that made the advent of democracy possible. The fifth section examines the effect of democratization on the structure of the welfare state in Spain.

A Story of Relative Political and Economic Failure

Until the second half of the 20th century, Spanish contemporary history was, broadly speaking, a tale of relative political and economic failure. After a period of territorial expansion and European hegemony in the early Modern Ages, Spain lapsed into economic decline and cultural stagnation in the following centuries (North and Thomas 1973). During most of the 19th century, Spain's industrial takeoff was blocked by considerable political instability, including three civil wars and frequent military *pronunciamientos*, inefficient legal institutions, substantial inequalities, and a poorly educated population. Eventually, conservatives and liberals, who had opposed each other for most of the century, reconciled their differences in the constitutional settlement of 1876 and agreed to take turns at governing the country through prearranged elections and an extended system of patron-client relations. The pacification of the country and the final creation of a relatively stable system of property rights eventually fostered a spur of growth.

As shown in figure 8.1, the Spanish per capita income doubled from less than US$1,400 (in constant 1990 dollars) in 1870 to about US$3,000 in 1929. However, that amount represented only two-fifths of the U.K. per capita income and less than two-thirds of the French one. Moreover, most of the growth was concentrated in Catalonia and the Basque country, which are north of the Iberian Peninsula. Finally, the increase implied only moderate change in the sectoral mix of the Spanish economy. Figure 8.2 reports the sectoral composition of the Spanish economy from 1850 to 1930. Growing at the same pace the economy did, services and construction generated about half of the total production throughout the period. Agricultural output roughly doubled in absolute terms but fell from 40 percent to 27 percent of the economy. The manufacturing sector, which multiplied by eight, claimed one-fourth of total output by 1930. Overall, Spain remained an agricultural country with almost 50 percent of the labor force employed in the primary sector (Nadal 1975; Tortella 1995).[1]

Democratic Transition and Civil War

The loss of the last two main Spanish colonies (Cuba and the Philippines) in 1898, the progressive organization of the trade union movement, and

Figure 8.1. Gross Domestic Product per Capita, 1820–1930

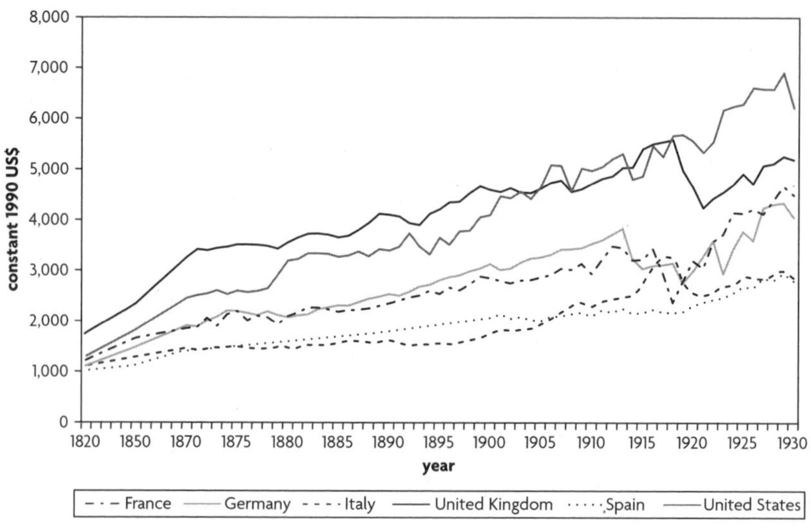

Source: Madison 1995.

Figure 8.2. Sectoral Distribution of Gross Domestic Product in Spain, 1850–1930

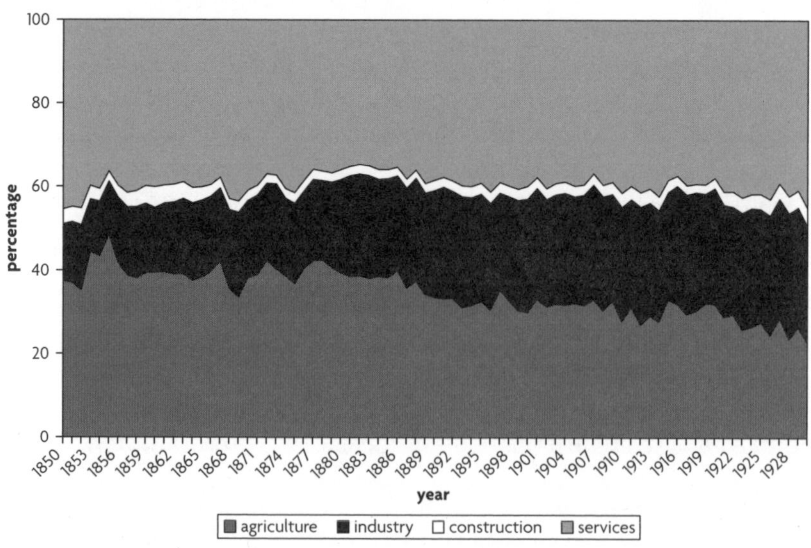

Source: Prados de la Escosura 2003.

the emergence of regionalist parties in Catalonia and the Basque country eroded the constitutional settlement of 1876 during the first two decades of the 20th century. In sync with the widespread political turmoil affecting Europe after World War I, Spain experienced substantial social unrest and political violence in the early 1920s. In 1923, to restore political stability, the monarchy supported a military coup d'état by Miguel Primo de Rivera. Seven years later, Alphonse XIII dismissed the latter and decided to democratize the country gradually through local elections. However, the victory of the Republican parties in the urban municipalities in April 1931 resulted in the king's abdication and in the introduction of democratic institutions in Spain.

The Spanish republic did not last long. Spain was polarized by considerable social and economic inequalities. In a country that was still eminently agrarian, the distribution of land was very unequal—particularly in the southern half of the peninsula: about 1 percent of the number of holdings occupied 50 percent of the land. Although arable land was more evenly distributed, the structure of holdings was considerable biased in favor of the largest ones. About one-third of the arable land was occupied by holdings of more than 100 hectares, while the proportion in Europe was around 10 percent (Merigó 1982). Urban workers, who were well organized into two trade unions, the socialist Workers' General Union and the anarchist National Confederation of Labor, espoused radical social and economic programs. Except for Catalonia and the Basque country, which had industrialized in the 19th century, the Spanish middle class was small and consisted of civil servants, military officers, and professionals (such as doctors and lawyers). In addition to highly charged economic differences, the republic had to cope with substantial territorial demands. The Catalan and Basque nationalist movements, which had become electorally mobilized at the turn of the 20th century to regain their own political institutions and the official recognition of their historic languages, met stiff resistance from large parts of Spanish society. Finally, Spaniards were intensely divided between the supporters of the Catholic Church, which aspired to maintain the educational quasi-monopoly and political recognition that it had secured in the previous regime, and a rabid anticlerical movement inspired by French radicals.

General elections were conducted under very acrimonious conditions and an electoral law that magnified small vote swings.[2] After left-wing parties lost two-thirds of their parliamentary seats in 1933 and as the main right-wing party, which ran as a pro-Church movement and favored a constitutional reform, was about to join the government, the radical Left and the Catalan regional government organized an insurrection a year later in 1934. The government had to call in the army to pacify the mining valleys of Asturias. A year and a half later, in the spring of 1936, new elections were held. A small swing in the popular vote resulted in a crushing victory for the left-wing parties in terms of parliamentary seats. In July 1936, General Franco launched a coup. This *pronunciamiento*, instead of leading to a bloodless change in regime, as had been the case with all Spanish military coups in the 19th century, was met with the active resistance of a fully mobilized union movement. Spain became engulfed in a three-year civil war that presaged the world war that would erupt in the summer of 1939.

Authoritarianism: From Autarky to Growth

With the defeat of the Republican government, Franco established an authoritarian regime that lasted until his death in 1975. The destruction caused by the civil war (and the world war that erupted a few months afterward) considerably depressed the Spanish economy. Per capita income fell to its 1900 level by 1938, and it did not reach its 1918 level until 1950. The proportion of active population in industry declined to 22 percent in 1940 (or the level of 1920), and the share of those employed in agriculture grew to more than 50 percent. Growth was feeble. The average annual rate was 1.25 percent in the 1940s.

The Autarkic Model and Its Breakdown

Spain's economic recovery was hampered, above all, by the heavily autarkic and statist policies pursued by the Franco regime. Inspired by the corporatist ideologies of Italian fascism and German nazism and, in part, compelled by its political isolation in the postwar European context, Franco's regime generalized a system of price controls and rationing, regulated foreign trade through quantitative controls, and monitored the allocation of financial credit. Public-owned firms were heavily supported and expanded, normally following political considerations.[3]

This intensely interventionist strategy was extended to the labor and housing market. To suppress one of the main forces that opposed the military insurrection, Franco outlawed any independent labor unions. Instead, workers and employers had to affiliate with a national trade union. In a concession to Falange, the fascist party that formed part of the Francoist coalition, this repressive stance was accompanied by very strict labor legislation that made it very hard for employers to dismiss workers or to hire them through temporary contracts. This state-based form of protection offered to employees was balanced with similar regulations in the housing market to cheapen rentals and to favor current tenants.

Although the Spanish economy experienced significant growth throughout the 1950s, it did so in a very volatile manner, constrained by important supply bottlenecks and subject to increasing inflationary pressures (see figure 8.3). After the government met a wave of illegal strikes with significant wage increases, inflation shot up to around 12 percent from 1956 to 1958. In addition, Spain faced a balance-of-payment crisis. Gold and foreign-currency reserves fell to an all-time low. Sizable short-term capital outflows took place in 1957 and 1958. More generally, Spain's economic structure remained stuck in an agrarian, underdevelopment trap. Although investment went up, it took place within a highly protectionist, import-substitution structure. Export-led growth was negligible. Imports as a share of national income remained flat during the 1950s, and exports actually fell by half. The structure of foreign trade reflected the structure of the Spanish economy. Exports were dominated by agricultural products and raw materials. By contrast, Spain mostly imported inputs for the productive sectors, particularly industry.

Figure 8.3. Annual Gross Domestic Product Growth Rates in Spain, 1930–2000

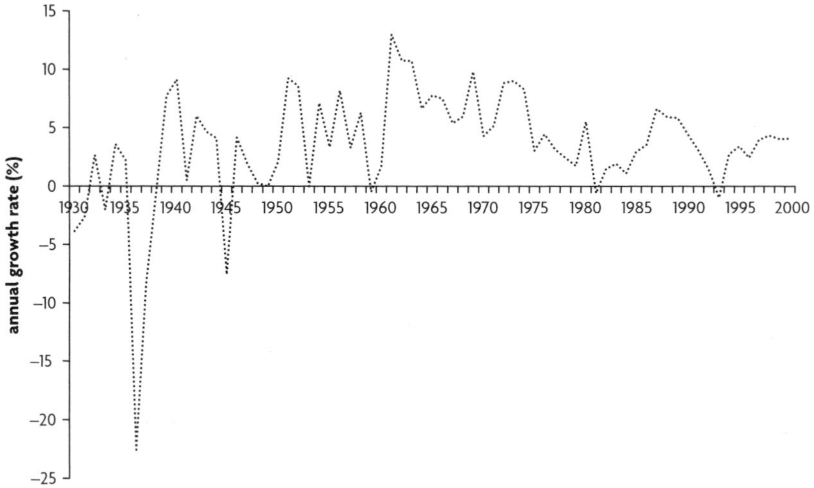

Source: Prados de la Escosura 2003.

In the late 1950s, after a prolonged period of stop-and-go policies, Spain eventually moved to break with its old interventionist system. In a rebuke to the core of Falangist and interventionist ministers who had dominated the social and economic departments of the Spanish government, Franco appointed two technocrats to head the economic ministries in February 1957. Their first attempt to impose contractionary policies and to overhaul and simplify the exchange rate system ended in failure. However, an acute political crisis, with a wave of strikes, and an economic recession, with zero growth rates and a severe balance-of-payment crisis, eventually forced the government to adopt a stabilization plan in March 1959. In addition to new fiscal and monetary measures to stabilize the economy, the plan included wide-ranging measures to liberalize the economy. At the behest of the International Monetary Fund and the Organisation of European Economic Co-operation, the government established a single exchange rate (accompanied by a significant devaluation), suppressed price controls over freely imported goods, reduced tariffs significantly, and liberalized foreign investment.

The stabilization plan was an outright success. Despite the devaluation and suppression of price controls, inflation remained subdued. The economy grew very quickly. From 1960 to the outbreak of the first oil crisis in 1973, output expanded at an average annual rate of more than 7 percent with very little interyear volatility. Per capita income more than doubled from about US$3,000 to US$8,500 (in 1990 dollars) in 15 years. In part because of emigration to northern European countries, unemployment was low at less than 3 percent. Economic growth was to some extent generated by a substantial increase in investment, which rose from 16 percent to 21.5 percent, but growth was mostly derived from considerable technological progress, which resulted from the incorporation of foreign "best practices" and foreign direct investment. Labor productivity in industry grew by 8.5 percent annually between 1960 and 1975. Growth also derived from a shift in employment from low-productivity sectors (agriculture) to high-productivity sectors (industry).

To understand why the reorientation of the Spanish macroeconomic policy framework took place, we should distinguish between the short-term factors that explain its adoption and the long-term causes of its consolidation. The framework was adopted primarily for domestic reasons. The lack of industry-led growth, the short-term difficulties in controlling prices and balancing the trade deficit, and the parlous condition of state finances made it possible for the reformist sectors of the regime to convince

Franco of the need to make a fresh break with past policies.[4] The Franco regime was an authoritarian, yet by no means monolithic, power structure. Although the 1936 insurrections was led by the army, it had relied on a coalition of diverse and heterogeneous interests: monarchists keen on overthrowing the republic, Catholics concerned with the anticlerical policies of the 1930s and frustrated by the de facto veto imposed by the left-wing parties to the entry of the right-wing parties in the Spanish government in 1933 and 1934, landowning families, important sectors of the Basque financial elite, some Catalan industrialists, and the fascist movement of Falange. For the first two decades of the regime, Falangists played a dominant role in the regime and shaped the economic policies of the state for two reasons: international conditions, which were defined by the strength of the Axis powers until 1944 and the isolation Spain experienced until 1953, and the Falangists' much better organizational strength (they controlled the quasi-party structures that underpinned the Francoist regime). However, the existence of non-Falangist supporters, who always retained a share of ministerial posts, gave Franco enough room to check Falange and to rely on alternative policies to overcome the economic and financial exhaustion experienced by the dictatorship in the late 1950s. In fact, it is likely that Franco decided to reinforce the presence of non-Falangist economists to check an aggressive campaign launched in the mid-1950s by some Falangists to strengthen the institutional and political role of Falange.

Whereas the timing of the policy shift of 1957 to 1959 may be thought of as random, the policy consolidation was not. The stabilization plan was not reversed (as many other stabilization plans have been worldwide) because several preexisting conditions (which are not present in countries that abandon their macroeconomic liberalization plans) made it immediately successful and, therefore, convinced Franco not to deviate from the new macroeconomic framework of 1959.

The Spanish economic miracle of the 1960s was made possible by three factors so far strangled by the interventionist schemes of postwar Spain. First, Spain already had a set of "virtuous" pockets, mostly concentrated in the Basque country and in Catalonia, which had industrialized in the past and, therefore, had enough managerial and technical know-how to respond quickly to the liberalization of markets. Second, the Spanish state had a relatively reliable legal and administrative structure, already established by the liberal governments of the 19th century and then explicitly modernized by the same technocratic cadres that engineered the stabilization plan of 1959. Finally, Spain could count on an extremely favorable foreign environment: for geopolitical considerations, the U.S. and European governments were keenly interested in a stable, rapidly growing Spain; foreign capital was available and ready to be invested in a potentially medium market located close to the European core; and the military ties with the United States acted as a mechanism to insure foreign investors against any policy reversals or confiscatory threats in the peninsula.

Social Consequences of Economic Liberalization and Growth

The transformation of the Spanish economy led to significant structural changes in Spanish society. Figure 8.4 shows the evolution of output shares of different economic sectors after 1930. Agriculture fell from 23 percent to 10 percent between 1960 and 1975, while industry remained at 30 percent. The service sector experienced an increase of 10 percentage points. Construction went up from 5 percent to 7 percent. In employment terms, the proportion working in agriculture dropped from 41 percent to 23 percent, while in industry, the proportion increased four percentage points to 27 percent. Most of the fall in agriculture was absorbed by a jump in the service sectors (employing 40 percent of the population in 1975).

The structural change in the economy was accompanied by strong migration flows. Between 1950 and 1975, the share of the three top

Figure 8.4. Sectoral Distribution of Gross Domestic Product in Spain, 1930–2000

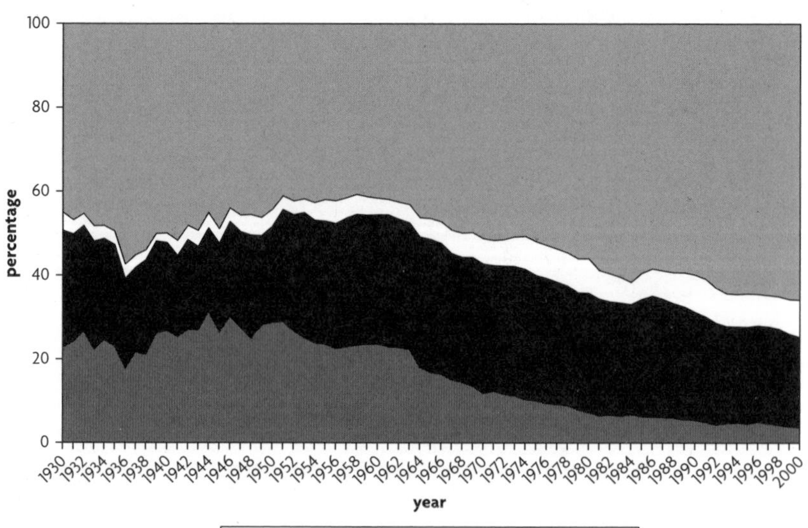

Source: Prados de la Escosura 2003.

destinations (Catalonia, Madrid, and the Basque country) rose from 20 percent to 32 percent of the population. By contrast, the southern part of the peninsula declined from 35 percent to 25 percent in the same period. Those migrations resulted in an unprecedented increase in urbanization. The proportion of Spaniards living in cities of more than 100,000 inhabitants climbed from 30 percent in 1940 to 50 percent in 1975.

The combination of economic growth, industrial expansion, and internal migration produced a substantial decline in the levels of interregional inequality. Figure 8.5 tracks the evolution of the coefficient of variation of per capita regional product from 1900 to 1990 and the standard deviation of regional per capita income after 1955. A dramatic fall in interregional inequality (from a standard deviation in per capita income of 0.37 in 1955 to 0.27 in 1973) took place during the Spanish miracle of the 1960s. A larger middle class emerged in Spain as a result of the growth. Using data from the Spanish national survey of salaries and the Spanish survey of household budgets, Revenga (1991) finds a significant decline in inequality from the early 1960s through the mid-1970s. The Gini index for the wages and salaries of (agrarian and industrial) employees declined from 0.294 in 1964 to 0.232 in 1973. The Gini index for household income fell from 0.393 in 1964 to 0.355 in 1974. The income share of the three central deciles rose from about 51 percent to 59 percent in that decade.

Figure 8.5. Interregional Inequality in Spain

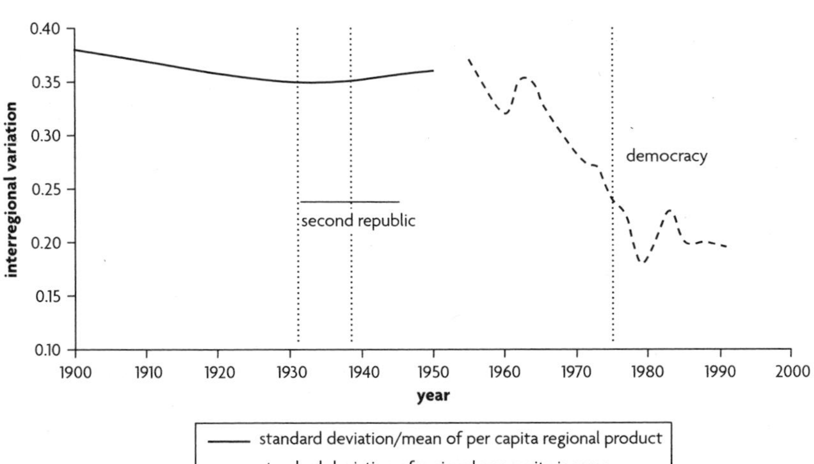

Sources: For per capita regional product, Prados de la Escosura 1992; for regional per capita income, Pérez, Goerlich, and Más 1996.

Table 8.1. Pretax and Posttax Income of Households

Country	Income quintile (% of income per quintile)				
	1	2	3	4	5
Pretax income					
Spain (1973–74)	1.0	10.3	16.8	24.4	47.4
France (1970)	4.3	9.9	15.8	23.0	47.0
Germany (1973)	5.9	10.1	15.1	22.1	46.8
Norway (1970)	4.9	13.6	18.0	24.6	40.9
Sweden (1972)	6.0	11.4	17.4	24.3	40.5
United Kingdom (1977–78)	6.1	10.5	16.4	24.4	42.5
Posttax income					
Spain (1973–74)	6.0	11.8	16.9	23.1	42.3
France (1970)	4.3	9.8	16.3	22.7	46.9
Germany (1973)	6.5	10.3	15.0	21.9	46.1
Norway (1970)	6.3	12.9	18.5	24.7	37.3
Sweden (1972)	6.6	13.1	18.5	24.8	37.0
United Kingdom (1977–78)	7.4	11.4	17.0	24.7	39.5

Source: Sawyer 1982.

By the early 1970s, Spanish income inequality was broadly in line with the largest European countries (see table 8.1). The Spanish Gini coefficient for household net income fluctuates around 0.37, which is similar to the German one, though higher than the Gini indexes in the U.K. (0.26) or Sweden (0.21).[5] A similar pattern emerges from data on consumption habits. By 1980, Spain had around 200 cars, 193 telephones lines, and 254 television sets per 1,000 inhabitants. Those figures were about three-fourths of the European average.

Still, significant social and economic inequities remained in place for three reasons. First, educational attainment was low. Although by 1970 the illiteracy rate had fallen to 10 percent, only 6 percent of the population had completed secondary studies by that year. Second, wages were dampened by excess labor supply and repressive labor institutions. Finally, taxation and public spending were low, and redistributive social programs were virtually absent. General government tax revenues fluctuated around 20 percent of gross domestic product (GDP) in the 1960s. Social spending was below 10 percent of GDP, less than half the European average.

Democratic Transition

General Franco died in November 1975. His successor, King Juan Carlos, the grandson of Alphonse XIII, who had renounced his crown in 1931, became the Spanish head of state according to the legal mechanisms put in place by Franco. The new monarch immediately launched a process of political change toward democratization. After some difficult and behind-the-scenes maneuvering, Juan Carlos succeeded in appointing a reformist cabinet in July 1976. Staffed by young politicians and civil servants who had worked within the Francoist regime, the new government moved swiftly to democratize Spain. In fall 1976, the government, using the legal mechanisms put in place by the very technocratic generation that had reformed the economy in the early 1960s and pointing to the existence of wide popular support for democracy, secured the consent of the old Francoist *Cortes* (the Spanish parliament) to establish a truly democratic parliament through direct, competitive elections. After the political reform was ratified with overwhelming popular support in a referendum in December 1976, the government engaged in informal conversations with the democratic opposition, legalized the Communist party, and granted a wide political amnesty. Although the transition to democracy was conducted in a climate of uncertainty, particularly over the reaction of the army and the extent to which terrorist violence or labor mobilization could disrupt the negotiation process, democratic elections were promptly held in June 1977.

This clean and competitive election returned representatives and parties that reflected the whole range of political preferences of Spaniards. The center-right government coalition obtained close to the majority of seats. The center-left Socialist party secured one-third of the parliament. Both the Francoist party and the Communist party received less than 10 percent of the vote, with about 5 percent of seats each. Catalan and Basque regionalist parties also entered the new parliament. Consensual politics dominated the transition to democracy. After protracted negotiations, a new constitution was approved in 1978 with almost unanimous support. The constitution established a parliamentary monarchy in which the king exercised only symbolic power, enshrined the existing social consensus around private property and the market economy and around the need to develop a welfare state to meet a generous list of social rights, and institutionalized the separation of church and state. Finally, it established a decentralized state to accommodate the political demands of the Catalan and Basque regions.[6]

An influential section of the scholarly literature has explained the success of the Spanish democratic transition as a result of a process of negotiation between enlightened elites who had learned the lessons of excessive confrontation the hard way—that is, through the hardship of war in the 1930s and economic stagnation until the 1950s. Nevertheless, the roots of democracy lay first and foremost on the changed economic and social conditions of Spain in the 1970s. According to estimations in Boix and Stokes (2003), which were based on panel data for all sovereign countries from 1850 to 2000, the annual probability of a democratic breakdown (that is, the transition to authoritarianism in a country that has started a democracy) is close to 5 percent with a per capita income of US$2,000 (the level of Spain in 1930) but 0 percent for income above US$7,000 (a level attained by Spain in 1974). Naturally, the level of per capita income simply proxies for the absence or presence of social conditions that make it reasonable for all the parties in contention to subject themselves to free elections and to the possibility of losing those elections and, therefore, power.

The rapid economic transformation of Spain, which revolved around industrialization and urbanization, had deflated past conflicts around the distribution of land. The extension of literacy and the adoption of advanced industrial technologies (with the correlated increase in productivity and incomes) had generated a strong middle class beyond the existing bourgeois strata in Catalonia and the Basque country. The very experience of sustained growth defused social conflict with the credible promise of higher incomes and more social mobility in the future. It is likely that the possibility of European integration reinforced the expectations of Spaniards about sustained growth. In short, Spain had overcome the zero-sum game in which it had been locked in during the past century and a half. This structural change explains why some timid attempts to open up the Francoist regime, entertained from 1945 to 1947 in the wake of the Allies' victory and again in the late 1950s, failed completely. True political reform had to wait until social and economic conditions were ripe for political change to occur. In addition to the transformation of material conditions for broad swaths of Spanish society, religious and cultural life experienced considerable change in the two decades preceding the transition to democracy. In the aftermath of Vatican II, the Spanish Catholic Church went through a thorough *aggiornamento* in both its leadership and ideological commitments. In addition to embracing the possibility of freedom of religion and political liberalization in the public arena, substantial parts of the Church's hierarchy and lay basis actively cooperated with a nascent union movement and the democratic opposition.

Ways to Build the Welfare State

As discussed earlier, economic growth resulted in a different economic structure and better distributional outcomes, and those outcomes created a swift and successful transition to democracy. In turn, the transition to democracy resulted in a larger public sector, with considerable transfers directed to lower income brackets.

As is apparent in figure 8.6, which reports public spending by general government, and figure 8.7, which displays current revenues of the general government, Spanish public expenditure fluctuated slightly over 20 percent of GDP or about two-thirds of the Organisation for Economic Co-operation and Development (OECD) average through the early 1970s. On the one hand, redistributive pressures were effectively suppressed through political means. On the other hand, the dictatorship met part of those demands through heavily regulated labor and housing markets that secured permanent jobs and cheap rentals to broad sectors of the labor force. The moderate growth of public spending until 1975 covered an increase in investment on education and roads needed to respond to

Figure 8.6. General Government Expenditure in Spain, 1970–98

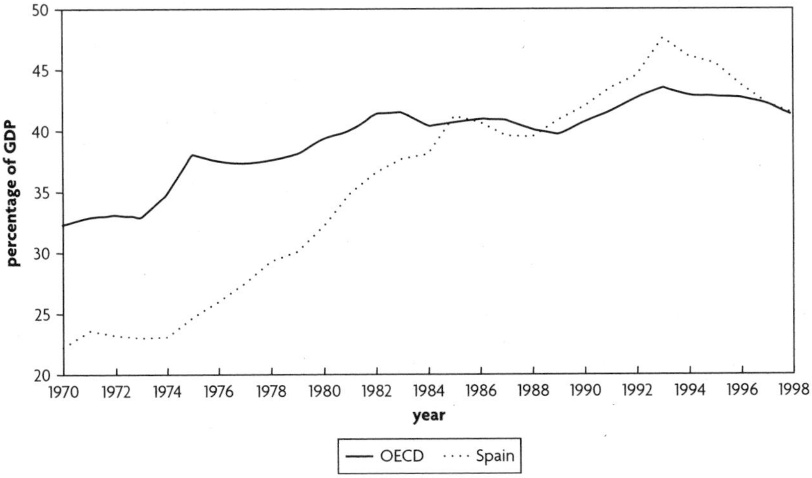

Source: Boix 2001.

Figure 8.7. General Government Current Revenues in Spain, 1970–98

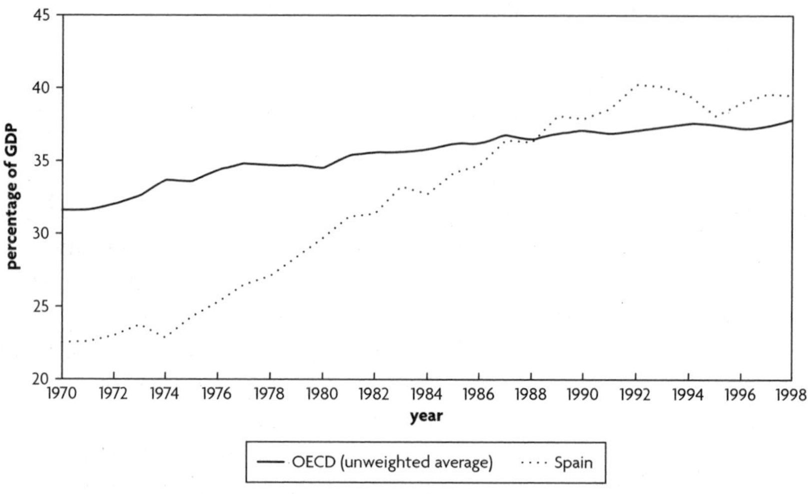

Source: Boix 2001.

rapid economic growth and to attract capital from more industrial countries. With the beginning of the democratic transition, public spending underwent a clear change. During the following 20 years, public spending grew by more than 1 percentage point of GDP per year in real terms to reach 49.6 percent of GDP in 1993.

The increase in public expenditure was first generated by two sequential trends: a rapid growth in social expenditure (in the form of unemployment benefits and pensions) in the second half of the 1970s and a significant rise in interest payments, which resulted from a growing public deficit (to pay for the expansion of social spending) in the first half of the 1980s. Because of the expansion of public spending, Spain had, by the mid-1980s, closed a historical gap with other industrial nations by building a public sector equal to the average OECD public sector and only slightly below the European average.

After experiencing a small decline, public spending grew again in the late 1980s to fund extensive social programs. By 1991, it had reached 43.5 percent of GDP. This percentage should be considered the equilibrium rate of public spending because, although the economic downturn of the early 1990s pushed public spending to around 48 percent of GDP in 1993, three years later public expenditure had declined to its level before the crisis.

The growth of public revenue and expenditure, as well as its internal structure, was a function of three factors. First, public expenditure

Figure 8.8. Public Revenue and per Capita Income in Spain, 1960–97

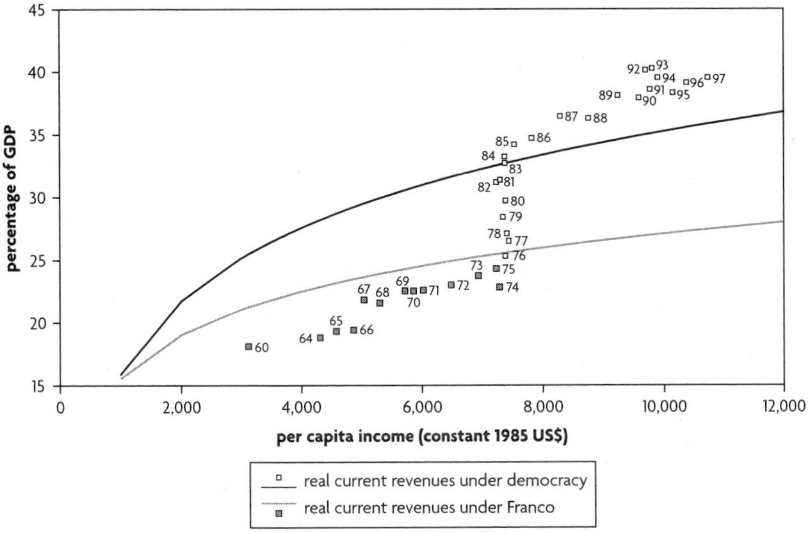

Source: Boix 2001.

responded to new social demands (related to the provision of public infrastructures and education as well as pensions and health) generated by the process of social and economic modernization of Spain. Second, growth in public expenditure emerged as a result of democratization, increased political participation, and electoral competition among parties. Finally, the transformation of the public sector was linked to the shift from a regulated state, in which protection came through permanent jobs and cheap rentals, to a liberal economy that had low tariffs and flexible markets and whose main mechanism to compensate losers and make them more competitive was public spending.

The interaction of development and democratization in shaping the Spanish public sector becomes apparent in figure 8.8, which reports the evolution of public revenue as a percentage of GDP and per capita income from 1960 to the late 1990s. Figure 8.8 also displays the predicted size of the public sector for different levels of per capita income and types of political regimes, on the basis of estimations in Boix (2001). The figure uses a panel of about 2,000 country-year observations for all countries for which data are available since the 1960s.

Until 1975, the public sector grew slowly and in perfect correlation with economic growth. In the mid-1970s, however, the economy stagnated for almost a decade. Spain had a per capita income of US$7,291 (in 1985 dollars) in 1974 and US$7,330 in 1984. By contrast, the political regime changed abruptly—and with it the size of the Spanish state.

The transition to democracy unleashed strong social demands for redistribution. Spaniards maintain a substantial egalitarian ideology and demand from the state a very active role in the reduction of inequality. In 1979, more than 70 percent of Spaniards agreed with the statement that "the distribution of wealth in this country is totally unjust." (Gunther, Montero, and Botella 2004: 173). As table 8.2 shows, support for redistributive policies is high in Spain: less than 3 percent of the population thought that the state should not be responsible for providing health services, pensions, and housing for the poor and for regulating the environment. With democracy and, hence, full political participation, the public sector quickly doubled in size—from 22.8 percent of GDP in 1974 to 34 percent in 1985 and then at a slower pace to about 40 percent by the late 1990s.[7] As democracy consolidated, public spending reached a plateau by the early 1990s.

Table 8.2. Spanish Support for the Welfare State

Speaking generally, do you think it should be the state's responsibility ...	Percentage of respondents			
	Yes, undoubtedly	It probably should	No, it shouldn't	Don't know
... to offer health coverage to everyone?	80	18	1	1
... to secure decent pensions to seniors?	79	19	1	1
... to offer scholarships to university students from low-income families?	74	23	2	2
... to facilitate decent housing to low-income families?	68	28	2	2
... to impose strict regulations on industry to reduce environmental damage?	66	27	3	4
... to give industry the support it needs in order to develop?	61	31	4	4
... to create a job for anyone demanding one?	60	29	9	3
... to provide decent subsidies to the unemployed?	57	33	6	4

Source: Centro de Investigaciones Sociológicas 1996.

Social Expenditure

Public expenditure grew first and foremost to fund new social programs. In response to electoral competition and to shore up support for the democratic process, the reformist government that presided over the political transition rapidly expanded the provision of unemployment benefits and increased the allocation of money to health and pensions. In 10 years, social expenditure almost doubled to reach about 18 percent of GDP in 1980 (see table 8.3), or about 80 percent of the European average. Pensions amounted to 6.4 percent of GDP, and public spending on health totaled 4.3 percent of GDP in 1980 (see table 8.4). By the early 1990s, Spain universalized the provision of public health, introduced old-age pensions for noncontributors, raised low-income pensions, and made unemployment benefits more generous.

As a result, by 2001, pensions were 8.9 percent of GDP, or 90 percent of the European average. Public health spending stood at 5.4 percent—again 90 percent of the European mean. Spending on unemployment benefits and active labor market programs matched the European level.

Capital Formation

Public spending made access to basic services more equitable, and it minimized the effects of economic volatility in an open economy in which standard macroeconomic policies were increasingly in the hands of European institutions. Public spending was also designed to bolster the competitiveness of the factors of production. Accordingly, the Spanish state directed

Table 8.3. Public Spending in Spain, 1953–2001

	Area of expenditure (as a % of GDP)		
Year	Education	Capital formation	Social expenditure
1953	0.7	n.a.	n.a.
1963	1.5	2.1	n.a.
1970	2.1	2.7	9.5
1975	2.2	2.7	12.1
1980	3.3	1.9	18.1
1985	3.6	3.7	19.5
1990	4.1	4.9	20.1
1995	4.5	6.1	20.4
2001	4.3	5.1	18.9

Sources: Boix 1998 and OECD 2004.

Note: n.a. = not available.

Table 8.4. Social Spending Programs in Spain and the OECD, 1980–2001

	Expenditure (% of GDP)				
Type of program	1980	1985	1990	1995	2001
All programs					
Spain	15.9	18.2	19.5	21.4	19.6
EU-15[a]	20.6	22.9	23.4	25.6	24.0
OECD-23[b]	17.9	19.8	20.9	22.9	22.1
Old-age programs					
Spain	6.4	7.7	8.3	9.3	8.9
EU-15[a]	8.1	9.0	9.3	10.2	9.9
OECD-23[b]	6.9	7.6	8.1	8.9	8.9
Health programs					
Spain	4.3	4.4	5.3	5.5	5.4
EU-15[a]	5.6	5.6	5.7	6.0	6.1
OECD-23[b]	5.1	5.2	5.5	5.8	6.1
... Unemployment and active labor policies					
Spain	2.2	3.1	3.1	2.8	2.1
EU-15[a]	1.7	2.7	2.3	2.9	2.1
OECD-23[b]	1.4	2.2	2.0	2.4	1.7
... Incapacity-related programs					
Spain	2.4	2.5	2.3	2.6	2.4
EU-15[a]	3.1	3.1	3.2	3.1	2.9
OECD-23[b]	2.5	2.5	2.7	2.7	2.6
Other programs					
Spain	0.5	0.3	0.5	1.1	0.8
EU-15[a]	2.6	2.7	2.9	3.3	3.0
OECD-23[b]	2.4	2.4	2.7	3.1	2.9

Source: OECD 2004.

a. The EU-15 refers to the member countries of the European Union until May 1, 2004: Austria, Belgium, Denmark, Finland, France, Germany, Greece, Ireland, Italy, the Netherlands, Luxembourg, Portugal, Spain, Sweden, and the United Kingdom.

b. The OECD-23 refers to Austria, Belgium, the Czech Republic, Denmark, Finland, France, Germany, Greece, Hungary, Iceland, Ireland, Italy, Luxembourg, the Netherlands, Norway, Poland, Portugal, the Slovak Republic, Spain, Sweden, Switzerland, Turkey, and the United Kingdom.

heavy sums of money to fixed and human capital formation. Fixed capital formation increased from about 2 percent of GDP in 1980 to around 5 percent in the mid-1990s. Most public investment was allocated to building or ameliorating those basic infrastructures that were thought to play a key role in linking the country (especially its less developed regions) to the European market, in increasing overall productivity, and in, therefore, offering more incentives to private investment. An ambitious construction program tripled the public highway network from 2,300 kilometers to 6,000 kilometers, revamped and expanded the metropolitan transportation system, and modernized the railroad system.

Human capital formation was also a central part in expanding the Spanish state. Public expenditure in education, which represented 2.2 percent of GDP in 1975, was steadily increased to 4.5 percent in 1995. The Spanish state reorganized primary and secondary education (through legislation in 1985 and 1990) and extended free and compulsory education until the age of 16 (in 1990). Combined with a decline in demographic growth, the rise in educational expenditure meant doubling the amount spent per student in real terms, vastly expanding the hiring of teachers, and extending education in secondary and university levels (Puerto 1991). The proportion of students age 14 to 18 years attending school increased from 50 percent in 1980 to 70 percent in the 1990s, and the proportion of students age 19 to 23 years rose from 22 percent to 33.1 percent during that same period. By 2001, almost 50 percent of the population had completed secondary education—10 times more than in the mid-1970s. The average number of years of education increased from 8.2 in 1977 to 11.4 in 1994. This increase was particularly marked in low-income sectors: the average number of years of education grew by 25 percent in the bottom income quintile but by less than 10 percent in the top income quintile (Oliver and Ramos 2001). Education policies were also complemented with active labor market policies, which rose from 0.2 percent of GDP in 1980 to 1 percent in the 1990s.

Conclusions

Spain stands as one of the few countries in the world that has completed a successful transition from authoritarianism and relative underdevelopment to democracy and economic abundance in the past half century. Most of today's wealthy democracies were already liberal and industrialized by the middle of the 20th century. The majority of countries that were poor in the 1950s are still part of the developing world today. The process of full economic and political modernization has taken place only in Southern Europe, in a few East Asian countries, and in sections of the former Soviet bloc.

With a few exceptions, preindustrial societies are characterized by the combination of low economic growth, authoritarianism, and inequality. In an agrarian, underdeveloped world, authoritarian rulers are the standard solution devised to protect any population against the raids of external bandits. Those rulers understand that the appropriation of land—and of fixed assets in general—is the only path to wealth and power. In this context, authoritarianism and inequality go hand in hand. In exchange for protection against bandits such as themselves, the rulers seize an important part of their subjects' assets. Moreover, subjects have no mechanisms to curb the expropriation they may suffer at the hands of their rulers. Growth is extremely unlikely to happen. Authoritarian rulers favor the maintenance of those noncommercial, pro-land policies that are the basis of their wealth. They mistrust and block the emergence of alternative sources of income generation that may eventually challenge their political preeminence.

Although coming in many forms and with different degrees of intensity, this political and economic landscape of stagnation dominated the whole world until the Modern Ages. Modern development—that is, the emergence of a commercial society, followed by an industrial takeoff—happened in a self-generating fashion in very few places—all of them located in the North Atlantic. Growth happened where monarchs were not able to suffocate some preexisting medieval and pluralistic institutions in the name of modern absolutism. In those places, governments sustained economic policies that protected the interests of merchants and investors and that allowed the latter to take advantage of the scientific revolution of the 17th and 18th centuries. With growth and higher productivity, inequality subsided. Inequality made possible the transition to political liberalism and democracy.

In those places where absolutism prevailed up to the contemporary period, development and democratization happened only (if at all) through one of two alternative paths. In some instances, the breakdown of the old authoritarian elite (and of the institutions that blocked growth) came as a result of war, defeat, and foreign occupation. This breakdown occurred in East Asia and Eastern Europe, where World War II—and particularly its victors—destroyed the *Ancien Régime* social coalitions and political institutions that hindered democracy and economic development. As those countries eventually became linked to the international economy (either in the 1950s and 1960s in East Asia or after the fall of the Berlin Wall in Eastern Europe), economic growth (followed by political liberalization in Asia and contemporaneous with democratization in Eastern Europe) took place. Alternatively, development happened through a more peaceful (but perhaps even less frequented) path. As capital accumulated in the already-developed core and began to suffer from growing congestion costs, it gradually spilled over to the near periphery—particularly if the country had either stable institutions or foreign military pacts that credibly protected capital against the threat of expropriation.

The Spanish case fits the second pattern. Its civil war did not transform the social and political structures of the country. If anything, it reasserted the old status quo the Second Republic had been unable to change. Nonetheless, prodded by the United States and stimulated by the formation of the European Union (EU), Spain embraced economic policies that fostered rapid growth and the social transformation of the country. European and U.S. capital flowed into Spain, and new industries, such as tourism, sprang up to cater to an increasingly well-off European population. Spain's full transit to the club of industrial nations comes with a caveat, which is already underlined in this chapter, to this story of foreign-induced growth (in the framework of a stable dictatorship). The economic miracle of the 1960s was made considerably easier by the presence of a few areas in the north of Spain that already had the skills and capital ready to take advantage of the stabilization program of 1959 because they had industrialized in the 19th century.

As Spaniards grew richer and joined an expanding middle class, past political and economic clashes mellowed. In the 1930s, most of the political and social conflict pivoted around the distribution of wealth in a poor economy. As the economy boomed, the past zero-sum game around property distribution lost steam. Instead, substantial numbers of Spaniards moved into new economic sectors that delivered growing incomes without having to expropriate well-off sectors. Those changing underlying conditions made it possible to push forward two broad institutional transformations in a peaceful and quite consensual manner. First, Spain managed to transition from authoritarianism to democracy. Once the stakes of the electoral game had changed in a way that made everyone ready to accept a defeat at the polls, democracy could be introduced and consolidated rather quickly. Second, Spain moved from a heavily regulated and closed economy to a regime defined by much more open and flexible markets, which are now fully integrated into the EU.

Although the political deal that paved the way to democracy and an internationalized economy was broadly successful, it is worth concluding this chapter by stressing one important economic quandary that remains unsolved in Spain. Spain has been systematically hailed as the model to which other countries should look at to complete a successful democratic transition. Less noticed, however, is that Spain also underwent an important transition in its overall economic policy framework. It went from a protectionist regime with thorough price controls, a bulky public enterprise sector, and regulated labor and housing markets to an internationalized economy with stable macroeconomic policies and essentially deregulated financial and product markets. Successive democratic governments deepened the process of economic reform that started in the late 1950s. Since the mid-1970s, the economy was further liberalized in preparation for the entry in the EU. In the mid-1980s, the Socialist government engaged in a painful adjustment of several industrial sectors to reduce the bloated labor force and considerable financial losses. The transition to democracy and the expansion of the welfare state were undeniably helpful in easing the costs of the economic transition in two senses. From a strict welfare point of view, the implementation of universalistic social policies in health, unemployment, education, and pensions minimized the losses that the industrial and economic transition carried for important sectors of the Spanish labor force. From a political point of view, the expansion of compensatory programs (as well as of policies directed toward education and human capital formation) extracted a much higher level of popular compliance with the general strategy of modernizing the Spanish economy than might have been possible otherwise.[8]

As is often the case in many economic reforms, the process of economic transition remained incomplete in one central sphere. In 1977, to shore up support for the new regime, the transition government struck an encompassing social and economic deal with left-wing parties, trade unions, and employers' associations. Yet instead of further liberalizing the Spanish labor system, that agreement and the legislation that was derived from it reinforced the stringent labor market regulations put in place by the Francoist regime. In the context of a country that still had a substantial part of the population employed in the primary sector and where most of the population was rather unskilled, that regulatory structure interacted with the skill-biased shock that most European economies suffered in the 1970s and 1980s, thereby causing unprecedented levels of unemployment. The Spanish unemployment rate shot upward to more than 20 percent in the mid-1980s (see figure 8.9).[9] More important, unemployment affected different social sectors very differently. Unionized male employees remained relatively protected by labor laws. By contrast, the unemployment rate reached more than 30 percent of women in the early 1990s and almost 45 percent of young people. Participation rates among women remained

Figure 8.9. Spanish Unemployment, 1979–2002

Source: OECD various years.

extremely low despite the extraordinary inflow of women in the educational system and in the job market. The welfare state smoothed the economic shock substantially, but the high level of unemployment had a considerable impact on Spain's economy and demography. First, the low level of workforce participation probably accounts for the fact that Spain's per capita income has not caught up with the European income significantly. Since the mid-1970s, Spain's per capita income has hovered at around three-fourths of the EU level. Second, in response to the structure of the labor market, with high unemployment and a sharp division between permanent jobs (mostly for old men) and temporary contracts (for young people and women), Spanish women postponed childbearing (Adsera 2004). The Spanish fertility rate dropped to 1.2 births per woman—one of the world's lowest levels for the past two decades. This rate, in turn, should have extraordinary consequences on the ability of Spain to finance its welfare state in the future.

Notes

1. Although the industrialization of the Basque country and Catalonia has been well studied (for example, Nadal 1975; Nadal and Carreras 1990), theoretical

accounts about its takeoff are scarce. Abundant natural resources did not seem to play an ultimate role: even though the Basque country was well endowed with coal and iron, Catalonia was not. It is more likely that the social composition of both regions (with an abundant artisan class and relatively equal farming and urban communities) favored their industrialization. Urban artisans had the basic know-how to adopt quite easily the new industrial technologies generated in the United Kingdom. The relatively larger number of farmers and urban strata could, in turn, absorb those new industrial products. The different Basque and Catalan social background may have derived from the continuity of medieval autonomous political institutions that made both regions less vulnerable to the failed economic policies of the Spanish state in the modern period. In fact, the industrial revolution emerged in the two areas where medieval parliamentary practices had lasted longer: the Catalan parliament was abolished in 1714 and the Basque institutions in 1876.

2. An analysis of the period can be found in Brennan (1990) and Malefakis (1970).
3. This section relies on Merigó (1982), Payne (1987), and Preston (1993).
4. It is also likely that some Spanish bureaucratic and economic elites became unsettled by the contemporary negotiations to establish the European Economic Community and by the effects that such a broad market might have on Spain.
5. An analogous outcome emerges from the more recent United Nations University/ World Institute for Development Economics Research–United Nations Development Programme database.
6. For an account of the period, see Gunther, Montero, and Botella (2004) and Maravall (1981).
7. The quick expansion of public spending was also related to the double shock of high unemployment and high inflation that characterized the stagflation crisis of the 1970s.
8. The lack of much broader compensatory policies may explain why popular support for reform fizzles so rapidly in developing countries whenever growth rates fall and unemployment goes up. For a theoretical discussion of this issue, in a context in which trade policy and public spending are endogenously determined, see Adsera and Boix (2002).
9. Bentolila and Jimeno (2003) estimate that 80 percent of the Spanish unemployment is explained by the interaction of the shock and the existing labor institutions.

References

Adsera, A. 2004. "Changing Fertility Rates in Developed Countries: The Impact of Labor Market Institutions," *Journal of Population Economics* 17 (1): 17–43.

Adsera, A., and C. Boix. 2002. "Trade, Democracy, and the Size of the Public Sector: The Political Underpinnings of Openness." *International Organization* 56 (2): 229–62.

Bentolila, S., and J. F. Jimeno. 2003. "Spanish Unemployment: The End of the Wilde Ride," Working Paper 0307, Centro de Estudios Monetarios y Financieros, Madrid.

Boix, C. 1998. *Political Parties, Growth, and Inequality*. New York: Cambridge University Press.

———. 2001. "Democracy, Development, and the Public Sector." *American Journal of Political Science* 45 (1): 1–17.

Boix, C., and S. Stokes. 2003. "Endogenous Democratization." *World Politics* 55 (4): 517–49.

Brennan, G. 1990. *The Spanish Labyrinth*. Cambridge, U.K.: Cambridge University Press.

Centro de Investigaciones Sociológicas. 1996. *Estudio 2206*. Madrid: Centro de Investigaciones Sociológicas.

Gunther, R., J. R. Montero, and J. Botella. 2004. *Democracy in Modern Spain*. New Haven, CT: Yale University Press.

Madison, Angus. 1995. *Monitoring the World Economy, 1820–1992*. Paris: OECD.

Malefakis, E. 1970. *Agrarian Reform and Peasant Revolution in Spain*. New Haven, CT: Yale University Press.

Maravall, J. M. 1981. *La política de la transición*. Madrid: Taurus.

Merigó, E. 1982. "Spain." In *The European Economy: Growth and Crisis*, ed. Andrea Boltho, 554–80. New York: Oxford University Press.

Nadal, J. 1975. *El fracaso de la revolución industrial en España, 1814–1913*. Esplugues de Llobregat, Spain: Ariel.

Nadal, J., and A. Carreras, eds. 1990. *Pautas regionales de la industrialización española (siglos XIX y XX)*. Barcelona, Spain: Ariel.

North, D. C., and R. P. Thomas. 1973. *The Rise of the Western World: A New Economic History*. Cambridge, U.K.: Cambridge University Press.

Oliver, J., and X. Ramos. 2001. "Capital humano y desigualdad en España 1985–1996," *Papeles de Economía Española* 88: 240–56.

OECD (Organisation for Economic Co-operation and Development). 2004. Social Expenditure Database. OECD, Paris. http: //www.oecd.org/els/social/expenditure.

———. Various years. *Labour Force Statistics*. Paris: OECD.

Payne, S. G. 1987. *The Franco Regime: 1936–1975*. Madison: University of Wisconsin Press.

Pérez, F., F. Goerlich, and M. Más. 1996 *Capitalización y crecimiento en España y sus regiones 1955–1995*. Madrid: Fundación BBV.

Prados de la Escosura, L. 1992. "Crecimiento, atraso y convergencia en España e Italia: Introducción." In *El desarrollo económico de la Europa del Sur: España e Italia en perspectiva histórica*, ed. L. Prados de la Escosura and V. Zamagni, 27–55. Madrid: Alianza.

———. 2003. *El progreso económico de España, 1850–2000*. Madrid: Fundación BBVA.

Preston, P. 1993. *Franco: A Biography*. London: HarperCollins.

Puerto, M. 1991. "La reforma de la enseñanza no universitaria: Aspectos económicos y presupuestarios." *Presupuesto y Gasto Público* 4: 153–70.

Revenga, A. 1991. "La liberalización económica y la distribución de la renta: La experiencia española," *Moneda y Crédito* 193: 179–224.

Sawyer, M. 1982. "Income Distribution and the Welfare State in Post-war Europe." In *The European Economy: Growth and Crisis*, ed. A. Boltho, 189–224. New York: Oxford University Press.

Tortella, G. 1995. *El desarrollo de la España contemporánea*. Madrid: Alianza Editorial.

INDEX

Boxes, figures, notes, and tables are indicated by b, f, n, and t.

A

M

N

O

P